PILGRIMAGE FROM DARKNESS

PILGRIMAGE
FROM DARKNESS

NUREMBERG TO JERUSALEM

DAVID E. FELDMAN

University Press of Mississippi   *Jackson*

Willie Morris Books in Memoir and Biography

www.upress.state.ms.us

The University Press of Mississippi is a member of the Association of American University Presses.

Manufactured in the United States of America

08 07 06 05 04   4 3 2 1

As in all biographical works, this book is dependent upon the memories of individuals who have done their best to remember circumstances accurately. Every effort has been made to research and check the veracity of those memories and the history surrounding them. Dialogue has been recalled and in some cases re-created as accurately as possible. In several instances details have been slightly altered for the sake of brevity or clarity, without the sacrifice of fundamental historical accuracy. We apologize for any inaccuracies that may have inadvertently occurred.

Epigraph from *East of Eden* by John Steinbeck, copyright © 1952 by John Steinbeck, renewed © 1980 by Elaine Steinbeck, John Steinbeck IV, and Thom Steinbeck. Used by permission of Viking Penguin, a division of Penguin Group (USA) Inc.

Library of Congress Cataloging-in-Publication Data

Feldman, David E.

Pilgrimage from darkness : nuremberg to jerusalem / David E. Feldman.

    p. cm.

ISBN 1-57806-619-0 (cloth : alk. paper)

1. Eder, Asher, 1925– 2. Jewish converts from Christianity—Israel—Biography.
3. Holocaust, Jewish (1939–1945)—Germany—Influence. 4. Israel—Biography.
5. Germany—Biography. I. Title.

CT1919.P38E5934 2004

940.53'18'092—dc22

2003019183

British Library Cataloging-in-Publication Data available

To my wonderful wife, Ellen (Toot was right)
To my sons
In memory of the beloved Nettie Hyman and Gail Gluck

"Don't you see?" he cried. "The American Standard translation *orders* men to triumph over sin, and you can call sin ignorance. The King James translation makes a promise in 'Thou shalt,' meaning that men will surely triumph over sin. But the Hebrew word, the word *timshel*—'Thou mayest'—that gives a choice. It might be the most important word in the world. That says the way is open. That throws it right back on a man."

—*East of Eden* by John Steinbeck

AUTHOR'S NOTE

In the summer of 2001, I received a phone call from a man I did not know who wanted to take me to lunch. He said his name was Leonard Levine and that he lived here in Long Beach, New York. He had just read a book I had written about American servicemen stationed in China during World War II, and he wanted to tell me of his own experiences, which had been similar, and to talk about a book he was hoping to find someone to write.

I had mixed feelings; his story might well be an interesting one, but many people had approached me with the notion that I should write about what they went through during World War II, and, as far as I was concerned, I had already done a book about the war and had moved on to other matters. We did meet, however, and, true to his word, after complimenting me on my work, Mr. Levine (now known to me as Lenny) did tell me a story that resembled what I had written about in *Born of War*. When I gently let him know that I was probably not going to be the one who would recount his experiences, he responded that he wasn't asking me to.

He then proceeded to relate the riveting tale of a Christian German boy named Oskar Eder who had become involved with the Hitler

Youth and the Luftwaffe. Late in the war, the young man learned the whole truth about the Nazis and was devastated. Deeply affected and spiritually bereft, he set out on a quest that introduced him to several branches of Islam, to Hinduism, to a variety of Christian groups, and finally to Judaism. Converted by a rabbinic court in Haifa and married to a Holocaust survivor, he is today an observant Jew living in Jerusalem.

That was the story Lenny Levine wanted me to write, and I eagerly agreed. I am grateful to Lenny and to Asher (formerly Oskar) Eder for trusting me with the telling.

PILGRIMAGE FROM DARKNESS

PROLOGUE

When the sun came up that morning in the late summer of 1969, it seemed to Leonard, as he stood at the hotel window, that the light shone up from the ground rather than down from the sky. The view from Jerusalem's King David Hotel was bathed in a soft yellow glow, the same light, he supposed, that had lit the site for centuries.

Captured in the luminescence were David's Tower and the ancient stone walls of the Old City across the valley, and in Leonard's mind, the centuries forged together into a single instant.

He turned to his wife, Judith, who was already dressed and ready for their tour. "Even a curmudgeonly old agnostic like me has to love this place. The history, the mix of sensitive people—and I'm not used to being in the majority!"

Judith gave him a dubious look, then joked, "A curmudgeonly old agnostic? You're not so old."

He threw back his head and laughed. His wide florid features melted into a loving smile. "If we don't hurry, we'll miss breakfast."

Several couples were already on the bus when they climbed up its metal steps, forty minutes later. "What is that sound?" Judith wanted to know. She looked around but could not spot the source of the continuous ethereal tone.

"It's coming from the top of that mosque." Leonard pointed. "It's a Muslim call to prayer. Get used to it. We're going to hear it five times every day." He looked around, took a deep breath, and closed his eyes with the exhale.

"I'm looking forward to some walking," Judith said. "I've never seen such a breakfast. Eggs, cereal, fruit, vegetables!" She wriggled in her seat. Seeing that she was comfortable and content, Leonard looked around the bus at the brightly clad American tourists in their multicolored shorts, with their dangling cameras. Despite their appearance and his preconceived notions, he had found most of them to be sensitive, well read, and educated.

Outside the bus several men wearing tourist guide badges were standing in a tight group and talking. Leonard opened his window and strained to hear what they were saying, but they were too far away for him to learn anything except that they were speaking Hebrew. One of the guides, a short, ruddy man with a thick red beard, left the group and stepped onto the bus. Leonard noticed a silver Star of David peeking through his beard. The man craned his neck and jabbed an index finger repeatedly over the tourists, counting to himself.

"Listen," Leonard said. "He's counting in German."

Judith sucked in a corner of her lip. "And I'll tell you something else. He isn't Jewish."

Leonard sat back and looked at his wife. "We're in Israel, dear. Jerusalem. He's wearing a Mogen David. He's a government official, an Israeli scholar, an educated Sabra. You don't think he's Jewish? What does he have to do, drop his pants?"

Judith gave him a withering look. "Leonard, please." She looked pointedly out the window.

The bus had lurched into the steaming morning traffic and was headed for its first stop. After a few minutes Judith turned to her husband. Her tone was no nonsense. "You forget where I grew up. In 1930s Hamburg you had to know who was Jewish . . . for survival. If you didn't pick up subtle tones, accents, how people carried themselves, if you didn't get off the sidewalk when certain people passed, if you didn't avoid eye contact and carry yourself in a slouching, shamed way, well, it was often the difference between life and death!"

Leonard thrust his head into the aisle and tried to inspect the guide more closely. The man's badge appeared to say "Asher," a common Jewish name which added nothing to their discussion. He had the appearance of an educated gentleman, a quiet man with cheerful, clear blue eyes and a thin nose. It occurred to Leonard that many German tour groups traversed Jerusalem, and many Jews had fled Germany for Israel.

He looked at his wife and knew there was something to what she said. In a matter such as this, Judith's sensitivity, honed from a childhood skilled in self-preservation, was probably accurate.

He looked beyond her, out the bus's window, at the throngs in the crowded, colorful streets. "Jew and Arab side by side, minding their own business. It's a satisfying thing to see."

"Let's hope the peace holds," said Judith. "Around here it can be a fragile thing."

"And I'm a lucky man"—Leonard turned to her, filled with awareness of the moment—"to have such an insightful wife."

The bus had pulled up in front of their first stop, the Holocaust memorial, Yad Vashem, and already their bearded guide had stepped down and was helping his charges off the bus.

As they waited for the crowd to make its way down the aisle and steps, Lenny tapped Judith's shoulder and pointed to a gathering of Chasidim. "Nothing's changed for them in centuries. Day-to-day life, religion. It's all the same now as it was then. Is that good, do you think, or dangerous?"

"It just is," replied Judith. "Come, our German non-Jewish guide is waiting."

As they stepped into the building, Judith turned to Leonard and handed him a handkerchief. "Cover your mouth with this."

"I'll be okay," he said, waving her away.

"You were retching the last time we were here, Leonard. Cover your mouth. Do you want to make someone else sick? In fact, I don't know why we come here."

He leaned close to her ear. "I did get sick last time, and I'm sure I will again. It's a horrific place, the saddest place in the world. But it's important to see . . . repeatedly. I also like to see its effect on other people."

They stepped into the darkened room filled with life-sized photographs of storm troopers brutalizing Jewish children. Judith took a deep breath and blinked. Leonard wiped his eyes, which had welled and brimmed immediately. He felt himself begin to gag.

"Photos from German newspapers . . ." Judith pointed, her voice small. Leonard nudged her with his hip and nodded toward their guide, who was off to one side, arms folded across his chest, intently watching his charges' reactions.

Leonard walked over to him. "Excuse me. I'm Leonard Levine, from New York. You're . . . Asher?" He pointed to the badge. Asher waited. "I hope you don't mind my asking, but you're about my age, so I was wondering where you might have been when all this"—he made a stirring motion with a finger—"was going on. I was home, soon to be in the Pacific."

Asher nodded. "I was in Germany."

Leonard nodded and paused. "Really? How did you manage in such circumstances?"

Asher looked at him; Leonard could not help noticing the deep blue of the tour guide's eyes. "I was sixteen in 1941. I lived in a very small town and I wasn't Jewish. In fact I had never seen a Jew before in my life, to my knowledge. Well, maybe one or two when I was very young. Excuse me." One of the tourists was beckoning, and Asher stepped in her direction.

For the next hour, though he and Judith followed the tour, Leonard saw little of what was being exhibited. He was concentrating on how he might gather further information about their enigmatic tour guide. Finally, at Judith's suggestion, he decided that the simplest, most direct approach was best.

"Asher, I would like very much to hear about your experiences during those years."

Asher shrugged. "As I said, I was in Germany, in a small town, like so many other people."

"But if you were in Germany and you weren't in a camp, you must have been . . ."

"German. Yes."

"Well, that's not what I meant."

Asher paused a long time. "Perhaps after the tour today, we might sit down at the hotel and have a cup of tea together."

"I would like that," said Leonard. He watched as Asher went back to his job.

"Well?" Judith asked.

"You were right, as usual. And he does seem very educated, quite refined," Leonard pointed out. "We're having tea later this afternoon."

"I'm sure he's a gentleman," Judith agreed. "But I'm equally sure there's more to it. Sit down with him, have your tea, and listen. Let me know what you find out."

Judith stayed upstairs, resting her feet, while Leonard took the corner table in the King David's busy dining room. The buzz of conversation mingled with the clatter of dishes and silverware around him. Most of what he heard was English, with a smattering of Hebrew and Yiddish. But he focused on none of it. Would Asher keep his agreement?

Perhaps there was nothing interesting in the man's story, as Asher himself suggested. A man in Germany during the Second World War. A German. How did he survive? Was he involved in what went on there? How could he not have been? And how had he come to be in Israel, apparently a Jew?

"I hope I haven't kept you waiting long." Asher stood formally next to the table.

"Not at all. I just got here." Leonard stood up, motioning to a chair.

"So? Tea?" Leonard said, beckoning to a waiter.

"Tea would be fine."

"Something else? You've been on your feet all day. What about some dinner?"

"No. Tea is fine."

"Two teas, then." The waiter nodded and left.

Leonard smiled tentatively. "Well, I'm interested in hearing about your life: how you survived during such a dangerous time; how you ended up here, doing this, with a Jewish star around your neck."

"It is unusual, yes," said Asher. "First of all, at that time, we were typical Germans."

"In 1941 . . ."

"Well," said Asher. "If you want an accurate picture of what happened, I think I should start before that. You have no . . . plans at the moment?"

"I'm all yours."

"Well, I spent many years searching. Originally I didn't even know I was searching. You see, I was for a long time . . ." He looked down at the tablecloth. "I was for a long time a part of the ignorance, the confusion of that time. My name then was not Asher; it was Oskar."

1

The thin four-year-old boy with the light blond hair sat cross-legged in a garden on a sloping hill amidst strawberries, carrots, peaches, and plums. He scrutinized pieces of fruit, reaching out with skinny arms, picking any he deemed ripe and placing them in a small wooden basket his mother had given him. It was the summer of 1929, and, as was often the case, the boy refused to eat anything but fruit from the garden. His mother had given up trying to feed him meat or cheese and his father had learned that beating the boy only steeled his resolve.

The boy's eyes traveled from the fruit to the swing and sandbox and back again. An ant crawled up his leg; he placed a finger in its path, and when the ant moved up it, he put his hand on the ground and allowed the ant to crawl off.

A reddish cat with white spots ambled over the footbridge that led from one of the flats in the four-family home. He had seen the cat often in the old woman's flat, had seen it ignore plates of meat and cheese put out for others, and had marveled at the cat's discipline.

"Tss, tss, tss," he called to the cat, which sauntered close to his hand, then reared back and made a lightning strike, slashing one of the boy's fingers. He yanked his hand back and sucked on the cut.

When the pain had dissipated, he went back to picking fruit and singing to himself. Beyond another footbridge, on the other side of a kitchen window, his mother stopped preparing meat for the rest of the family's supper and looked outside. She stood still for a moment, shushing her husband when he tried to catch her attention.

She broke into a sunny smile. "I love listening to him sing. He has such a sweet little voice." She held up a hand signalling her husband to wait while she listened some more. She sighed. "Of course, a little boy all alone in a garden day after day is a bit sad, don't you think?"

Her husband, who was tall and wore his hair so short it stood straight up on his head, adjusted his spectacles and folded his arms across his chest. "You cannot have it both ways, Sophie. If you keep him away from the tough boys, he will be by himself. If you don't want him to be lonely, he will be among those boys. Besides, Sophie, he has his sister."

"They're together in the yard, but they're not really together. Look at Hilde, trying to jump rope on the other side of the garden. It's hard enough to learn when you're three years old, but all alone . . ." She shook her head and waved the image away.

"I've seen them play together," Wilhelm protested. "But you can't expect brother and sister to be best friends."

Sophie looked at her husband. "So should we send him out—?" She nodded towards the front of the house. "You know what's out there."

"I'd be angry too if I had no work and had to hang around on street corners."

"They need someone to blame. They can't get their hands on the chancellor or the Reichstag, so they'll see our little Oggie playing . . ."

"The men won't bother him if he's with the other boys."

"The other boys are no bargain either. When I go to the butcher or to church I see the way they play, throwing each other around, taunting one another. Do you want Oggie to be like that?"

"I want to earn a living, Sophie." Wilhelm closed his eyes for a moment. "I want to go to the power plant every day and do my job, so you can put meat on the table, so we can have a place to live and that garden for our children. I want to teach Oggie to use my tools, so that he can someday do the same for himself and his family. I want to watch our children grow up honestly."

Sophie pressed her lips together. "If he is not safe, he may not live so long."

Wilhelm shrugged. "I'll admit Lauf and Nuremberg are poor, especially nowadays, but they are not dangerous. Not really. My father has had no trouble at the school he runs. The things you worry about are the same things all mothers worry about. The real concern should be eating and paying our bills . . . living a good, honest life."

". . . and the children," Sophie added.

Oskar looked up and glanced towards the house, as though sensing his name on his parents' lips, but after a moment he went back to singing and picking fruit for his lunch and dinner. He glanced at three-year-old Hilde, who was holding the rope with both hands and flipping it over her head, then stepping over it when it landed at her feet.

"That's fine for you," their father was saying; he had moved on to one of his favorite peeves. "To go and sit in church when there is no service—"

"It gives me comfort to just sit when the church is empty. Is there something wrong with—?"

"Not at all. But don't try to tell me the church is so wonderful. When they get involved in social issues, whose side are they on? As Voltaire said, they go to bed and wake up with the powers that be. All that talk on Sunday doesn't seem to mean much on Monday."

Sophie shook spices over the sliced beef on the white plate in front of her. "A person who says he wants only to earn money for his own flat and food should not criticize the church. Especially when he comes from good Catholic parents."

They both turned as the door opened and Oskar ran in and handed his basket to his mother, who nodded approvingly. "A lot of strawberries today, Oggie! Very good."

"They're my favorites. Now can I go out? The boys down the street told me they would be playing soccer this afternoon."

His mother looked concerned. "Oggie, you don't belong with those toughs."

"But I'm tough, aren't I?"

His mother laughed. "Of course, but not like those boys. Why not stay home and keep me company? Let your father be the one to go out for now." She gave her husband a serious look. "Even for your father, going across the street to run the power station or bowling once a week at the inn are quite enough contact with the lawless elements out there, thank you!"

Wilhelm shook his head. "What did we just finish saying about Lauf and Nuremberg? Poor? Yes. Dangerous? I don't think so. Those men are more sad about not having jobs than angry. They have nothing better to do than hang around." He shrugged and turned to his son. "But listen to your mother, Oggie. Be respectful."

On an evening not long afterward, when it was dark and quiet outside save for the occasional drunken shout, in the four-room flat there was a sweet smell of cooking jam and a din of kitchen clatter. Oskar's mother was bustling back and forth from countertop to stove and back again. The boy had been enthusiastic and proud to help prepare the fruit for cooking, but now there was nothing left to do but go to

bed. Hilde was already asleep along the other wall of their shared bedroom and, as usual, Oskar wanted company to help him get comfortable.

"Mama, tell me a story."

"Well." His mother sat down at the side of his bed and clapped her
hands in her lap. "What shall I tell you about?"

Oskar laughed. "You know!"

"Ahh. The ancient kings!"

Oskar nodded eagerly.

"All right, but only for a few minutes. A very short story. I have to
get back to the kitchen. Many years ago, in Bavaria, during a time of
great learning, great culture, great wealth, there was a beautiful castle. And in this castle lived a great king named Ludwig. It was a happy
time, a festive day, and he was a very kind king . . ."

When his mother finished the story, Oskar was not yet asleep.
"Sing to me, please, Mother," he begged.

His mother nodded, and in a soft voice began to sing an old lulla-
by. "Can you count the stars in the wide sky . . ."

Yet when she had finished, Oskar still had not fallen asleep.
"Tomorrow is Sunday, Oggie. You know what we do on Sundays?"

"Go to church?"

"Yes, and after church?"

Oskar's eyes lit up. "A ride on the train?"

She nodded. "That's right!"

The Eders often took Sunday excursions to nearby towns. Rail tickets were inexpensive, and Lauf's two rail stations, one on either side
of the river, connected with villages where a family might stroll and
shop for an afternoon.

On the train, Oskar would not sit still. He listened to his parents, who were discussing what they had just heard at church. Something about a "soul."

"Can I have a piece of paper and something to write with?" asked Oskar. Seated opposite, Hilde watched him, kicking her legs against the metal seat base.

Still talking, his mother found a paper and pencil in her bag, and Oskar began to draw. He thought a moment and peered down the front of his shirt. He had an idea. He drew two circles not far from one another, and surrounded them both with flames that formed a larger ellipse.

"Mother." He waved the picture. "Is this my soul?"

His parents looked at one another. His father said nothing; his mother smiled and appraised the drawing. "I suppose it will do for now." She patted his head and turned to her husband, shaking her head. "Our boy is thinking about souls!"

"Give him a piece of bread and jam," his father suggested. "Would you like that, Oggie?"

Oskar nodded. "You have the quince jam we made last night? That's my favorite."

His mother nodded. "But let's wait until we get off the train, so we don't make a mess here."

The village was even more rural than Lauf. Animals ran wild, and Hilde retched and Oggie wrinkled his nose at the smell of manure. Here, too, unemployed workers lounged in the streets, disheveled and wary, rarely meeting the eyes of passersby.

Oskar looked every which way, noticing farm animals rather than the faces of out-of-work men, happy to hold his mother's hand and eat his bread and quince jam.

As they walked and visited the tiny shops and Oskar's parents looked at the wares and goods the villagers were selling, Oskar tried to see everything at once, his head turning in all directions, his bread and jam waving.

His mother steered him away from a group of men in brown uniforms and towards a disorganized clutter of farm animals. In its midst, a chicken ran wildly back and forth, and Oskar paused, pulling on his mother's hand for her to stop, so he might watch. The chicken ran crazily in every direction, pausing now and then, head darting and poking, and then resuming its aimless running. Suddenly, the chicken ran right at Oskar, snatched his bread in its beak and ran off, its head jerking forward as it pulled its new meal down its gullet.

Hilde watched, her hand over her mouth.

Oskar began to wail and looked up at his parents. His father shook a finger at his son, then looked around at the people who had witnessed the scene. "You see this boy? A fool who lets a chicken steal his food!"

Sophie clutched his sleeve. "He is not a fool! Can't you see he gave that chicken his food out of generosity?" She reached into her bag and found the last bit of bread and jam and gave it to her son. "Don't listen to him!"

On the train ride home his parents did not speak. His mother handed Oskar a picture book. An aunt had given him the book months before. In it were pictures from faraway places with tall trees bearing huge pointed leaves. People worked under a tropical sun, on massive plantations.

"This is where I'm going to live someday, Mother." Oskar pointed at the pictures.

"Me too!" Hilde cried.

His father shook his head and groaned.

"I really am! You'll see!"

"That's fine, Oggie." His mother patted his arm.

His father brightened. "Never mind that. When we get home I'm going out to pick up a surprise for dinner!" His father tapped Oskar on the knee.

Two hours later Oskar was on the garden swing when he heard his mother's voice calling him and he realized how hungry he was. When he entered the kitchen he joined his mother and sister at the table and waited until his father brought in the steaming plate.

Oskar looked at the plate and put a hand to his mouth to keep from gagging. It was a pig, its head and legs intact, its skin charred.

"What a treat, eh!" his father said.

Oskar managed to nod, his body clenched, already rejecting the thought of eating what was so obviously a living thing.

His father carved the white meat and laid slices on each of their plates; his mother followed with potatoes, and his parents began to eat.

His father paused. "Well, go ahead."

Oskar looked at his plate, then at his father. With great resolve, and trying not to look at what was left of the pig, he forced himself to eat.

The Eders struggled to maintain a semblance of their normal lives while winds of change whipped around them. The schools, local shops, church, and Wilhelm's power plant were the limits of their experience, so the political firestorms made so plain by historical context and hindsight were not yet visible on the family's horizon.

Wilhelm Eder had little time for anything but work. Occasionally he bowled or played chess at the inn along with other Social Democrats, or attended church with his family, but as Sophie often pointed out, the streets were becoming less safe by the day. The loafers and unemployed had begun giving way to Brownshirts who were merciless under the guise of keeping order. So Wilhelm kept his family at home except for the occasional outing, most often to visit family. He went only to and from his job at the power station, across the street from the northern bank of the Pegnitz River. Inside the power station were a water wheel, a diesel engine, and other elements of engineering Oskar found fascinating. The boy enjoyed going to work with his father whenever he was allowed. He watched the men work, and asked whatever questions came to his fertile, curious mind. He liked the smell of oil and grease from the huge engine. By now he had forgotten his book about the tropics and was planning on following in his father's footsteps with a job at the municipal power station.

On one school holiday, he spent the entire day, or as long as his father could tolerate his curiosity, at the power plant.

"What does that switch do, and how does the power get from the wheel into everyone's house?"

Wilhelm, whose attention was on his work, explained as much as he thought Oggie would grasp, then suggested, "Why don't you go into the office, Oggie, and find the little toolbox I gave you and play with that? There are bolts and nails and some wood in the corner I left just for you."

Oskar was happy to do as he was told.

Twenty minutes later, his father came into the office looking for a spare part. He watched his son, who was hammering awkwardly with his left hand. "Why are you using your wrong hand?"

"I want to teach myself to use both hands."

"It's a waste of time. You'll never do as well with that hand."

"I can do it, Father, if I just keep working at it."

Shaking his head, Wilhelm went back to work. He turned around. "At lunchtime, we'll go home, then you'll stay with your mother for the afternoon."

Oskar thought a moment. "Can the warden's daughter come over to play?"

"We can ask, I suppose."

The warden lived in an apartment attached to the station. He was happy to give his daughter something to do on this school holiday. Oskar's mother prepared their lunch. Hilde joined them and the children ate quietly and were as well behaved as might be expected, given their ages.

Perhaps wanting to impress their visitor, who had brought her new teddy bear to show off, Oskar began interrupting his parents with observations. Finally his father turned to him and shook a finger in his face. "When elders are speaking you will be quiet, Oskar, or you will be punished!"

Oskar reddened and glanced at his guest. His mother sensed his embarrassment.

"I remember once, when I was a child," his mother said, "I was talking too much during my parents' lunchtime, just like some people I know. My father told us we must be quiet. Now, it happened that this day I was asked to go down into the cellar to get a cup of wine from the barrel to give to my father. When I returned, I tried to say something, but my father said I must be quiet. I was an obedient little girl so I listened and remained quiet, though I wanted very much to speak."

"You see?" said Wilhelm.

"Let me finish," said Sophie. "I told them that what I had to say was urgent, but my father would not let me say a word. He said I had to be respectful and wait until the meal was finished. Oh, I tried several times but was told each time to be quiet. Finally, when the meal was over, I told them through my tears that I had been unable to close the valve on the barrel and the wine was flowing out, all over the cellar. As you can imagine, my father's face turned very red and he jumped up, and ran down to the cellar without saying another word!"

She looked at her husband, who raised an eyebrow and went back to his meal.

After lunch the children were sent out into the garden. At first they took turns squeezing the teddy bear and swinging it around in the air, which made it growl, but after a few turns they grew tired of the game and looked around for something else to do.

"Let's play Life and Death," the little girl, whose name was Berta, suggested.

Hilde clapped her hands; she had no idea what Life and Death was, but she loved games and was delighted to be included in this one.

"What kind of game is that?" asked Oskar.

"It's a game of pretending," Berta explained. "We take turns being different kinds of dead. First we roll dice, which I have in my pocket, then . . ."

"I didn't know there were different kinds of dead," Oskar said, trying to remember if he had heard such a thing at school or from his parents.

"There are stages of death, really," Berta said. "There's half dead, almost all dead, dead like a mouse, and completely dead. You can think of more if you like."

"Can I try?" Hilde wanted to know.

"We roll the dice to see who goes first." Berta took out the dice and each child rolled. Berta's roll was highest, so she went into the middle of the garden and laid her head on a cluster of leaves surrounded by purple flowers. She groaned and turned her head from side to side, then smiled up at her hosts. "This is half dead."

"Can I go now?" Hilde cried, waving her hand as though in school.

"My roll was next highest so I'm next," Oskar said, with an air of importance. He rolled onto his side in the planting area, one hand waving behind his rump, as though he had a tail. He gave off high-pitched squeaks and then was silent. "This is dead like a mouse," he said solemnly, as he got up and brushed himself off.

"But these aren't real deaths," Hilde said. "You're still alive! Let me take my turn!" She ran to the footbridge, where they had left the teddy bear. She picked it up and ran over to the watering can, which was at the edge of the garden and filled nearly to the top with water. She dropped the bear in, then reached in and lifted it, dripping wet, from the can. "This is drowned dead. It's completely dead!" she cried, triumphantly waving the bear in the air. This time it did not growl.

"You've spoiled my bear!" Berta cried.

"No," Oskar said, looking at his sister and then back at Berta. "She killed it. Completely dead."

After Berta went home, Oskar sat at the kitchen window, watching his sister play on the swing. A fly had been buzzing around the room; it was a big, slow-moving, green-headed fly, and when it landed on the sill, he was able to stealthily slip a glass over it. After watching the fly buzz up and down the inside of the glass, he trapped it in his palm, then managed to grab one of its legs. He held the fly up in front of his face, wondering why it had so many legs when he had only two. He began pulling legs from the fly with his other hand.

"Oggie! What are you doing!" His mother had come into the kitchen.

When he explained his curiosity, his mother put a hand to her mouth, then sat down next to him, her voice softening. "This is a living thing, Oggie. You must not torture it. It feels pain, you see."

Oskar looked at the fly, which was writhing frantically. His mother's words sank in and he burst into tears.

His mother hugged him to her, holding him for a long moment. Together they rocked back and forth. "Oh, my boy," she whispered, holding him at arm's length.

2

Lauf's elementary school was a fifteen-minute walk from Oskar's home, and until his sister was old enough to come with him, Oskar usually made the trip alone. He was not allowed to socialize or play with the other boys. He agreed with his mother's assessment of them as too rough, yet he admired their athleticism and hardiness. Shy and quiet from years alone in his garden, Oskar did not have the assertiveness to approach them. His lone friend was Konrad, a boy who lived not far from the Eders. Konrad's father owned a small paper mill and knew Oskar's father from the Social Democrat center.

Each grade was seated in its own row in the one-room school, the youngest in front. Oskar listened attentively during the secular studies. When the teacher spoke, Oskar thought of his mother's bedtime stories and pictured tall, ornate castles in Bavaria, where great men sat at fine desks and wrote with long feather pens. The individual contributions of such cultural icons did not mean much to a six-year-old, but Oskar remembered their names and the fact that they were German. He did not fully comprehend even the simplified history lessons in which the Holy Roman Empire was decimated by revolutionary events in France.

Some of what Oskar learned did make sense. Because he had been on trains, he could envision in a basic, abstract, childlike way some of the industrialization of the mid-1800s, with its railroad construction and cultural growth. He learned that museums had been built and that zoos, theaters, and art galleries had flourished.

His mind soaked up information and imagery the way his body soaked up food, water, and sunshine. It was in religion class, when the priest took over, that the child began to assert himself more creatively.

"And on the seventh day, the Lord rested," the priest explained. "This is why it is important for us to rest on Sunday. It is mandated in the Decalogue, the Ten Commandments."

Oskar raised his hand. The priest pointed to him.

"We observe the seventh day on Sunday?"

"We sanctify that day as the Lord's Day."

"But on our calendars Sunday is the first day. So shouldn't Saturday be the seventh?"

"Sunday," the priest explained, "is the day of the Resurrection of the Lord."

"But you just said the seventh day we are commanded to rest and the seventh day is Saturday. If you look at the calendar . . ."

"That was changed," the priest interrupted.

"Why?"

The priest, a pale, paunchy man with thinning hair and bright red cheeks, stepped close to Oskar and touched him on the head with a heavy finger. "The old law is the law of the Jews, and the church was authorized to change that law."

"Really?" Little Oskar looked up at the priest. "By who?"

"The Holy Spirit."

"Ohhh." He was quiet after that; Oskar would not dare argue with the Holy Spirit.

The following week however, he had more questions for the priest, who was giving a lesson on the commandments.

"You must love thy neighbor as thyself," the priest explained.

Oskar's eyes began darting from side to side as his mind tried to grasp the concept. His hand shot up. "Love my neighbor as myself?" he repeated.

"Well, don't you like yourself?" the priest asked. The boy nodded. "Then you should like your neighbor too."

"But we don't all like everything and everyone the same way. My father likes spaghetti noodles, and I hate them," Oskar said. Some of the older boys in the back row began to laugh.

Oskar went on. "And he forces them down my throat. So, maybe my father doesn't love me!"

The priest saw that tears had come into the boy's eyes. "Your father wants you to be strong and healthy, and sometimes that means eating foods you may not like so much. That is a kind of love, and you should obey him, Oskar."

Several inches of snow had fallen the previous night followed by a fresh dusting during the school day. The wind bit into Oskar's cheeks and swirled around him, trying to find its way between the folds of his coat as he and Konrad struggled homeward. Crowds of boys congregated up and down the streets, wrestling and throwing snowballs. The girls clustered in smaller, more steadily moving groups. Outside one of the shops three boys bounced on their toes against the cold, their hands in their pockets. One nudged another and nodded toward the two approaching children.

"Look what we found," the first boy said to Oskar. He pointed to a frost-covered iron railing around a storefront window. "It's a special kind of ice cream: delicious . . . and free."

Oskar looked up at the window. Sun glinted off the frost and he had to shade his eyes with one hand.

"All you have to do is lick it."

"It doesn't cost anything?" Oskar wanted to be sure. "And it tastes good?"

"Just like ice cream," said another boy. "We'll let you try it, even though this batch is ours." They stood aside, making room for Oskar, who walked up close to the frozen iron, and was about to lick it when Konrad interrupted him.

"Don't! Your tongue will stick to the metal!" Oskar looked at his friend, then at the older boys' faces. He ran, with Konrad close behind.

The boys chased Oskar and Konrad, but only for a few feet, deciding instead to go back and wait for another victim.

Around the next corner was a much larger crowd of boys throwing each other into snowdrifts. As Oskar and Konrad passed, an arm reached out and pulled Oskar in. Instantly the air was knocked from his lungs by a blow to the back, and for a few moments he was trapped in the struggling mass of flailing bodies. Punches grazed his head, an icy boot kicked his side, and when he finally staggered to his feet, Konrad was nowhere to be seen. He gathered his school materials from where they were strewn—some were in the street, some where the boys had been fighting, some were missing entirely—and made his way home, dirty and bleeding. He made up his mind not to tell his mother that with the pain and blood and humiliation came the new thrill of being part of a tangle of arms and legs he had only watched until today, the thrill of being covered with dirt and grime from the same wrestling match as the older, tougher boys he had only admired before now.

"Oggie!" His mother's hand covered her mouth. "This is what

happens when I let you . . . now you'll stay home!" She marched him
to the sink in the kitchen and cleaned his wounds. "Now go in the
salon," she said when she was finished, "and play with your trains."
She folded her arms against the pain in her chest.

"Why don't you come over to my house this afternoon?" Konrad
asked. It was the following Tuesday, a sunny morning in 1932, and he
and Oskar were walking to school, struggling to keep stacks of books
under their arms. "We can go fishing on my father's boat."

"Don't I need a license for that?" Oskar asked.

Konrad gave him a knowing look. "I'll help you get a license."

Normally a focused student, Oskar had difficulty paying attention
that morning. He had questions for Konrad. Was there a fishing rod
for him? What kind of fish were in the river?

As usual Oskar gave away his snack bread during recess and went
outside to find his friend. He found Konrad in the playground, playing tag with a half dozen of the boys in his class.

"Can I play?" Oskar asked.

"Sure," said one of the boys, "but you have to be it!" The boy ran
toward him, but Oskar was light and quick, and he sped away, running in a tight circle, avoiding the boy's reaching fingers. He headed
for the nearest wall of the school, and at the last possible instant
veered away. The boy chasing him wasn't as quick and he crashed
through one of the lower-level windows.

All motion on the playground stopped as the boy gingerly climbed
back out, peering at a rip in his coat sleeve and a dark, spreading
bloodstain on one shoulder.

The school door flew open, banging against the bricks, and the
school's warden rushed into the yard, screaming. "Who broke my
window? Come on. Who broke it?"

The warden ran to the boy, who was still examining his arm, and began slapping his face, back and forth, the sound echoing across the playground.

"Who asked you to come here and break my windows? You filthy Jew! What is the matter with you dirty, disgusting Jews!"

Oskar turned to Konrad, who had come over and was standing next to him. "What exactly is a Jew?" Oskar wanted to know.

Konrad looked at him for a long moment, started to say something, then stopped; he stared hard at the boy, who seemed like any other boy. He shrugged. "I have no idea."

Religion class was held after recess and once the priest had presented the lesson and settled at his desk, allowing the class time to copy what he had written on the board, Oskar raised a hand. "I was wondering, sir, can you tell me what a Jew is, and why it's bad to be one?"

The priest considered the question. He looked down at his desk, then scanned the young faces in the room. "The Jews are the people from whom our Lord Jesus Christ was descended." He sighed. "But they killed him, you see, so now they have to suffer for it."

Oskar looked down at his desk, then at his friend to see what he made of this, but Konrad was sitting with his elbows on the desk, his hands over his eyes, as though trying to shut out the news.

After school and before fishing, Oskar had to go home to do his homework, but promised to meet Konrad in an hour at the dock. On his way home, his thoughts were of fresh air and a full bucket of fish. Oskar passed an inn and heard men's voices singing inside. He walked nearer to the window to hear what they were singing.

"Brown as the soil is our clothing . . ."

True to his word, Konrad was able to get Oskar a fishing license, and his father did indeed have a small fishing boat complete with several sets of gear. The boys wasted no time in setting up their gear and shoving off into the little river. Within a few minutes, Oskar felt a tug on his line, then a harder bite, and finally an enormous pull, which he returned in kind, setting the hook. He gave the fish enough play to tire it out and never pulled hard enough to snap the line until, with Konrad's help, he pulled in a seven-pound carp. People in other boats and along the sides of the river pointed and cheered, and someone must have told the local newspaper, because a representative was dispatched to Konrad's house to interview Oskar, who had become an instant celebrity.

Oskar carried the fish home, where his mother explained that she would prepare it in a soup with potatoes and other vegetables. Konrad was invited to stay for dinner, but declined, as he was expected at home.

"We're going to the store, Oggie," his mother said. "Once we have vegetables and spices, you can help me prepare your catch."

"First I want to ask Father about something that happened today at school." He related the broken window incident and his conversation with the priest about Jews.

His parents looked at one another. His father spoke carefully. "You know I have Jewish friends in town . . ." He looked at his wife, who shook her head. Wilhelm paused before going on. "I will talk to the priest about this when I have a chance, Oggie, but I must ask you not to bring up such things." Abruptly he changed the subject. "Do you know who I'm going to invite over to share your fish? Grandfather Anton and Nikki."

Oskar smiled. "I'm going downtown to help Mother pick out vegetables."

In the darkening afternoon, Lauf's little grocery store filled with wives using whatever meager marks their husbands could spare for potatoes, which were inexpensive and filling.

The women chatted and gossiped. A heavy woman in a grey coat had captured the attention of the rest. "My husband was at one of their rallies last weekend." She closed her eyes and shook her head. "Magnificent! The pageantry, the marching, the banners! It was like a dream! And then there he was! He had only been a name to me, this Hitler! *Ach*, he was captivating! Like a reincarnation of the Holy Roman Emperor. I never heard anyone speak like that. It was as though he knew what my heart wanted to hear before I myself did!"

One of the women laughed. "She's in love," she said.

The first woman shook a finger at her. "You would be too, if you heard him. The women were fainting, the men were shouting and stamping their feet. I tell you it was the event of the century! And when he finished speaking, your ears rang, the cheering was so deafening. And then I realized I was shouting too!" Her face glowed with excitement. "I would go again tomorrow, and the next day!"

The person behind the counter was whispering and looking in their direction, and Sophie's head cocked to one side as she tried to hear.

"It's Sophie Eder!" the counterman whispered, and Sophie looked down to see if Oskar noticed. He was looking at the woman in the grey coat.

"Her sister was that pregnant schoolteacher who committed suicide from the shame of it. I just now heard about it."

The counterman's wife shook her head, her voice barely audible. "Terrible, but who could blame her? An unmarried pregnant schoolteacher is impossible to hide."

Sophie paid for her vegetables, took Oskar by the hand, and rushed from the store. Down the street, outside the inn, three men leaned against the building, watching them pass. Sophie overheard one of them say to another, as they approached, "Here is a question for you: a passenger liner sinks in the ocean, and hundreds of people die. Who should be punished?"

"I dunno," said another man. "The captain?"

"The bike drivers and the Jews!"

"I don't get it," said the second man. "Why the bike drivers?"

All three laughed and watched Oskar and his mother pass.

Grandfather Anton and his wife, Nikki, had arrived and were seated at the table when they came in.

"Is what the storekeeper said true?" Sophie breathlessly asked her father, who nodded slowly without asking what they had heard. Oskar's mother cupped both hands to her mouth. Tears ran down her cheeks. "How could they have known?"

"Anton came to get the doctor, who was visiting in Lauf when it happened," said Nikki. "That's how the storekeeper knew first." She bit her lip. "We didn't want to concern you. We weren't sure . . ."

Sophie was shaking; Oskar hugged his mother's leg.

His father struggled to find appropriate words. "Was her pregnancy . . . ?" he began clumsily.

"There was no pregnancy," Anton interrupted. "That's what everyone assumed. She had dropsy. Her legs were as swollen as her belly."

"Oskar," his mother said, collecting herself and glancing out the window. "Keep your sister company outside until I call you for dinner."

"But you were going to let me help you prepare my fish! Grandpa, did you see my fish?"

Anton managed an absentminded half smile. "I understand you are now a celebrity, even in Nuremberg! Sophie, let him help."

"Only if you change the subject."

Oskar looked at his mother. "We're not going to see Aunt Mathilde anymore, are we?"

"No, she was very sick. Now I need your help, Oggie, so please put that out of your mind and concentrate on cutting vegetables like a big boy, all right?"

Oskar nodded. "But first I have to wash my hands."

By the time he returned, his parents and grandfather had changed the subject.

"We see them nearly every day at the railway station," Anton was saying. "They're everywhere."

Sophie nodded. "We saw some of them on the way home."

"Brownshirts? I heard them singing in the inn," Oskar said.

"Just cut the vegetables and put them in nice piles on the side of the cutting board," his mother directed.

Wilhelm stroked his chin. "Oggie, if you want to stay healthy, remember three things: keep your feet warm, your digestives working well, and your head cool. You know what that means, keeping your head cool?"

"It means don't wear too many hats!" Oskar answered.

"It means to consider carefully before you make decisions. Don't make rash judgments." He turned back to Anton. "The Social Democrats in Lauf feel the same way, things are getting dangerous. Not many cool heads around anymore, that's for sure, at least that's the word at the power plant and downtown at the club. You know, my father has been talking about organizing a demonstration. With the election coming . . ."

"*Ach*, another election," said Nikki, disgusted. "Every day, it seems, another election."

"Well, if my father's right we can contribute to this one in more ways than one," said Wilhelm. "As the director of a respected Nuremberg school, he has a lot of friends and more than a little influence."

"A demonstration?" Anton was surprised. "He should listen to his own son's advice about having a cool head. These Brownshirts, or white shirts, or whatever they call themselves today, won't see that as a joke!"

"Well, he's a member of the Bavarian People's Party. So if the demonstration were in the form of a Bavarian parade, with Bavarian flags . . ." Wilhelm smiled to himself. "It would, on the one hand, be for Bavarian pride, yet I think a message would be sent: that we're not afraid to stand up with something besides a swastika on a flagpole."

Anton saw his point. "I'm sure it will have some support from any Catholics and Social Democrats who aren't afraid. People are looking for a reason to show the Nazis something, anything."

"And giving the children little Bavarian flags," Sophie pointed out, "can be a kind of protection. Even the Nazis wouldn't attack children."

"I'm not so sure," said Anton. "You tell your father, Wilhelm, tell Julius I said to be careful!"

"Can I go? Please? I want a flag!"

"Oggie! Back to chopping!" his father ordered.

3

One of the priests at school was explaining the meaning of the Lord's Prayer; Oskar's hand shot up.

"Please, sir, what does the word 'hallowed' mean?"

"It means 'holy.' We are asked to live a life that contributes to the holiness of his name by being a good person, you see."

Oskar's hand went up again; this time he called out his question without waiting to be asked. "Why does the Lord need us to make his name holy?" His expression was so serious, his mouth so set, and his eyes so focused, that, though weary of the child's questions, the priest had to smile. "The way the Lord's Prayer is written, we are encouraged to contribute to the holiness of the Lord's name with our words, deeds, and actions."

Oskar shook his head. "I don't understand this at all! The Lord's name is *already* holy."

A bit less taken with the boy's charm now, the priest looked at him for a long moment. "Some things, young man, you have to take on faith." He let out a long breath and continued with his lesson.

Oskar arrived home and put his books on the table; he wrinkled his nose. His father sat opposite him, smoking and turning newspaper pages. His mother was hovering over a large cardboard box on the countertop. Hilde was bending over the edge of the box, reaching inside, exclaiming, "Look! Look!"

Oskar came over and looked. In the box were two plump, furry white rabbits, their sides heaving, noses twitching. One had a black patch on its side, and the other was entirely white; both had pink eyes and ears. Hilde was dropping bits of carrot onto the straw around them.

"Ooh, they're so soft," Hilde said, stroking the white rabbit's side with a fingertip.

"Look at the way their little mouths move when they chew, side to side, faster and faster!" Oskar laughed; something about their chewing struck him as hilarious.

"Just like this." Sophie moved her mouth in quick, tiny chews and twitched her nose, holding the rest of her head perfectly still.

"That's it!" Oskar cried, pointing at his mother and laughing so hard he nearly lost his balance.

"Mama's a rabbit!" Hilde said.

"Maybe we'll call her 'our little rabbit' from now on," said Wilhelm, smiling because his wife did indeed look like a large plump rabbit. "Enjoy them for a few days," he said to the children. "On Saturday, we'll enjoy them another way."

Oskar stopped laughing. "You want to have them for supper?"

"Of course," his father said. His mother continued to wiggle her imaginary whiskers.

Oskar couldn't take his eyes off the rabbits. Directly behind them stood the oven, and the two images combined in his mind, forcing his memory back two months to an inn where his family had stayed in a picturesque village a short train ride away. As dusk gathered outside, the owner of the inn had announced that he would slaughter a pig for supper and could he please have some help from a few of the guests? As Oskar and his family watched, the owner and two volunteers bound the pig's feet and the owner raised a hammer and struck the pig on the head. The man's aim had been poor or his attention distracted, because the blow only glanced off the side of the pig's snout. As Oskar looked on, the man rained blows on the animal's head, which jerked every which way as it desperately tried to avoid the heavy hammer. Finally, the inn owner took out a long knife and began slicing and carving.

Oskar looked forward to going back to school the following term, running and playing with his friends in the playground. As he grew more confident in his physical abilities, his social confidence grew as well, until he became one of the more popular boys. The following school year would be more fun, more exciting than the last.

But fear of the Nazis, who ascended to power in early 1933, had finally begun to filter into the small towns, until even the most sheltered of families was affected. When he shared his excitement about the coming school year with his parents, they glanced at one another and his mother launched into an earnest explanation.

"We have decided to send you to a boarding school this year, Oggie."

"A what?"

"A Catholic school in a place called Cham, near the Czechoslovakian border. You will live there."

Oskar shook his head and looked at his father.

"It's too dangerous for you here, Oggie," his mother went on. She considered how to put her fears, which she barely understood, into words a child might grasp. "The robberies, fighting in the streets, in the schools. The Nazis send thugs around, who—"

Wilhelm shook his head at his wife.

Oskar was clutching himself, arms folded across his chest, fighting back tears. "But you're letting Hilde stay, aren't you? You just don't want me around!"

"Hilde is too young to go away to school."

Sophie reached out to him, but Oskar backed away. "It's not what you think at all. We hope the Nazis won't last. Perhaps in a year . . ."

"A year!" The boy turned his back. "That's forever! I won't go!"

"You have to go," his father said, albeit gently.

Beyond the train station, at the edge of the tiny town of Cham, the school was surrounded by tree-covered hills. During the train ride, Oskar watched the countryside and the animals and people that came and went from his view. But when they stepped from the train, the reality of being away from his parents for the first time overwhelmed him, and he sobbed and clutched at his mother's coat.

"Why don't you want me? Why? Why!"

His mother swept him into her arms and whirled him around, hugging him to her, their tears mingling as their cheeks pressed together. "We're doing this *because* we love you so much. We want you safe!"

Oskar stopped crying. "It's because you love me?" He turned this new idea over in his mind, examining it with analytical curiosity.

His mother's chin quivered. "We'll all be here for your Communion. Ah," she brightened, "you forgot about your Communion. I can see it on your face."

"Can I have a bicycle? Can I have an air rifle?"

"You have quite a sense of timing, don't you?"

The dormitory held twenty-five boys. Once the lights were out, they introduced themselves, described their families and friends, told jokes, and speculated about their new school. Falling asleep took nearly an hour.

In the morning, they awoke to a stern monk striding up and down the aisles between the beds, bidding them all wake up and get on with the responsibilities of the day. He stopped in front of one of the boys, examined the boy's face, and tore his blanket from the bed. He ran his hand over the sheet and began slapping the boy, back and forth, with either side of his hand. The slaps echoed in the otherwise silent bed chamber.

The boy, whose name was Gustav, neither flinched nor cried out. The monk shook his finger at the silent children.

"There will be no wet beds in my school! Understand?" He turned on his heels and strode from the room, which was silent for a full minute.

"You took that awfully well," Oskar said finally.

"I have a nerve condition," Gustav explained. "I can't feel pain, or hardly at all, anyway. Come here, I'll show you. Pinch me." He allowed the boys to take turns pinching him, and Gustav instantly became a celebrity and rallying point among the boys.

Oskar developed friendships at his new school, but as in Lauf he shied away from the roughest of the bunch. He did not share their cruelty and was too sympathetic to their human and animal victims to be a wholehearted participant in their troublemaking. What he did share was their boisterous independence, which now and then landed him in trouble with the monks.

One monk in particular cast a cold eye toward Oskar. His name was Kunibert, and early on he noticed that the thin, fair boy from Lauf was often distracted, rarely focused on his lessons. The monk's rebukes did nothing for the boy's attention span.

One day before Kunibert arrived, Oskar was in the front row, where the monk had put him to keep an eye on him, but Oskar had turned around in his seat and was pretending to be the monk, calling himself *Gummipferd*, which sounded like the monk's name but meant rubber horse.

The boys' laughter died away. He turned; Kunibert was behind him.

"*Gummipferd*, is it?" The monk advanced toward him, a sly smile creeping over his face.

"It was only a game, sir. I'm sorry."

"I've finally caught you."

"I, I—" Whatever Oskar had intended to say was lost as the monk whipped a backhand slap that began at his waist and ended flush on the side of Oskar's face.

"You have to learn respect! Discipline!" the monk roared; then his voice dropped. "But I don't suppose beating it into you will do it, do you? Do you?"

Not wanting a further beating, Oskar shook his head.

"Ah. Then you will write out the Lord's Prayer one hundred times, to be completed by first thing tomorrow." The priest smiled. "And if you do not have the entire hundred finished, even if you have ninety-nine, you will do it again from the beginning, and so on, every day until you have done the assignment and can behave yourself."

"Yes, sir."

That night, Gustav asked him what he was going to do. "How are you going to manage to write the Lord's Prayer one hundred times? You'll have to stay up all night."

Oskar nodded. "I guess I will, then."

In the morning, Oskar was still writing when the sun came up. Every few minutes he had to stop and shake his fingers or press his palms together to stretch out his hands.

He heard yelling coming from the dorm and ran in to find the wake-up monk slapping Gustav again, screaming about wet sheets. Unable to feel the pain, Gustav merely took the slaps. After nearly a dozen, he smiled at the monk, who reached out, half blind with fury, and with a quick swipe, tore the bottom of Gustav's ear. Now the boy did scream, from a pain beyond his affliction, and from the sight of the monk's bloody fingers.

The monk registered brief satisfaction, then realized the trouble he might be in, as Gustav appeared ready to run from the room.

"All right. Enough. You'll need medical attention and we have to have a talk." As he prepared to take Gustav out, the monk turned to the rest of the boys, who were white-faced and queasy. "Please, boys. Don't mention this to anyone. I'll be more gentle in the morning from now on. All the Nazis need is another reason to notice a Catholic school. They'll shut us down and maybe worse. So promise me you won't say anything, even to your parents?"

The monk's brutality led to more questions in Oskar's mind. Religious leaders, beacons of that segment of society representing the best of humanity, showed themselves to be impatient, cruel, even brutal— rarely the bastions of understanding and love they purported to be.

The year's shining light was his tenth birthday and Holy Communion, a day on which the harsh reality of daily life in Cham was suspended in favor of festive celebration. And best of all, his parents and sister were to visit.

The day lived up to its promise; his family doted on him and the feast after the ceremony enabled Oskar to forget his homesickness and enjoy his surroundings for the first time. The promise of special gifts upon his return home was a bittersweet reminder, sweet in that he had longed for a new bicycle and air rifle, bitter in that he could neither receive nor enjoy them while at parochial school.

When his parents left, the stark reality of his spartan life returned. As he laid his head on the pillow that night, he found the pageantry and honor a warm but fading memory, and realized that tomorrow promised hard work and the added responsibility that came with the status of his age.

Oskar arrived home two days before Christmas, happy to smell his mother's cooking and feeling a little estranged from his sister, who had grown independent and no longer looked to her big brother for all of her answers. As he came in the front door, he noticed a tall fir tree, as yet undecorated, in one corner, its top brushing the ceiling. The "angels" who did the Christmas decorating had apparently not yet arrived.

His father had passed wires through a hole he had bored through the salon wall. His mother shook her finger. "Now you stay out of the salon this afternoon. And you, too, Hilde!"

In the kitchen, over heaping plates of butter creme torte, his mother asked about school and exclaimed how wonderful it was that they were together again.

Later that afternoon, Oskar looked out over the garden and remembered how he had once sat so innocently, surrounded by fruit and flowers. He heard a banging noise and remembered the hole in the wall bordering the salon. He went to the wall, put his ear to it, bent low and angled his eye to the opening. His father was stringing lights and decorations onto the fir tree, turning it into the vision of light he and Hilde had seen every year of their lives.

"What are you doing?"

He rolled backwards and looked up at his mother.

"But that's . . . Father. The tree . . . But, I thought . . . the angels!"

His mother laughed. "A grown-up boy like you still believes in angels?"

"Father's always put up the lights?" Oskar remained on the floor; it was as though heaven itself had fallen on him.

"Get yourself dressed. We have things to discuss at dinner."

Oskar stayed on the floor, crushed by the weight of fallen myths and idols. Like many boys in Germany in the 1930s, he had little to believe in: his mother's bedtime stories of Bavarian kings were ancient parchment memories.

But he was grateful for his family, for being able to sit at the holiday table next to his ever-changing sister, opposite his mother and father, who were so obviously delighted to have him home, even for a short while.

"Oggie, we have something to tell you," his father began.

"Let me, Wilhelm. It is more gentle coming from a mother."

"All right then."

"You know we sent you to Cham so you could be away from certain things that were happening at school. Many of the teachers and administrators who did not see things the government's way, well, they were"—she waved her hand as though releasing a small bird—"they are no longer with the school. We had hoped that after this year it would blow over."

"What would. . . ?"

"This Nazi popularity. We thought maybe it was a trend that would collapse."

His father looked him in the eye. Man to man. "We were wrong, Oggie. Now even the church approves of them."

His mother's words rushed at him. "We see no point in sending you back to Cham next year."

"No point . . . and no money," his father said.

"Nothing has changed here," she said. "In fact, the Nazis are becoming more popular. I don't know if it is coincidence or they have something to do with it, but some things are a little better, and they are getting the credit. Unemployed workers are no longer all over the streets. In fact many of them have been hired as Nazi thugs. There is a little more food perhaps, and the prices are not quite so high."

"Ah, but it is not the price of food that is the problem," Wilhelm said. "It is the price we're all going to have to pay for these changes. Just wait."

Oskar squinted, trying to make sense of his father's words. He turned back to his mother. "So I will not be going back next year?" He tried to keep the rising joy in his belly from showing on his face.

4

"How long did you say the train ride to Hersbruck is?" Oskar had come into the kitchen, turned the radio to a classical station, and was spreading honey on a roll. He nodded when his mother held up the kettle of malt coffee.

"Not long, Oggie. Perhaps twenty minutes."

"I think I'll like this school better than I would have liked the Gymnasium. Those ancient languages . . ." He made a sour face.

His father, who had finished breakfast, poked his head into the kitchen. "You have a good head for science and math. The *Realschule* is just the place for you, Oggie. Enjoy your first day. Okay, I'm off to work."

A few faces on the train were familiar, but Oskar kept to himself most of the day, concentrating on his studies, listening to the teachers, and avoiding the rough boys.

He had heard rumors of what were referred to as government-sponsored scout organizations—the *Jugend*, for boys over fourteen, the *Jungvolk*, for boys ten and older, and a separate organization for the girls. But he was never approached directly, and with the more pressing business of finding his way around a new school and attending to his work, Oskar thought no more about them.

He had one especially interesting teacher. Not a church adherent, this teacher admired the ancient Germanic religions and was a vegetarian, a combination which fascinated ten-year-old Oskar. When pressed, the teacher explained that the ancient Germanic peoples did not eat pig because it was unclean, but, rather, ate horse, because the horse was thought to be strong.

Oskar raised his hand and asked why the practice had changed.

"When missionaries came west to central Europe, one such missionary from Ireland, Bonifazius we call him here, labelled the Germanic peoples idolators for revering the horse. The Germans ought to eat pig instead, the missionary explained, to show our religious independence, to show the Jews we are free from their old law. The Jews, you see, also do not eat the pig."

Oskar had been keeping personal notes in a little journal he had hidden in his room. He wrote about his schools, teachers, and friends, as well as the people he avoided. The journal was not a central part of his life; he did not rush home to write in it, since he was well adjusted enough to cope with most everyday circumstances without his feelings and frustrations needing any outside outlet. He had, however, been a sheltered boy, a private child, outside the mainstream. He was thoughtful and analytical, not only about physical phenomena but about morals and ethics, and he found that writing down his thoughts helped him organize them and make sense of what otherwise seemed confusing.

When he found the journal on Hilde's bed one evening, he was embarrassed and enraged, and shook it in her face, demanding that she never touch his things. He then locked himself in and Hilde out of their room. He did not hear her crying and asking their mother that they have separate rooms. He opened the journal and wrote in it that his sister had become a stranger, perhaps while he was at Cham the previous year. She was no longer the loving baby girl he remembered.

At dinner the next night his sister was talking about a girls' youth movement she had been asked to join at school: the *Jungmädel*, the equivalent of the *Jungvolk*, the younger branch of the boys' Hitler Youth. She refused to join, she insisted, her voice rising. Oskar listened, astonished and with more than a little grudging admiration at this independent person his sister had become. On the other hand, the resentment of the previous night remained, so much so that he began to be interested in the boys' group. He knew nothing of what they stood for, but perhaps they might be a doorway to the world of the rougher boys, whom he had long avoided yet secretly admired.

The conversation and fantasy were short-lived because their father came in, white-faced, and rushed into the bathroom, their mother close behind. They heard only his stern order: "Just sit down at the table and leave me alone."

Their mother came in and silently set supper on the table. In a few minutes their father followed, washed, his hair in place, wearing a new shirt. He turned the radio off. "I need to talk to your mother, children. Please go into the salon with a board game, or if you have homework . . ."

The children went to the salon and pressed their ears to the kitchen wall.

"We had an accident . . ."

"Start from the beginning, Willie."

"One of the transmission belts was weak. I knew it for a few days. I can tell with these machines, you know? I can hear the difference."

"I know. Calm down."

"So I called for repair. This was yesterday. Well, the repairman came this morning, first thing. And he fixed the belt."

"Good!"

"Not so good. We were testing it, and it must have still been weak in a spot, because it broke . . . and tore off part of Otto's thumb."

The children didn't hear any response, so Oskar peeked around the corner of the doorway and saw his mother holding her hand to her mouth; their father's head was down.

"Well, Otto will be out of work now. I feel terrible, of course. But that's not the worst of it. The officials came right away to look into the situation. They looked at Otto after he went to the doctor, and they accused me . . ."

"Accused you? Of what? It was an accident!"

"Of course, but you know Otto is a Socialist . . ."

"I didn't know. Did you?"

"Of course."

"Did they know you. . . ?"

"No, but almost as bad. The Nazis think I hired Otto knowing he was a Socialist, and arranged the accident on purpose, to get him a pension!"

"Ridiculous!"

"Well, I told those officials what I thought of their theory. We had quite an argument."

"Willie, your temper!"

Oskar came out from behind the door. "Father, why do we have to stay in the salon? Why can't we hear. . . ?"

"It's too dangerous!" came the shouted answer. "If you speak of this at school or on the street, I could lose my job or go to prison! Better you don't know."

Oskar had never seen his father frightened; the sight both terrified and inspired him. He stood up straighter. "Father, if it's dangerous I won't speak of it. I promise."

"Oskar, Hilde, come here." Sophie gathered the children into her arms. "Sometimes the adults need to keep things just between themselves. Sometimes we have to speak privately, for your own good, for your own protection."

"And sometimes," Wilhelm said, "children say things without thinking or realizing they are saying them. Words slip out. You have to trust us."

With a pat on the head and a kiss from their mother, the children were sent to their room. Oskar ignored his sister and retired to a corner of his bed with his journal.

He could not be trusted? No one must be allowed to know these feelings, he vowed. He was not allowed to know the secrets of his own family? Well, then, he decided after a moment's thought, he would not share his own secrets with his parents. He would keep to himself.

He would have his revenge.

Before his teenage years, a boy naturally begins to feel an independence that is nature's way of sending him out on his own, of freeing him from his parents' tutelage and protection. Often the feeling is bittersweet, conflicting, and difficult to understand, the result of changes in his body as much as events themselves. And so young Oskar, who had enjoyed the protection of the enclosed garden in Lauf and his mother's stories, who had feared the rough boys, began to change. The brutal incidents at boarding school and his parents' choice not to include him in their decision making began to inspire something other than fear: a mistrust of adults. His change of perspective extended also to the rough-and-tumble boys on the street and in school. Oskar began to observe them more carefully, and his fear diminished while his admiration of their physical abilities and camaraderie increased.

For these reasons the salon wall outside the kitchen, where a small person might press his or her ear, became familiar and well worn. He was sitting there one evening, careful to remain utterly silent, when he overheard his parents' furtive whispering.

"We cannot stay here, Sophie. It's too dangerous. Once the local Nazis are out to get you, there's nothing you can do."

"Where could we go?"

"There is a job in Upper Franconia, a town called Forchheim, running another power station."

Sophie paused. "You've been looking, asking around all this time?"

Oskar heard his father chuckle. "I knew I had better have a solution before telling you we had to move the family. Forchheim is more Catholic, less Nazi-influenced than Lauf."

"I suppose you've found a house as well, and a school, and . . ."

"Some things I leave to you, but I do know of a flat in a two-family house that belongs to a shop owner there, the lower flat. It's actually just a bit outside the town, with a nice garden, though I'm not sure we have use of it."

"We can look at the garden, no? Our eyes will have use of it. The children no longer need to play in one."

"I know how much you like Lauf . . ."

"Lauf is just a place, a name. If the Nazis have singled you out, we have to leave."

Forchheim was a very old, moderately sized town of about fifteen thousand, north of Nuremberg, with medieval roots; its oldest buildings dated back to Charlemagne. As the family walked from the train, Oskar noticed the remains of an old city wall that he later learned dated to the Middle Ages, while the town hall and the administrative buildings were ancient stone Gothic structures. The new Eder family home was at the foot of the road to Nuremberg, called Nuremberg Strasse, or Nuremberg Street.

An immediate perquisite as far as Oskar was concerned was having his own room. No more stolen journals or lack of privacy. The situation fit perfectly with his new independent attitude.

While he had begun to admire the older, more athletic boys, he remained cautious and held back in his new surroundings to acclimate himself. He did not develop friendships quickly, save with one boy, who had contracted polio at an early age and who walked with a pronounced limp.

Despite his physical handicap, or possibly because of it, Willie was quick-witted and assertive, and shared with his new friend from Lauf a natural, boyish mischievousness and inclination toward pranks and practical jokes. At school they managed to exploit a subtle rift they sensed between their chemistry and physics teachers by sneaking into the chemistry laboratory and mixing chemicals that ought to have been kept separate. Upon learning of the dangerous use of classroom material, the chemistry teacher blamed his colleague in the physics department.

Later, the boys would learn that they shared a compassionate side.

It was a year in which pressure was increasingly applied on boys to join the growing ranks of the *Jungvolk*, the branch of Hitler Youth for those below the age of fourteen, with their uniformed pageantry, marching, and war games.

Oskar spent nearly half of his free time with his new bicycle, hurtling up the hill at the outskirts of town. Along with many of the other boys and their bikes, he worked at bicycle acrobatics, jumping, spinning, and riding in tight circles. While he didn't know the other boys, there was an unspoken friendship that came from shared experience and informal competition. One regularly saw the same faces on the same bikes, and the shared skill and competence created a respect that led to a bonding, not the kind directed by authority, as in the Hitler Youth, but another, more natural kinship.

The other half of his time Oskar focused on his skill with his new BB rifle. He put his independent streak to good use, training in private, aiming at flies on walls and blades of grass. He practiced and honed his skill until, at a church picnic, he took part in a competition, hitting a small ball that danced on a water fountain five times in a row. The prize was to have been awarded for six consecutive hits, but his gun misfired on the sixth shot and the owner of the kiosk refused to recognize his feat. The other boys in the competition, some of whom were Oskar's acquaintances, insisted he have another shot. Seeing the crowd's opinion, the kiosk owner allowed him another turn, and Oskar hit the ball again and was awarded the prize: a cuckoo clock.

The bicycle and rifle kept Oskar busy and temporarily away from the negative influences his family's move was designed to avoid. They also temporarily thawed his anger toward his parents.

At school, his biology teacher was constantly discussing the future of science. Someday, he promised, one would no longer have to eat. One would ingest two pills each day, one for nourishment, the other for filling one's stomach. Science and research would enhance our lives; the future would hold benefits for all.

Early in the year, Oskar visited his friend Willie at his home on the other side of Forchheim. The boys played in Willie's bedroom, where Oskar noticed a large, wooden writing desk with an enormous crack running through its writing surface. "Why would you keep a broken desk? You have a nice house; you can afford . . ."

"Do you believe in the supernatural?" Willie asked, looking at Oskar with wide brown eyes. "Do you believe in a person's death reaching out and touching another person?"

Oskar shook his head, but without much conviction. "What do you mean?"

"I had an uncle, my favorite. Ever since I was a little boy, he and I were very close. Last year he was on a business trip, in Australia. One night, while he was gone, I heard this loud noise and woke up, turned on the light, and saw this crack in the middle of my desk."

"How. . . ?"

"I still don't know, but a few days later, I learned that my uncle had been killed that very hour."

"They don't teach that sort of thing at school, do they? Only strict science, and order and morality. What do you think?"

"That and how it's all being degraded by the Jews."

"Yes, the Jews." Oskar had heard about these Jews and the way they were supposedly invading and debasing Germany's culture, particularly music and theatre; with their licentiousness, they were said to be betraying the very heart of Germany, simply by virtue of their existence. Strange, Oskar thought, remembering the boy who had been slapped in the schoolyard in Lauf. Had that boy been a danger to society? And how was it that he looked no different from the rest of the boys?

"Well," he said, after a moment. "Destroying our tradition of music and poetry would be a horrible crime, I suppose. But how, I wonder, are they managing it?"

"I don't know," said Willie. "It seems to be okay for us to correspond with French children. Our class writes them postcards every week and they write back. It's an official project! You have a good point. With all this contact with French boys, how is it that the Jews, whom we never see, are destroying our whole culture?"

Oskar thought very hard. "They must be terribly clever."

The following month, Oskar's class was taken to see a movie about a boy who had become a member of the Hitler *Jugend*, and was proudly wearing his uniform, marching, and playing war games with the other boys. Hitler was his hero and the boy worked hard to follow his hero's directives: learn fearlessness, duty to the Fatherland, discipline—important characteristics for all German boys.

The boy began to suspect that his parents were not quite as enthusiastic as he was. They were, in fact, rather bourgeois, less patriotic to the Nazi cause and therefore to Germany, as far as he was concerned. It seemed obvious to the boy in the movie that it was more important to have allegiance to the führer than to one's parents, particularly since their attitude was so complacent, so inappropriate.

The movie disturbed Oskar. His own parents did not like the Nazis, and he was angry with them because he felt left out, not trusted, and rejected. The Hitler Youth beckoned to him. There was a seductiveness to a group that included the elite boys and yet invited him. That the *Jungvolk* had uniforms, songs, and activities that unified German boys was a further seduction.

Some boys' fathers were full-fledged hundred-percenters, unquestioning Nazi supporters, but others, like Wilhelm Eder, questioned, even criticized, albeit privately, the gathering groundswell of propaganda and enormous social pressures.

The disappearance of Socialist and Communist leaders dampened any criticism on Oskar's parents' part, and criticism was further quelled by the pressure on children to inform on their parents.

Questions about the Hitler Youth and the acceptability of joining the ubiquitous Nazi organizations became all but moot, as membership in the *Jungvolk* became compulsory for boys who reached the age of ten. Oskar's father, suspected of being linked with the Social Democrats and of having staged the work accident, registered his only son.

At school Oskar learned to apply the English saying "my country, right or wrong" to his own country. Why should only the English boast such patriotism? History as taught in school became primarily military history. Social and cultural details of the school curriculum were de-emphasized. The focus was on the strongest and fittest, the heroes most beneficial to the Fatherland.

The *Jungvolk* meetings were held weekly, and readings were given out praising ancient Germanic virtues. Some of these reminded Oskar of his mother's bedtime stories and other legends of his earliest youth, and he enjoyed the sense of shared identity that pervaded the crowded rooms.

Other aspects of *Jungvolk* were more difficult to accept, and Oskar was less comfortable with them. Athletic competition, the bearing of pain, and war games were all much less to Oskar's liking, but he rationalized his participation, deciding that such exercises were probably healthy for his growth and development, for shedding his "mama's boy" self-image.

At home his parents vacillated, at times expressing their disapproval of the *Jungvolk*; Hilde patently refused to participate in the girls' affiliate. If need be, she would stop attending school altogether, she insisted. Publicly, however, the Eders were too frightened to offer resistance. They watched as neighbors disappeared and, since they had children, they saw no choice, no place to go; they had no historical perspective demonstrating what the Nazis would someday do to Germany and the world. To them, the Nazis were a distasteful political trend that brought a growing social pressure, rather like McCarthyism in 1950s America, though more pervasive and life threatening.

Given the fact that Oskar's entrance into the *Jungvolk* came on the heels of an incident that inspired distrust of his parents, he was perhaps more open-minded to the group's message than he might otherwise have been. Or, perhaps this is too optimistic a view, as the Hitler

Youth were so widespread, so quickly and firmly enmeshed in every aspect of the children's lives, that for Oskar (more so for boys than girls) there may have been no avoiding them.

In his view, the government had been proven acceptable by the world's authorities. The Vatican had endorsed it in the recent concordat, and the rest of the world had gotten over an early hesitation and followed suit, joining the Nazis' pageantry at the 1936 Olympic Games in Berlin. Even France, who had never respected the weak Weimar Republic, showed deference to the strength of Germany's new government, standing by as the German Reich reoccupied and swallowed up territories it considered its own, including the coal-rich Saarland and demilitarized Rhineland. Who was Oskar to ignore such evidence?

One of his favorite places was the repair shop at the power station his father managed. Doubling as a kind of hardware store, the shop stocked a variety of tools and parts one might need to fix household items. The rows and aisles of materials and hardware were impressive to the eager child's mind.

Oskar was browsing one afternoon among the shelves, examining boxes of tools, thinking about the word "Reich." What exactly did the term "Third Reich" mean? he wondered. The word meant kingdom, though he knew Germany was not a kingdom in the usual sense. The Holy Roman Empire had been the First Reich, and then there had been Bismarck, the Second Reich. Each had been geographically extensive, while this Reich was not. This was simply Germany. So what, exactly, was the Third Reich? He was confused, and tried to use logic to find an answer. He had heard something about the Pope making some kind of proclamation about the German government, or perhaps it had been vice versa.

On the other hand, *The Reich* was the name of a well-known news-paper.

The door opened and the factory supplier came into the room. He remembered his father's frequent complaints about the difficulties of acquiring supplies, so the man's arrival appeared to Oskar to be good news.

He crept close to the counter to hear what his father and the sales-man were saying. For the first few minutes there was no discussion; Wilhelm examined the price sheets, his glasses low on his nose. He looked from the sheet to the salesman, and back again.

"How is it that your prices, which are supposed to be wholesale, are higher than the retail prices in Nuremberg? I'm a seller. I have to offer a competitive price."

The man shook his head. "Those are larger stores that buy in bulk; you only want two or three of each item at most. Buy in quantity and the price goes down. Of course, you could find some other way to lower your costs."

Oskar glanced at Bernhard, Wilhelm's employee, to see if he had heard. But he was stocking shelves in the back of the store, opening cartons, removing products, walking them up the ladder to the top of the shelf, and setting them out for display.

Oskar watched his father begin to nod. "Whatever I do, people will just take the train to Nuremberg. Even if you add the train ticket to the price of their part, the result is still lower than what I can offer. I will have to close my shop."

"I daresay," said the salesman, glancing at Bernhard, "you have a dilemma, since layoffs are forbidden." He smiled suddenly. "We wouldn't want to contribute to unemployment."

Wilhelm didn't answer. He knew the edict well.

After the man left and once Bernhard was out of earshot, Oskar approached his father.

"What will you do?"

"I cannot run a repair shop and store at a loss, Oskar. I will have to give Bernhard some other job in the power station to save money. I don't want to break the law."

"It's a good law, isn't it, Father?"

Wilhelm looked at his son for a long moment. "There are a lot of poor people, Oskar. It is a difficult time, and the government says it means well to forbid layoffs. It is a difficult law, because the work I will give Bernhard is work I could do myself without too much trouble."

Oskar thought about this. "But the government does other good things, don't they? You know the way they have us put all our food in a big pot once a month so we can eat like the poor people? And how we give what we save that way to the poor? That's a good thing, Father, isn't it?"

But his father didn't answer directly. He tousled Oskar's hair. "Your mother's right. You're a good boy, Oggie, with a good heart."

5

"I could use some help fixing that broken cabinet, Oggie. What about tomorrow, after school?"

"Can't do it."

His mother put down her fork. "But you love helping your father fix things."

"I didn't say I wouldn't love it. I said I can't."

"Why not?" his father asked quietly.

Oskar continued to chew. His sister had stopped eating and was looking curiously at her brother, who seemed entirely absorbed with eating: he watched his fork dive at the noodles on his plate, pierce a few, and raise them up and into his mouth. All apparently fascinating.

"Just can't. Busy."

"Oggie's joined the *Jungvolk*," Hilde said. Now she had his attention.

"What business is it of yours? Since when are you interested in social groups?"

"I'm surprised, that's all. And the *Jungvolk* are not a social group."

He could feel his parents looking at him.

"Is this truc?" his mother asked. "The Hitler Youth?"

He didn't answer; he was fed up with his parents' picking at him. His father had stopped eating, his fork midway between the plate and his mouth, gravy dripping ridiculously. Oskar watched the brown drops splatter on the white plate.

"I have a note from the director at school."

"Why didn't you tell us?" his mother wanted to know. "What were you waiting for? Christmas?"

Oskar smiled at the absurdity of this letter being a Christmas gift to his parents.

"It's a funny letter?" his father wanted to know.

He held out the envelope. His father put down his dripping fork, wiped his hands and mouth, and tore it open.

"So, you don't behave any better at school than you do at home." He turned to his wife. "The director wishes to see me tomorrow."

"You know your father would rather be working," said Sophie.

Oskar shrugged. "So? I didn't tell him to take the day off, the director did."

His mother shook her fork at him. "You are becoming more argumentative every day."

"You've always encouraged me to question, to be inquisitive—"

"But always respectful! A bad attitude can get you in trouble." Her eyes flitted from her son to her husband and then blinked away, toward the salon; Oskar saw fear in them, a fear he did not understand. "*Jungvolk*," she muttered. "*Ach!*"

The next day Oggie and his father waited on the green cushioned chairs in the director's outer office, which smelled of fresh paper and polished wood. His father wore his Sunday suit, and sat with eyes glued to the far wall, now and then glancing at the clock. Oskar wondered what his new friends were doing after school, and tried to see into the hallway outside the office as his feet dangled over the edge of the chair, bumping its legs.

Finally the door opened and they were called inside.

"Mr. Eder," the balding, bespectacled director began, from behind his desk. "Your son is impertinent and arrogant. This is not the first time he has questioned his teachers or openly disagreed with them in front of the class. Oskar does not respect authority, in fact"—the director paused to take a long look at some documents on his desk, then rose from his chair—"in fact, I have never seen such a situation in all my years in Catholic Bavaria! Imagine! A boy with the worst marks of the year in both religion *and* behavior! Both at once! The boy must have really worked for such an achievement!"

How odd, Oskar thought, that the director, whom everyone knew to be affiliated with the Nazi SA, would concern himself with Catholic Bavaria. Oskar glanced at his father out of the corner of his eye and saw, to his surprise, that his father was trying not to laugh.

"I'm shocked," Wilhelm said drily. "I have always thought of Oggie as very bright. At his schools in Cham and Lauf his teachers said he was one of the more intelligent, even gifted children. If here, you say he is not, well, perhaps the problem is not so much with Oggie . . ."

"I did not say he was not intelligent," the director replied. "That is not the point. To tell you the truth, I would like very much to have this arrogant young man dismissed entirely. Fortunately for him, his other grades are too high." The director leaned forward, toward Oskar's father, palms flat on his desk. "He's *too* smart." He looked hard at Wilhelm, as though the father, not the son, might have been the root of the problem.

Wilhelm's eyes strayed to the photo of Adolph Hitler on the wall and to the papers on the director's desk, each stamped with a swastika. A tall red, white, and black Nazi flag stood in the far corner of the room.

Wilhelm began to nod. "I will have a talk with Oskar," he said, his voice subdued. "His mother and I will make sure he behaves." He gave the boy a look that conveyed more than words, and Oggie understood that misbehaving in school again could mean trouble for the whole family. "Oggie," he said.

"I'm sorry, sir," Oskar said, in a barely audible voice.

His father went home and Oskar was sent back to class.

On the way, he heard a voice singing, and he poked his head into the music room. A thin older boy was sitting alone, a notebook in his lap.

"What are you doing?"

The boy shook his head. "Nothing. Getting ready to go back to class."

"It's okay," Oskar assured him. "I won't say anything. I was just curious."

The boy gave a diffident shrug. "I write poems, songs. I wrote an operetta once."

"Really?"

The boy nodded. "Would you like to hear some?"

"I haven't time now. I've got to get back to class. What's your name?"

"Schwalb. You know, swallow, like the bird. Yours?"

"Eder. Oskar Eder." He waved and headed back to class.

The *Jungvolk* began to take up more of Oskar's time. He was satisfied to wear their uniform and blend in with the other boys, marching and singing and studying their shared Viking and ancient Germanic origins. Occasionally he took part in their athletic competitions, and his wiry body, nimble feet, and quick hands served him well. He excelled, often winning, even at wrestling, where he found ways to out-think his opponents, using their size and momentum against them. What had been engaged curiosity and independent thought began to be perceived as leadership qualities in this first tier of the youth movement. With his quiet confidence, quick mind, and facility with words, he was looked up to by other children, and perhaps his newfound popularity endeared the *Jungvolk* to him more than their policies and affiliations might have otherwise.

As Oskar's self-confidence and status within the *Jungvolk* grew, his relationship with his parents and sister cooled. He remembered and resented his parents' lack of trust in him and nurtured it as a personal slight, oblivious to the protective intentions behind it. He had depended on his parents to provide a feeling of safety but no longer felt he needed that protection. He was part of something bigger now, and what greater safety was there than numbers, especially when that was added to a growing confidence in his newly discovered abilities? He had heard recently that "freedom is the insight into the necessity." Wasn't Germany's struggle for recovery exactly such a necessity?

Hilde Eder had long looked up to her brother as a source of intelligence and wisdom. His seduction by the *Jungvolk* was a betrayal as far as she was concerned, a failure on her brother's part to see through a deception. Without a young boy's hungry, fragile adolescent ego, Hilde, even as a schoolgirl, saw only empty pageantry and promises in the group's rapidly swelling ranks.

Yet even while Oskar's commitment to the *Jungvolk* grew in time and depth, he had reservations. Their rhetoric at this point spoke more of Fatherland and patriotism than incitements to violence, but some notes in their songs rang false; racial references and claims of biological superiority set off alarms in the independently thinking part of his mind, though, as yet, those alarms were not loud enough to drown out the allure of a Greater Germany.

Oskar noticed a change in his parents. They were less outspoken in their dislike for the Nazis. Oskar's father was especially remote, perhaps because his job as the manager of the Forchheim power plant was a public one; he was essentially a government technocrat. Oskar felt the subtle undercurrent of dissatisfaction running through his household and the town. He would find his parents whispering when he entered a room, and when he was noticed, the whispering would stop. He sensed similar subtle misgivings about the government in some neighbors, and without an adult's perspective, without being subjected to the same pressures and intimidations suffered by those neighbors, the boy saw only the dishonesty, the deception, the evasion of the patriotism he was learning at and after school. He learned to sense shallow, insincere conformity, and to despise it, less for its nonconformity than for its insincerity.

Oskar had seen unemployment and street crime wiped out, national pride restored, unifying social programs instituted and, more recently, territories such as Austria and the Sudetenland, which he had learned were historically German, restored to German ownership. The result of all this was a blossoming patriotism in the young man that was less the emotional exhilaration of some of the youth leaders than a more calculated loyalty. Seeing a choice between publicly parroting the government's line while privately disagreeing, on the one hand, and genuinely supporting that which seemed supportable, given the evidence available to a boy his age, Oskar decided in favor of the latter.

Once war broke out, this would all become academic. In Oskar's view, strict patriotism was required by war. The German word for war, *Krieg*, is derived from *kriegen*, meaning to get or make one's bread, to struggle for survival. War took the decision making out of the equation. War, as Clausewitz, the Prussian military thinker, had observed, is the father of all things.

On a bright spring morning in 1938, Oskar was lying in bed, reading one of the Karl May books he had accumulated in recent weeks, looking up now and then, listening to a flock of finches arguing in the trees across the street.

From his Saxon village, Karl May wrote of wild Kurdistan and charming Arabia, of American cowboys and Indians, and of the German-born pioneer Old Shatterhand and his Apache friend Winnetou, bringing German flavor to the American West. The books' heroes seemed to Oskar to be average people in extraordinary circumstances. The panoramas and vistas took on a reality, transporting him to a place where the good guys always won and evil was always defeated.

He looked up. The birds had been drowned out by another sound, a low persistent growl which grew slowly to a grinding roar. He went to the window and watched long lines of army trucks file slowly past. He carefully laid the open book on his pillow and hurried into the kitchen.

"What's going on? What does it mean?"

"Austria has asked for an alliance with Germany. So the army is moving in. Peacefully, they say."

Oskar noticed his mother and Hilde exchanging glances. He returned to his room, his disgust and bewilderment with his parents adding to his growing store of mistrust. Within minutes his mind again roamed free in Karl May's vaguely German version of the American frontier.

Every now and then, he looked up, thoughts intruding on his mind's eye. Ever since the harnessman's accident, his parents had become insincere in public, and as frightened at home as that rabbit who had once been his mother's namesake. With a shake of his head he dismissed these thoughts and forced himself to return to his book.

Class was over; crowds of students, Oskar among them, carried their books outside and waited at a corner of the building.

Animosity had been building towards one of their classmates. Theo was from a pious, Catholic family and was something of a teacher's pet, eager to please his instructors and inform them of other students' misbehavior.

So Oskar and his friends waited, and when Theo appeared, they fell on him, kicking and punching and shouting, "Traitor! Informer!"

By the time the young mob was finished with Theo, the *Jungvolk* meeting was about to start, and Oskar looked over the members of his group, his brood. The *Jugend*, the older Hitler Youth, who wore the increasingly familiar black and red swastikas on their arms, was meeting at the same time, and he made sure to keep out of their way while chatting casually with a few of the others.

A noise behind him made Oskar wheel around. One of the older boys was charging into the crowd, sending children sprawling. He had been nicknamed Betz, or Ram, because he took such pleasure in charging into the unwary, punching and kicking and flailing.

Oskar made sure to keep his distance from Betz and boys like him; their admiration for fighting and tackling played a part in his trying to hold onto his leadership in the younger group, the *Jungvolk*, rather than moving up to join the older boys in the *Jugend*.

Oskar edged in the other direction and glanced again towards the building's entrance.

"Hey, Oskar!"

He turned. "Willie! I looked for you at school today but didn't see you. I was hoping later on we might . . ." He stopped. Willie's eyes were wide, startled and focused on something behind Oskar. Instinctively, Oskar whirled and stepped to one side, just as Betz flew by and tumbled to the ground. The older boys, the *Jugend* leadership, were lined up watching and laughing. They applauded Oskar and ridiculed Betz, who rolled over, and leaned up on one hand.

"How'd you do that?"

Oskar held his breath for a moment, was relieved when Betz turned away, then gratified at the subtle and respectful nods that came his way from the *Jugend* leaders.

After an hour of reading and discussion, Oskar took his *Jungvolk* charges out into the streets for a series of paramilitary exercises. Up and down the streets they ran, singing, hiding behind anything big enough to shield a little body, calling out signals and salutes, and all with the earnest urgency of children playing adult games. As they passed shops and Oskar saw his reflection in the glass windows, he remembered the words of one of his teachers. Theirs had been a lesson in German cultural history, of Germany's historical greatness and richness of culture. But somehow the tenor of the lecture had changed to a familiar refrain: the disintegration of their culture and society, and how it was all the fault of the Jews.

The Jews, the boys had been told, had infected the arts and business world; these creeping parasites were said to be everywhere. Oskar was told that some even had shops in town. One, a textile shop, was on the main street, near the open square where the youth groups met and were inspected before beginning their activities. Oskar passed the store frequently but never noticed anything strange or suspicious. Its owners appeared to be normal people, not at all the "ugly Jews" shown so frequently on wall posters or in newspapers.

The boy's mind was a confused swirl of ideas and suspicions: perhaps the store's owners were masters of the art of deception, hiding their "Jewness" behind pleasant masks. On the other hand he had noticed "good Aryans" who appeared to kowtow, whose public opinions and posturing were different from what they whispered in their own homes.

Which was the deception? Which was to be applauded, which vilified?

He looked back and saw some of his charges lagging and called to them, ordering them to catch up . . . for the Fatherland!

The hysteria that November evening in 1938 began with a radio bulletin on the national radio network, the *Deutschlandsender*, about a seventeen-year-old Jew named Herschel Greynszpan who was said to have murdered a German diplomat in Paris. Oskar's father seemed obsessed with the story and with the growing, nearly hysterical rumblings against the Jews.

The following morning Wilhelm listened to the radio while eating his breakfast. People were said to have risen up, and, in a spontaneous outburst of rage, demolished shops and synagogues all over the country. More than 230 had been killed, three times that maimed and nine of Berlin's twelve synagogues burned.

Wilhelm put down his spoon and turned off the radio. "Oskar, Hilde! You will be staying home from school the next two or three days. Stay indoors. No school, no marketplace, no shopping, no visits with friends and no *Jungvolk*." He waved away questions, his face a strange mixture of impatience and fear. He would, he explained, get them each doctor's notes, legitimizing their absences.

Oskar and Hilde looked at one another. The next day, when Oskar tried to sneak out to satisfy his curiosity, his mother grabbed him by his hair. "Can't you obey your father?" she shouted at him, and he discerned in her voice that same strange fear.

After a few days Oskar and Hilde returned to school, and their lessons went on as if nothing had happened. His friends asked whether he had seen the demolished shops and homes of the Jews and when he admitted he hadn't, they went together to the textile shop on the square and stood silently; its main display window had been smashed and the store had been ransacked. The windows of a second-floor apartment opposite the shop were broken, too.

"If you see something you want in there, just take it," one of the boys said. "It's free!"

Oskar ran home, found his parents, and told them what he had seen. His father looked up from his newspaper; for some reason he was furious. "Why can't you obey? Didn't I tell you to return home from school immediately, no delay, no detour? I don't want to tell you again: don't go near those places. Stay away from those stores!"

"You'd better start listening to your father, instead of your class-mates," Sophie added, the color drained from her face.

His father went back to his newspaper. "Listen to this, Sophie. They say it was a popular uprising over this, what was his name, Gru-enspan?"

"Popular?" mused Sophie. "But it was in the middle of the night! And everywhere. Oh, please, Wilhelm. It was anything but. The government created the whole thing. It's plain as that plate in front of you."

"If we know what's good for us, we'll keep the children home, our mouths closed and eyes open. Oggie, you and your sister go do your homework. Right now!"

Oskar's mind refused to accept that the incident was the government's work. Hadn't the government already restored much of their pride, the safety of their streets, many jobs? Hadn't the government given them the *Jungvolk*, which had lifted him out of his own fears and inhibitions?

But the persistent thought remained: even if they had not been responsible, why had the government been unable to prevent what had happened, to stop the violence? The thought was not really a thought, but an inkling, a hint of a germ of a seed that would grow years later. Something, somehow, was slipping out of control.

On his way to class he heard a melody coming from the music room, peeked in and saw Schwalb, fingers tapping on each beat, singing and writing in a notebook.

"That's good, did you write it?"

The boy was startled. "Oh, hi. You're . . ."

"Eder. Oskar."

"I would have remembered if you'd given me another minute. Thanks. It's about swallows flying to warmer weather."

"Swallows, like your name. Go on. Don't let me interrupt."

Schwalb went back to singing and composing. The song was about longing for a warmer climate, but it did not seem to really be about swallows. It was about wishing for a better life, pretending and acting happy. Smile, the song said, always smile, and never, ever show your feelings.

6

A new, government-sponsored program had been announced. Individual families from one village would swap children with those from the next. The interchangeability of children and parents would demonstrate that children do not belong to the parents, but to greater Germany . . . to the Reich.

Oskar's newly cultivated indifference towards his parents joined with his enthusiasm for the *Jungvolk* to ward off all but the vaguest remnant of homesickness he might have felt. And even that melted away when he tasted the food his new "mother" cooked, which was entirely different from his own mother's food. Her sauces and spices, even the way she set her table—all were new and refreshing. The novelties of his new family and neighborhood dominated his stay: a new house with new furniture, new habits and rules, a new neighborhood to be explored, different local boys with new games played. Long forgotten were the days when he was too shy and intimidated to extend himself out of doors.

And at night, when he might have missed his parents and the comfort of his own bed, he buried himself in Karl May's vision of Old Shatterhand and Winnetou, of Hadj Abu Alif Omar, and the *Lost Treasure in the Silver Lake*.

When he returned home, Oskar asked his mother to prepare his food the way his new "mother" had. Happy and relieved at her son's return, Sophie did as he asked, but was not surprised when, after a day or two, he asked her to return to her old cooking.

During the next year, their parents' conversations would confuse Oskar and Hilde, whose responses would be mixed brews of shock, fear, curiosity, revulsion, and, on Oskar's part, a determined patriotism.

It was on a bright March morning in 1939 that his father was reading about Germany's annexation of Czechoslovakia.

Sophie shook her head. "It's a terrible shame."

"A shame?" Oskar asked.

"To dismantle Czechoslovakia."

The boy shook his head, disappointed that his mother's words flew in the face of everything he had been taught. "But can't you read the map? Doesn't Czechoslovakia look like a dagger in Germany's belly? And haven't they badly mistreated the Germans who lived among them? At school we're told that the French boys who had been writing us don't want to anymore. Not very nice, is it?"

His mother looked at him with her familiar mixture of impatience and fear. "Do you really believe this is the boys' idea?" she asked.

A half year later, another morning began much the same way, with Wilhelm quietly reading his newspaper, Oskar greeting him and going into his room to get dressed. It was cool for late summer, and he had just opened a window to enjoy the fresh air when he heard his mother scream. He ran to the kitchen.

"It will never end!" she cried, palms to the sides of her face.

"What?" Oggie looked around but saw only his sister, eating her breakfast, and his father still reading the newspaper.

"It's worse than 1918, you have to admit it now, Wilhelm! We're all going to suffer! *Ach*, the criminals!"

"What happened?" he demanded to know.

His father held open the paper for him to read.

"So?" Oskar shrugged. "The Poles deserved it. They probably learned from the Czechs. Why should we tolerate the mistreatment of Germans?"

His mother looked him up and down; her eyes narrowed. "Why aren't you wearing long trousers? I will not allow you to go to school looking like that! And where's your tie?"

"Mother, this is the way I go to school every day. I can wear shorts or I can wear lederhosen. I'll tell you what, you make the choice."

His mother looked at him for a long time. Finally, she shook her head. "What happened, Oggie? *Ach*, what has happened to us? We've become . . . I don't know what! Oggie, don't you see this?"

"Shorts or lederhosen?" He smiled at his mother. "It will be okay."

"Such puffed-up words . . . those bandits." His mother turned away, shaking her head. "No, Oggie, it will not be okay. It will never be okay."

A few days later, Wilhelm Eder was drafted.

On the radio and in the newspapers Hitler declared that he had worked tirelessly for peace; he had tried to talk with the Poles, proposing, cajoling, but without success. The Polish government had refused to negotiate.

Once Poland was attacked, Britain and France briefly hesitated before honoring their commitment to defend their ally. After a few days of debate and wrangling, on September 3, a beautiful late summer morning, a clear day fit for strolling by glittering waters or inhaling fragrant pine forest air, the major European powers did finally fulfill their obligation to Poland and declare war on Germany.

The second world war in twenty years had begun.

Unless they are in a battle zone, as they were in London and Berlin during the bombings of those cities, the enormity of war may be lost on children. But when a parent goes to war, the conflict becomes personal and a hole appears in the family's home life. In the Eder household, there was some small comfort taken because of Wilhelm's age, which would, Sophie hoped, keep him out of combat, and his skill, which would keep him employed where he was most needed, running power plants. Despite his mother's attempts at reassurance, fourteen-year-old Oskar couldn't help seeing the effect of his father's absence on his mother and sister.

Initially, he would be in Czechoslovakia, and, within a year, transferred to France; finally would come the transfer bringing the deeper, unspoken fear: to Russia, as the war opened on a second front. After the tide of the war turned, in the winter of 1944–1945, Wilhelm would fall into the hands of the French army, somewhere in southwest Germany, and would lose contact with his family.

Sophie grew stoic and silent during the war, tending the daily needs of her family, her jolly, "rabbit" qualities a bittersweet memory. She rarely spoke of their father, and when the children asked, she would say, her eyes looking through them, that he was missing.

Initially, the government encouraged cautious optimism and hearty industriousness. Everyone was to help with the 1940 harvest, as Germany's industrial machinery turned to war.

For the Eder family, that meant a month of Oskar helping farmers in a small village in Middle Franconia; they were relatives of his paternal grandparents, Julius and Pauline. For a boy who had loved nature all his life, the visit amounted to a vacation. He bounded through yellow and green fields and shaded woods, forgetting his concern about whom to trust, happy to meet boys his own age who seemed to grow right up out of the ground, boys toughened by nature rather than the streets. He tried to copy them, running barefoot over fallen leaves and twigs, but his village feet were too tender and he went back to his shoes, still watching the boys with admiration, enjoying their company without jealousy or politics. The 1940 harvest was a farewell to nature, as troubling, difficult years loomed, but it was also a time he would return to later. Nature and forests would be spiritual touchstones for Oskar, providing comfort and relief at times from the violence and trauma of men.

One day as he approached the farmer's house after helping with the harvest for a few hours and then playing exhilarating forest games, he found his grandfather standing outside with the farmer, a man of about sixty. Oskar slowed to hear what they were saying. Something about "the front" and France.

The farmer looked at Oskar, who was not quite sure the man was speaking to him.

"Big mistake," the man said.

"Excuse me?"

The farmer shook his head and looked at the ground. "I say it was Bavaria's big mistake joining Bismarck's Second Reich while we could have joined up with Austria and France instead."

Oskar looked around to see if anyone else had heard this heresy, then laughed self-consciously, and went into the house. As he washed for supper, the man's words echoed in his mind, and his derision turned to unease and discomfort. Later he would remember the farmer's words, and agree.

With the escalation of conflicts and annexations into full-fledged war, a rationing system was instituted and ration cards doled out. Oskar used his card to buy bread, which he meticulously sliced into seven portions, one for each day of the week. With care and discipline, he lived on his allotments. Others, meanwhile, were less comfortable with the new system.

A chilly wind blew through the house; the kitchen curtains fluttered and Oskar's mother pulled her sweater close around her shoulders. Oskar took his time eating his bread; Hilde looked down at her plate of potatoes with disgust.

"I cannot and will not eat another potato!" she declared.

"Well, where's your bread then?" Oskar asked.

"You know very well where it is. I ate it yesterday."

"Why would you do that, knowing you'd be hungry today?"

Instead of answering, Hilde began to cry, tears spilling from the corners of her eyes and running in tiny rivers down the sides of her mottled cheeks. "I've become a potato-eating animal! My whole life is nothing but potatoes!"

"You should have saved your bread, Hilde."

"Enough, Oggie." Their mother stood over them, stern but shaken. "It's not her fault, it's mine. It was my decision to give you your own ration cards instead of taking care of the food myself. When your father left it was too much for me. What a disaster the whole business has been! What a mistake!"

Not sure if she meant giving the children their own ration cards or the war itself, Oskar snorted, assuming the former. "I'll tell you what was a mistake: that Hilde didn't join the youth movement to begin with." He shook his head at his sister. "They would have toughened you up the way they did me. I'm in twice the physical condition I was in last year." He smiled at his mother, hoping to cheer her up. "And she would have learned enough discipline there to ration for herself without bothering you or whining about being a potato baby."

Hilde stopped crying suddenly. "I'll eat potatoes for the rest of my life before I join. I will!"

Oskar laughed to hide his annoyance. "Joining's required. You have to do what the government . . ."

"Let them kick me out of school!"

Sophie looked at them both, then pointedly at Oskar. "She doesn't have to go because I say she doesn't have to go. So enough!"

Oskar shrugged and returned to the bit of crust on his plate. "She's only beating her head against a wall. It's her stomach she has to listen to." What he didn't say was that in a corner of his mind as yet untouched by Nazi propaganda, he admired his sister's independence.

When they went to market the following day, Oskar agreed to go along to help carry groceries on the way home.

On the way, his mother greeted acquaintances with the traditional Bavarian salutations "Grace of God" or "Greetings of God," but when she entered the butcher shop, ration cards in hand, and cheerfully spoke to the woman who owned the shop, a young man who was being waited on turned, and shook his head.

"This is an improper greeting now. You must say 'Heil Hitler.'"

Oskar looked up at his mother, who was staring at the man. She quickly regained her composure. "Don't tell me how to greet people, young man!" She allowed her voice to slowly rise.

Fearful of any confrontation that might attract attention, the woman who owned the shop retreated to the back of the store.

The man leaned towards Sophie. "How would you like it if I reported you to the SS?"

A spark came into Sophie's eyes; she could not control herself. "And how would you like it if I reported that you molested me?"

The man's mouth opened and he backed away, looking wildly behind the counter, as though for some authority who might have witnessed such an outrage.

As the door slammed behind him, the shop's owner returned. She smiled at Sophie, her hand to her throat. "Oh, Grace God, I admire your courage! Listen, I have to follow the rationing system, but anything I can spare I will give you when I can. Of course," she added, "I have to charge for it."

Thereafter, Sophie came home on occasion with some extra bones or meat scraps to add to the family's meager rations.

At school, the tension of the war was demonstrated and dissipated through a rash of jokes, both pro- and anti-Nazi, that were whispered in hallways and on playgrounds.

"Hitler and Goebbels took a train to Paris. When they got off the train, they saw a porter coming towards them shouting, 'Baggage! Baggage!' So Goebbels grabbed Hitler and pulled him back onto the train. 'Better we get out of here,' he said, looking around. 'They've already recognized us!'"

A more political joke referred to the Austrian Nazi Party asking for Hitler's help prior to that country's annexation: "Hitler and some of his advisers stood over a fish pond. His advisers threw stones at a fish, trying to catch it. But Hitler rebuked them, calling them crude, and said there are better ways to catch fish. He opened the water outlet, draining the pond, and when the pond was empty, the advisers wanted to grab the fish, but again Hitler rebuked them, and said, 'Why should we appear to be robbers? Let's wait until the fish cry for help, and only then extend our helping hand.'"

Yet another joke poked fun at the known proclivities of Nazi leaders: "The Nazi minister of labor, Robert Ley, was known to be a drunkard, and Goebbels was known to chase young ladies. Both passed away and in paradise each received a fitting present: Goebbels was given a lovely angel, and Ley a big beer mug. They rejoiced, until they found out that the mug had a hole in its bottom, while the angel had none."

To teenage boys, wars, especially when they are not local wars, can be black-and-white melodramas. Victory, defeat, and glory are the stuff of wars, and to many German boys, the quick defeat of France was evidence of victory and glory. The jokes were less a real criticism than a natural outlet of teenage energy towards anything they might not understand, a way, perhaps, of coping. For the moment, Sophie's fears of "a disaster" were not shared by most citizens, certainly not by boys in the *Jugend* or *Jungvolk*.

Most of the young men who had been the boys' teachers at school disappeared that year, swallowed up by a rapidly swelling armed forces. Volunteers and retirees were brought in to teach the boys, who were quick to find fault with their new teachers, perhaps because of the disruption of their routines and the excitement of what was occurring outside the classroom.

One of the new teachers was an elderly, nearly blind man who had been brought in as a math instructor. He doddered into the room, and the boys watched as he felt his way from the doorway to desks, his hands moving along their tops, until he arrived at the front of the room.

The following day, some of the boys arrived early and smeared the tops of the desks and the backs of chairs with ink. When the new teacher felt his way towards the front of the room, he stopped halfway and commented that the furniture seemed wet. The comedy went on for days, with the teacher carrying on his lessons with blackened hands and smudged face, until, before class one day, one boy limped to the head of the class.

"No ink on the desks today!" he declared. Oskar saw that it was his old friend Willie. "This man volunteered to teach us and we should respect him. He really should be retired now, a grandfather playing in the park with his grandchildren. But instead he volunteers his time to come and teach us mathematics. Shouldn't he be safe here from this kind of mischief? We've had our fun now, haven't we?"

At first, the boys seemed uncertain. Two boys in the back laughed, and one of them stood up and began to shout something, but Oskar found himself shouting that boy down. He got up and stood next to Willie.

"He's right. Let's leave the teacher alone. Give him a chance."

During that day's class, the teacher seemed to brighten; he was more engaged and animated, as though he knew the boys had taken a liking to him, and as they put their books away, he commented that this class had been a pleasure to teach.

In English class, Oskar's influence was different. The English teacher was a known drunk, seen at taverns until late in the evening, often still showing the effects of the previous night in class the next day.

A discussion one day involved an English description of the desert, populated, the teacher explained, with Bedouins and camels, which he said were stupid, boorish animals.

"Stupid, yes!" shouted Oskar. "But they know where the water spots and wells are, and can always find their way back to them."

The teacher paled, as though he understood the inference, and said, "Yes, I know what you mean." The class burst into laughter.

By mid-1941, soon after the war with Russia began, prisoners of war began appearing around town. The lack of able-bodied men and the plethora of prisoners soon led to an arrangement with the local authorities whereby one was allowed to apply to have a prisoner work at one's home.

Oskar and Hilde's mother applied, and soon three gaunt, haggard Russian POWs could be seen dragging coal into the basement to feed the furnace. They also peeled potatoes and helped to harvest the garden.

Occasionally, Sophie would offer one something to eat, which was strictly forbidden, and, terrified of a trap, the prisoner would turn away. Over time, however, she won them over, bringing the half-starved men down to the basement and feeding them cooked vegetables. When they recognized her kindness, Oskar saw and never forgot the stark gratitude that lit their faces.

The middle school Oskar attended in Forchheim had only six grades, so the following year he was enrolled in the seventh at an upper school in Erlangen, which was a few miles and one train stop in the direction of Nuremberg.

"Everyone talks about 'order,'" Oskar complained one day after school. "Order at home, order in the classroom. There is even the Holy Order Blessed Daughters of Heaven. We have to write an essay about it as part of our homework."

His mother turned off the radio. Hilde looked up from her studies.

"Order is a tradition handed down from Frederick the Great," Sophie explained. "It can be a virtue, a comfort. It can help you get your work done, to be industrious. Of course you have to master it by putting in effort. Perhaps that is where the problem—"

"We also learned about the beauty of the tank and artillery corps. Are they examples of 'good' order?"

His mother and sister exchanged glances. "Well . . . ," Sophie began.

But Oskar didn't let her finish. "The artillery corps does seem as though they have to be orderly, to keep the equipment clean and working. And in combat there is an exact procedure that ensures the most orderly, effective use of the guns. In the tank corps it's much the same. Efficiency in the military is crucial to the success of any campaign. But at home, I'm not at all sure it's so important. After all, how I put my books and clothes away is not really—"

"You found their talk of artillery and tanks attractive?" his mother asked, half holding her breath.

"Oh, I'm not so interested in artillery or tanks. They aren't half as interesting as they are made to sound," Oskar proclaimed, and his mother sighed with relief; his sister, too, for all their differences, seemed to relax, if only to see their mother happy.

"No, I'm going to be a pilot," Oskar announced, beaming. "And join the engineer corps. So instead of being drafted into the infantry, or the tanks corps, I'll have the double benefit of flying like a bird, and getting trained as an engineer."

Sophie was mortified.

"You know that song, the one about becoming a new kind of man by learning to fly?"

"Excuse me, I'm not feeling so well." Sophie covered her mouth and hurried from the room.

"Oggie!" Hilde gave her brother a sour look. "You've made our mother sick."

He gave his sister a secretive look. "The boys on the train all smoke. Well, they don't really; they pretend, collecting dried grass and trying to smoke it. I even tried a little." He made a face. "It burned and scratched my throat. I don't know why anyone smokes. I'm going out. There's a Youth Group meeting in an hour."

"You're really going to be a pilot?" When her brother nodded and headed for the door, she called after him. "I'll bet you'll find plenty of real cigarettes in the Luftwaffe."

Late that night Oskar was roused violently from a sound sleep by a cacophony of screaming sirens, yelling, and footsteps. He heard his mother shouting that he had to get dressed and get out of the house. The civilian guard was coming around to supervise the drill. He hopped frantically in the darkness, trying to find his clothes and one of his shoes, an odd image in his mind's eye of his blind mathematics teacher. He was the last to stumble outside, where he found his mother, his sister, and what looked like half of Forchheim waiting.

"There's something to be said for order at home," his mother whispered, as he took his place for the civilian guard's inspection. "Helps you find your clothes."

The following evening he remembered, and was careful to stack his books where he would find them, to fold his clothes in a neat pile, and to leave his shoes together under his bed.

7

On an overcast afternoon in 1942 Oskar jumped off the train, ran all the way home, and found his mother sitting at the table with his sister, exactly as they did every day, the radio blaring what he considered to be BBC propaganda.

"I've got something to tell you, Mother," he crowed. "And you, too, Hilde. Do you know what they gave me for my leadership in the *Jungvolk*?"

Neither answered. His mother gave an annoyed wave.

"Mother! I'm talking to you!" His voice grew proud and patriotic. Now she looked up, giving him a look only a mother could give an aberrant son.

"I'm sorry, Mother. I was so excited. They've invited me to join the civilian guard. I'll be guarding you and Hilde and everyone else at night! Some nights, anyway. And the best is, they've given me a motorbike!"

His mother pointed to the radio. "Listen."

Though he usually refused, on principle, to listen to the English broadcasts, he did as he was asked.

The announcer was talking about prisoners of war, as well as Jews and Communists, being killed in German "detention camps."

Oskar sighed and sat down. "You are so gullible, Mother. And Hilde, why do you encourage her? This is wartime and you believe the enemy! Think about it. They sneer at us and we at them. You think the enemy does nothing wrong? Of course they are going to make these claims. It was you, mother, who told me we were descended from Frederick and Ludwig, and also Kant and Beethoven. Open your eyes. In wartime, we defend our country, any way we can. The enemy does the same."

"So you're in the civilian patrol now?" his mother mused. "And with a motorbike!" She tipped her head to either side, pretending to be impressed.

"Well, I have to go to Nuremberg tomorrow to pick it up. I start patrol tonight."

Sophie took a deep breath and gave a quick exhale. "And if you catch someone who isn't where he is supposed to be?"

"I'll do my job."

A few nights later a patrol which included Oskar rounded a corner and came across a young man they had never seen before, a rarity in Forchheim. When they asked who he was, he stamped his feet and refused to answer. Oskar demanded an identity card, but the man could produce none.

"If you will not open your mouth, I will help you," Oskar shouted, and slapped him across the face. "Still nothing? Well then. We're taking you to the police."

Dragging the man by the collar, the patrol arrived at the police station, where it was eventually discovered that the man, who must have been too terrified to speak, was from the next village and was staying with a local family while helping out in the butcher shop.

The next day Oskar waited, braced, to hear the lecture from his mother, the teasing from his sister. His overzealousness had been proven wrong, and had made him look foolish. In his mind he had prepared arguments, pointing out the greater perspective, the protection and safety he was affording so many, and how they were worth the risk of a mistake which, after all, had ultimately harmed no one except, however briefly, a foolish young man.

But the criticism, the teasing, the lectures never came. Despite the newly fallen snow and temperatures below freezing, his mother was outside stamping the cold from her feet with a group of neighbors, all of whom were incensed. Hilde was with them, her cheeks flushed with anger and the cold. Oskar remained just inside the door, listening.

"We just won't do it," his mother was insisting. "If we stay together on this, there's nothing the government can do."

"I'll be the first to admit the Nazis have done a good thing or two, but they can't do this," another neighbor was saying, her voice rising sharply. "Just let them try."

"I'm with you," said a third. "My Werner wouldn't stand for it and neither will I. Of course, he's at the front, but if he were here, ooh, I don't want to think about it!"

"How can they expect us to fight an atheistic enemy to support another atheistic regime?"

"I don't know," said a fourth voice. "Maybe it's only rumor. I tell you, if it's true, we'll be no different from the Bolsheviks! They'd never!"

"Hilde!" Oskar whispered. "What's going on?"

She rushed to him, her voice a secretive whisper. "A new government order. We have to take down every crucifix in the whole town. In the school, in the court, in every official building."

Oskar didn't answer. The order was unexpected, but what followed two days later galvanized the town.

The mothers of Forchheim turned out in a demonstration,

carrying banners, signs, slogans, and crucifixes of every size and material. They then went a step further, directing the local politicians to inform their superiors that the mothers of Forchheim would write their sons at the front, telling them to put down their arms and return home. They would tell the young soldiers, the pride of the Nazi regime, that the government had forbidden their own mothers' crucifixes.

"I tell you, Willie," Oskar breathed when he saw his friend at school, "I wouldn't have believed it if I hadn't seen it for myself. The mothers intimidated the government."

Willie did not seem impressed. "We're seeing new things every day. Have you been approached by the SS to bring your *Jungvolk* to SS headquarters on certain afternoons?"

"No, but I know it's done in other places. They have parties."

"Recruitment parties," Willie corrected. "And they're not exactly voluntary. The boys are given a lot of beer and told how wonderful the SS is, and when they are good and drunk they're coerced to sign up. The question is, are you going to do it with your group?"

Oskar shrugged. "I can only tell my boys to ask me before they sign anything. I can also ask that no official meeting be arranged without my knowledge and consent." He made an openhanded gesture. "Look, I'm not against the SS, particularly. I don't really know much about them. But this practice"—he clucked and shook his head—"it's against everything we're taught to believe about having honor, being German. Getting kids drunk and signing them up for the rest of their lives? Dishonest, and pretty disgusting if you ask me."

Once his father was gone, Oskar had no access to information on the progress of the war; he refused to believe what his mother heard on the radio, nor was he aware of events in Asia or the United States.

He knew of German victories because they were trumpeted in newspapers and on the radio. He knew that Germany's nonaggression pact with Russia was followed by the invasion of Poland. He was aware that resistance by armies once touted as the mightiest on earth had been feeble. In June of 1940, France surrendered, followed soon after by the relentless bombing of England. And Churchill's famous vow never to give up was, of course, ridiculed in German radio broadcasts.

Only those facts that would reflect positively on the Fatherland were left intact in German news reports. When, by the summer of 1942, the tide of the war turned on both fronts, and the Russian winter halted at Stalingrad what had been an inexorable German advance, the German newspapers reported what facts they had, while editorials urged unity and patriotism.

Oskar understood and accepted what he believed to be his duty to the Bavaria he had been taught to love. Even had he learned of the turning tide, he would not have believed it. He knew only that his application to become a new kind of man, a man of the future, a flying man and, later, he hoped, an engineer, had finally been accepted.

The very real possibility of combat and perhaps even death was heroized by the Nazi propaganda machine; the horrors of war were so garlanded with laurels of glory that their bitterness was rendered palatable. In theory, at least, Oskar was ready to do his duty.

The *Jungvolk* had prepared him, to a degree, for basic training: he was used to the need for physical fitness and to the order, the regimentation, and the smell of grease and machinery, which, he hoped, would stand him in good stead as an engineer after the war.

All new recruits, regardless of their destination, trained together. Future pilots, infantrymen, and tank corps commanders all were treated as one.

An officer lectured the men on the benefits of vegetarianism. The thin, agile, middle-aged career soldier exhorted the men to follow his healthy example, promising that they too would be able to train longer and harder without tiring. Oskar watched him with little interest, hearing nothing in the man's arguments to convince him to change his diet.

Within several months he and many others were transferred to Gatow, a small town not far from Berlin, to begin flight training.

It had been Sophie Eder's hope that her son would wait as long as possible to enlist or that the government would be delayed in drafting him. His intention to become a pilot may or may not have been attributable to an idealistic song; however, the choice met with Sophie's approval. While she privately grieved over her husband's enlistment and feared for her son's safety in combat, once Sophie accepted the fact of Oskar's military service, his choice of the Luftwaffe may well have been due to her influence. Pilot training was, after all, time consuming, exacting. If it would delay his departure for active combat, she was for it, especially once she saw the tide of the war turning. Perhaps, she hoped, Oskar might escape combat entirely.

The planes of the Luftwaffe varied widely in their technology and purpose. There were Messerschmitts, bombers and the more famous fighters; there were Buckers and Arado training planes, as well as Heinkel bombers and Focke-Wulfs. A host of Junkers planes included the Junkers W34, referred to as the Ju34, a single-engine transport, which would eventually be one of Oskar's training planes.

The men had been at pilot training school nearly a week. Oskar had heard that the British and Americans trained their pilots by placing them directly in the aircraft they would fly in combat or transport. The Luftwaffe's system was different; pilots were initially taught to fly gliders, like the DFS 230 or 331 or the Gotha 242. Once mastered, the gliders were followed by small, single-engine planes, and then by a progression of more complex and powerful aircraft, until the pilots were adept and comfortable in whatever plane the Luftwaffe had chosen for their permanent assignments.

He sat in the tiny glider, the front of which was affixed to a rope, while the other end was wound around a mechanical winch. The spool turned, the rope wrapped around it, and the glider was reeled in at increasing speed until it was airborne, whereupon the rope fell away.

Except for the rush of the wind in his ears, Oskar flew in breathtaking silence. He looked up and saw only clouds, while, below, the land stretched out in tiny parcels, each with its own color, hue, and texture. He felt a brief unease; the German saying "air has no beams" crept into his thoughts. He wondered if he would complete his circuit and land safely.

But exhilaration took over and he was on top of the world, filled with the joy of achievement, remembering the old song and feeling he truly was a new kind of man, a flying man, whose home was in the air. The song ran through his mind, accompanied by the wind's music. Man's nature seemed to have changed, becoming bigger by incorporating the sky into his domain. He was no longer a ground creature; he had dragged himself up and become a creature of the sky.

He would quickly graduate to the larger gliders, which were towed behind planes, and then to small-engine aircraft. Oskar's love for flying grew with each challenge and the knowledge of each new plane. His interest in the mechanical and engineering aspects of the aircraft, their function and maintenance, was a mature version of the curiosity he had exhibited as a child at his father's electric plant, and perhaps a result of his father's encouragement of it. He remembered his father's confident "Oggie can do it!," and now, in his new life as a flying man, he was himself confident and was indeed able to learn and demonstrate a facility with all he was asked to do.

With small-engine planes came a different kind of exhilaration, one of power. While the luscious silence of the gliders was gone, it had been replaced by a mastery of motion. In the air, acrobatics, loops, twists, turns, and rolls were thrilling possibilities, though of course not all right away.

During the winter of 1943 and the spring of 1944, as Oskar learned about single- and dual-engine planes, the excitement of training was often interrupted by English and American air attacks.

The men were smoking, which bothered Oskar; he remembered the weeds and grass the boys had smoked on the train to Erlangen only a few years before, and how it had burned his throat when he tried it himself. He had just returned from sending his mother his extra ration of chocolate, an alternative preferable to cigarettes. He had heard that chocolate, especially the very rich variety available to the pilots, was good for a man's nerves, so he had quickly ended his smoking career and taken up the sweet dessert, much of which he sent home to his mother.

He was walking across the grass not far from one of the airstrips when he heard the alarm and crouched, searching the sky for American or British fighters. He saw one of the German novices in a lightweight training plane, twisting and turning the craft as a British fighter closed in on its tail and fired. The pilot managed to bail out as his plane crashed and burst into flames.

Shading his eyes with his palm, Oskar saw that the pilot's parachute must have become doused with gasoline as he jumped. It was now a useless inferno. As the man fell, burning and screaming, the English fighter came about, trained its sights on the man, and put him out of his misery.

Oskar was rooted to the spot as the English fighter came about again, guns chattering.

Other than overhearing his mother listening to the BBC, Oskar had no experience with the British. He had never met an Englishman, and now had seen this one kill a helpless pilot. All he had learned as a child in the *Jungvolk* and more recently in the army about the superiority of the German was confirmed in Oskar's mind.

The number of British and American planes in German skies increased as the war continued to turn against Germany. The German high command had no reason to inform the average soldier, or even the lower ranks of officers, of the war's status. Keeping what little morale there was had become a priority, along with the most effective use of Germany's waning manpower. The Russian front and the equally dangerous Russian winter had exacted a high toll in German lives, and struggles for manpower frequently arose between branches of the military.

One morning, Oskar was ordered to copilot a training flight to Posen. For that flight, he was told, Hennig would be the primary pilot.

Oskar hoped to fly due east over Berlin, although there had been instructions not to fly over the larger towns and cities. Rain was forecast for Berlin; Posen was expected to be clear and sunny. He hoped Hennig would agree. When he approached the Ju34, he found Hennig, whom he barely knew, already there. Oskar saluted and introduced himself, trying to ignore Hennig's bottle-thick eyeglasses.

Once the engine was started, they waited and checked the

propeller's rotation speed. An average speed of 2200 revolutions per minute was best, the minimum being 1900. Theirs was just over 1900. "Perhaps we ought to visit the repair shop," Hennig suggested.

Oskar considered the suggestion. "How would you feel about spending the day doing infantry exercises in the mud? That's where we'll end up if we put in for repairs." They looked at one another and climbed aboard, reading the smiles on one another's faces, seeing the specks of fear behind them, as well as the choice to fly despite the fear. That brief moment made them more than acquaintances. Seated beside one another, they exchanged nods.

The little transport plane slowly gained altitude, its engine struggling. "Perhaps we should fly over Berlin," Oskar offered.

"It's off limits," said Hennig. "There are so many enemy aircraft over the city, we'll be taken as one and shot down. At the very least the sirens will sound, don't you think?"

Oskar shrugged more bravely than he felt. "Who could mistake this old bird for an enemy aircraft? We'll be fine. Trust me."

As they reached Berlin, which was a bombed-out shell of the proud city it had once been, their propeller sputtered, caught, sputtered again, and managed to keep turning at 1400 rpm.

The plane dropped as though it had hit an air pocket. Below, the streets were covered with debris. The propeller speed dropped to 1200.

Oskar began looking around on either side of the plane, not telling Hennig that he was trying to find a place to put down, but broken concrete and debris littered the shattered streets. The plane dropped again, more sharply.

Oskar looked at Hennig and saw that his glasses had come off and his face had turned a light shade of gray. His eyes were glazed with fear.

The plane nosed down and went into a dive.

Until this point they had shared control of the plane, but now Oskar took control and banked to one side, desperately searching for an open area. Finally he spotted a wide wheat field between concentrations of houses and made for it, his hands working the controls as though the knowledge were somehow in his fingertips. The plane landed remarkably smoothly. Oskar jumped out and looked the aircraft over, astonished that it was undamaged, then helped Hennig from the plane. After a short rest, he radioed their base.

The following day they were called before their commanding officer. Oskar was prepared for a long, loud dressing-down, at the very least.

Their commanding officer looked from Oskar to Hennig and back again. "Which one of you made the decision to pilot this plane into a civilian backyard? Who was at the controls?"

Hennig answered, without looking at Oskar. "It was him."

"I see," said the officer. "Well, Eder. Is this true?"

Oskar nodded. "Yes, sir, but it was only to save lives, sir. There was no intention to—"

"That's enough, Eder. I asked a simple question and you answered it. That will do."

"Yes, sir."

"You are to be commended. Both of you, for making such a difficult landing without damaging the plane. As you know, we have fewer and fewer training flights; the infantry wants you, all of you, to leave the Luftwaffe. They need you on the ground." The officer turned away, took a few steps, then spun to face them. "But my duty is not to make such value judgments. I am an officer and you are cadet officers."

"Not yet, sir," Oskar began. "Actually we are only . . ."

"You are cadet officers," the commander repeated. "As of today."

The fuel shortage grounded much of the German air force, and newly promoted Cadet Officer Eder experienced a short but frightening stay north of Berlin, near Stralsund, which was barraged constantly by the Americans and British. Rumors among the men were that this was where the new V rockets were produced, including the *Vergeltungswaffen*, known as the vengeance weapons, the forerunners of modern rockets. This terrifying prospect explained the ferocious enemy fire.

To Oskar's great relief, his unit was split in half, with his group transferred southeast, to a place near Velke Mezerice in Bohemia, in what later would become the Czech Republic, where Oskar would see no actual combat. As the war drew to a close, the German air force tried to retain its men, keeping them busy with infantry exercises and theoretical study, but eventually, because of the threat posed by advancing Russians, pilots were transferred to ground forces, though here again, Oskar's luck would hold.

Oskar met Heinz, a *Gefreiter* (a rank somewhat equivalent to a private first class), who was something of a philosopher. Heinz would have a long-lasting influence on Oskar's future, as would a jarring, shocking sight and an introduction to a new kind of person.

8

The village was quiet, except for early morning birdsongs and the voices of women on their way to market, sounds Oskar was happy to hear. The silence was pleasant after Stralsund, and could be enjoyed rather than waited out as a lull between sorties and attacks.

The day went by quickly and in late afternoon there was time to walk in the hills with Heinz, his new, well-read friend. "Do you hear it?" Heinz looked at Oskar, who was instantly on the alert, down in a crouch.

"What? Where is it?"

"No," Heinz laughed. "The soft lapping of a lake's waves. It's coming from over there." He ran around a stand of fir trees and Oskar followed. His footfalls on the beds of rust-colored pine needles blended with the rustling of the wind. He found Heinz standing at the edge of a pond, enjoying the moment.

"Think about it," Heinz offered. "Give this all a little thought."

"Think about what?"

"What's happening around us."

Oskar looked around, then upward, towards the bits of white sky visible through the tops of the crowded fir trees. "I like it."

"I mean out there." Heinz sat down, his knees drawn up to his chest, a pine needle between his front teeth. "There's something wrong with us."

"With us? How do you mean?"

"I mean with us. With Germans."

"You mean because the war is going so badly?"

Heinz gave a sad laugh. "Maybe it's good that the war goes badly." He got up and began striding between the trees. Oskar struggled to keep up; Heinz was taller, and took longer steps. His opinions were different, not those of a typical soldier or a typical German. They reminded him of someone, someone he liked but who annoyed him now and then. Someone he could not quite remember . . .

Heinz turned suddenly. "Think of what Goethe meant in *Prometheus*. Don't listen so blindly to the rational ideal. Listen to your heart, what you believe in. You're a smart fellow, Oskar. Look around and think about what Germany's doing. I don't mean how we're doing in the war; I mean the bigger picture, starting five years ago, ten years ago. Use your brain. Think of Hegel. What would the dialectic tell you?"

Not used to such philosophical references in everyday conversation, Oskar was momentarily speechless. "Isn't the dialectic the root of Marxism? And aren't we fighting the Russians? Sounds a bit traitorous to me."

Heinz grinned and slapped Oskar on the shoulder. "My friend. You have quite a sense of humor! What I'm telling you is that there is something wrong with Germany. Dreadfully wrong, and in a very basic way. I suppose it is treasonous to say it, so don't repeat what I'm saying around the base, all right? But it's true nonetheless. Listen, there are some people I want you to meet."

Oskar looked around.

"Not in the middle of the forest. You should be a comedian. I mean downtown. Some friends. You'll see. And I want to bring them a little something. You'll help me, won't you?"

Oskar didn't answer, but was intrigued. He remembered who it was he had been trying to think of. "Heinz, wait." Heinz slowed so that Oskar could catch up with him. "You know, you sound a lot like my mother."

That night, Oskar helped his new friend discreetly carry concealed packages off the base. He knew they were doing something at least mildly forbidden, but he liked Heinz, his independence, his thoughtfulness; he was not simply a disobedient adventurer. He had reasons for whatever he was doing, and Oskar had learned in the short time they had been acquainted that he admired his new friend's values.

He realized after they had walked for a while that they were heading for a group of houses.

"You're bringing me to meet Czech civilians?" he asked, not sure he believed what his friend appeared to be doing. "But what about the no-fraternization rules?"

"So go back if that's the way you feel. But I think you'll like these people. Just some folks and their nice old grandma. Besides, how will anyone know?" Heinz gave him a merry smile. "Were you going to tell the major?"

Oskar waited while Heinz knocked on a door, which was answered by a young man who smiled at first, then saw Oskar and looked frightened and concerned. He and Heinz had a short, fierce discussion after which the two soldiers were beckoned into the house, the young man peering anxiously around outside before closing the door behind them.

He led them into a back room where a group of a half dozen

waited: four men, an elderly woman, and another woman who was obviously her daughter. They, too, were startled by Oskar's presence, but relaxed somewhat after the young man offered soothing and conciliatory words. Oskar felt rather than saw the eyes dart his way whenever his attention was elsewhere.

Heinz began pulling food from packages and handing it out. Everyone spoke in a foreign language, which Oskar quickly realized was Czech. He could feel their camaraderie and his exclusion, but after a time, the elderly woman gave Oskar a tentative smile. She tapped her chest and said something in Czech.

"Grandma," translated the young woman. "Call her Mamushka."

Mamushka's eyes brightened, silently asking who he was.

"Oskar," he said.

Mamushka said something else and nodded toward the young woman, who bowed her head slightly.

"She's explaining that I am her daughter." She shrugged. "I teach school, so I know a little German."

Mamushka said something else, then looked at Oskar as though waiting for an answer.

"She wants to know if you are married." Before he could respond, the teacher answered her back and they both laughed. "I scolded her for not seeing that you are too young."

Oskar gave a self-effacing shrug towards the older woman. "Tell her I have a sister and mother in Forchheim, in Germany. Does she know where that is? And my father is in the army. Somewhere in Russia, I think."

Mamushka listened attentively, then set about helping the men distribute rations while carrying on a spirited conversation with her daughter in Czech, some of which was translated for the benefit of the two Germans.

Mamushka appeared to be the leader, and her questions and comments concerned day-to-day matters rather than policies or philosophies. Food, plumbing, family, conditions in the town, and the circumstances of particular people Oskar had never heard of all were questioned, commented upon, and discussed with an openness and ease refreshing to a boy who had been surrounded by fearful friends and neighbors. As Mamushka became more comfortable and appeared to accept Oskar's presence, the men, who for the most part had kept silent, seemed to relax as well.

Finally Heinz stood to leave, holding his hands out first to the teacher and then her mother, who turned from Heinz to Oskar, spoke a few words and took both his hands with her thick fingers.

Her daughter laughed. "She says, 'Darling, I love you. Give me a kiss.'"

Before he could respond, Mamushka had pulled him to her and given him a sloppy kiss on the side of his face.

"Thank you," he said to them all, looking each in the eyes. He touched his own fingertips to the place where Mamushka had kissed him, and followed Heinz to the door. One of the men bade them wait while he opened the door a crack, peered outside, then opened it a bit more, and thrust his head out. Finally, they were motioned through.

Oskar had to hurry, even run, to keep up.

"That was pretty interesting," he panted.

Heinz laughed and glanced back at him. "They're with the Czech resistance."

They walked on in silence broken only by chirping crickets. "But they only spoke about everyday trivialities."

"We don't speak enough Czech, nor they enough German to say much else. I just know they need food, so I bring it to them." He waited for Oskar to catch up, clapping him on the arm. "But you can tell they're good people, right? And they're not the only ones, so think about what Germany is doing."

"The old lady," Oskar said, after they had walked at least another mile. "She has a husband?"

Heinz looked at Oskar with a raised eyebrow. "What do you think?"

A week later, Heinz asked Oskar to return with him to Mamushka's. Oskar readily agreed, but at the last minute was called into the major's office, where he was told he was to leave immediately for a mission in Berlin.

Traveling by train, he took in the charred trees, demolished neighborhoods, and streets covered with chunks of bombed buildings. While he had seen hints of the remnants of the war, nothing he had seen so far had been on so large a scale. It was as though some huge calamity, some plague affecting only concrete and steel, had overrun the city and its suburbs.

When he arrived at the train station, the illusion was broken in a way that would remain with him for the rest of his life. He was walking quickly, head down, concentrating on where he was going and whom he was expected to see, when a commotion distracted him and drew his attention to one side. A crowd had gathered, citizens as well as military personnel, and everyone was talking at such a volume that he was pulled in that direction. But he looked only forward, at the crowd, not understanding exactly what they were doing or what their exclamations referred to.

Finally, he followed their eyes, looked up, and stopped midstep. A chill started in his shoulders and ran down his arms. His legs became cement.

Hanging by a thick rope over the crowd, swaying slightly in what little breeze there was that balmy afternoon, was a German officer. One end of the rope had bitten into the man's neck; the other end was affixed to the ceiling. He had been a major; his uniform was covered with medals over which a placard had been hung.

It read: "I am hanging here because I declared that the war will be lost."

Oskar dragged himself back a step, in part from the force of the words, which were like a hammer against a part of his mind, against what was left of his childhood, his days in youth groups, his years of believing everything he had been told by the authorities. He also recoiled from the smell. The rot and decay had finally reached him.

Speeches rang in his memory, promises shouted by Hitler in years past, about the new kind of man who would rise from the ashes of the old, the new kind of man who would march Germany into the future.

Well, here he was—rotting, decaying, and swaying in the soft breeze.

And Heinz's words, which he had been so quick to dismiss, came back to him.

Something was fundamentally wrong with Germany.

He went on with his assignment but with barely more life than this officer, this man of new Germany. He returned to the camp and for the next few days kept to himself, not answering the questioning looks from the other men, Heinz included.

"You missed a good visit with Mamushka," Heinz said a few days later. Oskar was grateful that his friend did not ask what had been on his mind. He had no interest, indeed no ability, to explain what he had seen or its effect on him. The experience was not only beyond words, it was beyond understanding—a watershed moment in his life he would not fully grasp until many years later.

So he waited.

"They want us to come back, tomorrow. But Mamushka told me not to come unless I bring their new friend: you. What do you say?"

Oskar shrugged. "Maybe." It was the best he could offer.

"Be ready by four. You know where to meet me."

But when they arrived at the house, one of the men took Oskar out again. At first he was concerned that he had somehow been rejected.

The man, who was one of those he had seen on the previous visit, took him to a street corner where they waited. Eventually, in broken German, his companion explained that they were looking for a particular man, a short dark man, probably thin, possibly ill.

Finally, they were hesitantly approached by just such a person, a man whose enormous brown eyes would not meet their gaze, but stared downwards and to one side. The man coughed horribly, at times unable to stop. Oskar looked around, expecting to be accosted by the authorities, feeling odd since technically he was himself an authority.

They returned to the house and one of the men explained that they would like Oskar to return the next day. No further explanation was given.

So the next day, he returned to the house, curious, interested, still deeply affected by his experience at the Berlin railroad station. He was brought into a room with the same shy, coughing man, and left there.

He spoke to the man, who appeared not to understand. After a while, the man made it clear that he had nowhere to go, no food or clothing. He was from Silesia, he said, dropping the name Hirschberg. Oskar did not quite understand whether this was his family name or that of the town he had come from. The man went silent after that. Either he was too sick to talk or conversation did not interest him.

After a long while, during which time Oskar wondered where the rest of the house's occupants were and why Heinz had not been invited along today, he thought of something to offer this suffering man.

"Why don't you contact the Red Cross?"

The man looked at him as though he were crazy.

"They'll give you help, find you shelter."

"I wouldn't dare!"

"Well, I see you speak a little German, anyway. I really do think you should contact the Red Cross." He leaned toward the man. "You're not a criminal, are you?"

Mustering what indignation his condition allowed, the man drew himself up. "I've done nothing wrong. Nothing!"

And then he knew. Oskar sat back. "You are . . . a Jew."

The man hung his head, as though this were an accusation. Then he looked Oskar in the face, eyes bright, his fear drained away. "Yes. I am a Jew."

After a long moment, during which memories, stories, his very education and experience battled with reality, he finally answered, very softly. "But . . . you are a human being." The words were a revelation to himself. "You'll be helped."

The sickly man gave Oskar a look accusing him of terrible naïveté, followed by a bitter laugh. "That's what you think."

"Then I will help you," Oskar announced. "When we meet again, I will bring food."

"But all I can give you in return is this." The man removed his gold watch and held it out. "It's all I have left."

Oskar shook his head. "Use it later, when you need food and there's no one to help."

As he hurried back to his unit, a thunderstorm crashed and sizzled in his mind. Far from being a monster, this Jew, this man, was sick, and terrified of the Red Cross. Wasn't helping people the Red Cross's job?

This emaciated coughing man was the monster responsible for every wound Germany had suffered over the last thirty years, and perhaps for generations?

A single thought rained into his mind, which lit up suddenly, illuminated by a lightning idea . . . Heinz had been right.

The four or five visits he paid the Czech underground cell after that day were much more cordial and open. With her daughter's help, the old woman with the sloppy kisses taught Oskar to say "good morning" and "good night." Though Oskar brought food intended for him, he never did see the coughing Jewish man again.

A tiny seed had been planted. It was likely always there, existing even before his mother's anti-Nazi influence, which she had never seen take root. The seed was planted in the boy who sobbed with guilt after pulling the wings off a fly. But before it could grow unimpeded, a forest that stood in its way had to be razed, a forest planted by the German educational system of the late 1920s and early 1930s, a forest planted by monks and neighbors, by newspapers and radio broadcasts. And by the Hitler Youth.

Heinz had helped, and so had the sight of the man hanging in the Berlin rail station; the Czech underground cell with its Jewish refugee had finished the job, allowing the seed to start its upward crawl. It was a seed of horror, a seed of hope; more than anything it was a seed of knowledge. It would be watered, encouraged, and coaxed by people and circumstances in the coming years, and by Oskar himself, who was learning that he could take some measure of control over his own life and opinions. Still, the roots of the old were difficult to excavate, and vestiges remained, to be struggled with on other days, as the seed would grow to a sapling, requiring pruning and occasional cutting back so that it might grow and blossom to its fullest potential, ever striving for light.

9

The back of the truck stank from sweat; no one spoke. Oskar could tell from the sun's position that they were heading east, which worried him. A vision of the coughing Jew appeared now and then in his mind, but Oskar was too caught up with his new circumstances to dwell on recent acquaintances.

He climbed down from the back of the truck and stretched the kinks from his legs, then glanced at one of the men nearest him. "Vienna?" he said.

"More or less," the man answered.

"Between Vienna and Linz," someone offered.

"Closer to Vienna," said the first man.

"Don't get too comfortable," said a major, who was now their commanding officer and who had been riding up front. "We're getting back on the truck right away."

"Russian front," someone muttered.

"That's right. A battlefield east of Vienna."

The men milled and shuffled, some smoked, waiting for the next transport trucks to be readied.

"When you signed up to be a pilot," said the man who had been sitting nearest Oskar, "did you ever think you'd find yourself at the Russian front? Above it, yes, but on the ground?"

The major glared at him. "Anything we can throw in the Russians' paths will do. Pilots, sea captains, infantry. It doesn't matter anymore. They've marched all the way through Hungary and we've got to stop them now."

Transport trucks had begun rolling up and now stood idling and shaking, thin trails of smoke rising from their tailpipes.

The words were just beginning to sink in, forming a kind of paralysis in all of Oskar's muscles except those of his stomach, which had begun performing some kind of gymnastics. He looked around for a bathroom and heard his name called. Considering the situation—that they were all boarding and departing on trucks at once without special designations or jobs—the idea struck him as impossible, a delusion perhaps, brought on by impending death.

Then he heard it again. "Eder! Oskar Eder!"

Another officer, his boots caked with mud, was presenting Oskar's commanding officer with a piece of paper. The two huddled for a moment, and then his own commander began to sputter. "Impossible! The man is to board this truck and travel to the front, right away!" The two argued again, and, finally, Oskar's commander crooked a finger at Oskar.

"Eder! You are to go with this major!"

Oskar did as he was told, standing next to the major's truck while everyone else boarded the transports, which roared away, leaving behind the smell of oil and cold earth. Not wanting to appear insubordinate, Oskar watched the major's face, but it was a blank mask. "Come on," the man said, finally. "Get in."

He did as he was told and together they drove towards Linz. "Do you have special orders for me, sir?"

The major smiled. "We have a friend in common. Heinz recommended you to me."

"How did you convince that major to give me up to you?"

The major laughed. "I outrank him. We'll stay the night in Linz and I'll introduce you to . . . well, to your new commanding officer. We have a sort of unofficial plan."

The next morning, the major woke Oskar up early and bade him get washed and dressed right away. "I received news about your prior unit a few hours ago," he said, over breakfast. He looked Oskar in the eyes. "They were killed last night by the Russians."

Oskar sat back, the breath knocked from his chest. "All of them?"

The major sipped his coffee. "A few were taken prisoner." He continued in the same breath. "Before heading out I want you to meet your new commander. Put down that spoon and come with me."

The major led Oskar into a small barracks, little more than a hut. As they waited just inside the door, Oskar could see a man in a bathroom, shaving. When called by the major, the man came in and gave a halfhearted Nazi salute.

"It'll be just the two of us, now, eh?" said the man. Oskar glanced at the uniform hanging in the corner and saw that the man was a captain. "Pretty good pilot, are you? And I know you feel as we do."

"As you do, sir?"

"I'll take you down to see the plane if you like. Just give me a minute." Oskar nodded, then turned to see what the major thought, but the major was gone. "She's a four-engine and entirely for my own use. You know how to copilot her? Of course you do."

Once he was finished shaving, the captain led Oskar to the runway. "The idea is that even though Germany is finished, Japan might win—probably will. They don't give up over there, do they? So if . . . when Germany collapses, we'll be over there, get it?"

"Over there?"

"In Japan."

"You want me to copilot this . . ."

"It's a Condor. Focke-Wulf FW 200."

The plane was now in sight. Oskar swallowed; the paralysis had returned to his extremities, the gymnastics to his stomach. The plane in front of him would never carry half the fuel to fly to Japan. The captain was laughing and Oskar took a step back. He sounded slightly delirious. "We'll be well received, don't you think?"

Oskar stopped walking. "Listen to me. We can't carry nearly enough fuel and still have the machine guns necessary to fight off an attack. We'll never make it."

"Oh, please. We can sneak out under cover of night and refuel in Iraq. I have pro-Nazi friends there who would be delighted to help us. Then we could make our way to India and finally Japan. It's a perfect plan. I've been thinking it up for—"

"It's a ridiculous plan. We'll be shot down over the ocean in this flying bull's-eye. Better to fall into Russian or American hands. At least we'd be alive. A much better plan would be to retreat into the Alps." He could see the captain's immediate interest in his idea and rushed on, trying to convince him. "There's a German fortress up a ways. I'm sure I can find it. Then, if Germany does collapse, as you're so sure of, you can bet that the Americans will run into the Russians and who knows, probably fight them. Our best bet would be to avoid the whole thing. Forget Japan, forget your pro-Nazi friends. In fact, let's forget this joke of a plane, and take two smaller planes. We'll each fly one and we'll load them with enough food to survive in the mountains until things clear up here."

"You're right. Yours is a better plan. We'll go right away."

After filling dozens of boxes with supplies and loading them into two light transport planes, similar to those in which he was first trained, Oskar waited for the captain to take off. Once the captain was airborne, Oskar began to taxi towards the start of the runway. The steering seemed sluggish, and, after struggling to keep the plane in line, Oskar realized that it was overloaded and would only turn to the left. He stopped his aircraft, losing sight of the captain, who was gradually gaining altitude.

Oskar rearranged the boxes as best he could, and resumed his takeoff.

As the plane struggled to climb, two agile American fighters, P38 Lightnings, made for the little transport. His overloaded aircraft had no chance to outmaneuver them, so he tipped his wings to either side, in the internationally recognized greeting. Neither American responded and Oskar waited to be shot down. But the fighters passed without firing a shot. In the distance ahead, he saw the captain, heading for a meadow.

Oskar landed without difficulty and jumped from his aircraft. They were in southern Austria, near the Yugoslavian border. The captain was struggling with a huge roll of barbed wire he had taken from his plane. He beckoned to Oskar.

"We'll hike up into the mountains. I need you to carry this for me."

"All the way up there?" He pointed up the mountain, which disappeared into the clouds. "Why?"

The officer faced Oskar, squared his shoulders, and put a tense hand on the revolver in his belt. "Do what I say."

They scrambled up the wooded slope, and Oskar fell behind as he struggled with his prickly burden. An idea came to him. He began panting, feigning exhaustion. "Wait," he called. "I've got to take a few breaths!"

But the officer didn't wait. He called back impatiently for him to follow.

"I'm doing the best I can!"

"Hurry up!" The officer waved his pistol. "Run!"

Oskar began to run, but as soon as he entered a wooded area, he dropped the barbed wire and began zigzagging down the hill, dodging between trees, staying low to the ground.

Beyond the aircraft, at the bottom of the hill, stood a villa, and Oskar ran up to its front door and pounded his fist against it, glancing behind him, half expecting the captain to emerge, firing his pistol, from the wooded slope. The door was opened by a slim, elegant man who invited Oskar in, and listened politely to his desperate story.

"I'm an author," the man explained, as Oskar looked around the attractive salon. The man's hand swept over several shelves. "I'm Austrian, and these are some of my books and articles. The Nazis haven't much liked what I've had to say about them; in fact they threw me in prison two or three times. I consider myself lucky to have lived until the regime collapsed in Austria, which in fact is what precipitated my release."

Oskar smiled breathlessly. "I have also been friendly with the underground. In Czechoslovakia. I was trying to get away . . ." He nodded towards the front door.

"So I see," said his host, with a raised eyebrow. He appraised Oskar's muddy uniform. "You're not the usual Luftwaffe pilot, are you? Why not stay here as my guest until things cool off a bit?" He extended an arm towards a sofa.

After a few surreal hours of tea in the author's salon, a convoy of trucks approached and Oskar saw they were German, so he went outside and flagged one down. "That's a mobile engineering workshop you're hauling, isn't it?" Oskar asked. "With some pretty nice precision tools. It would be a shame to see it fall into American or Russian hands. Why not keep it, take it home, start a business? We could do it together."

"I think it's a bit late for that," said the driver. "Or maybe you hadn't heard. We surrendered. The whole country is occupied by French, English, American, and Russian troops."

The news sank in. "Maybe we can slip by them."

As he spoke, an American unit appeared and a huge officer ran up to Oskar.

"What do you think you're doing?"

"I was just about to turn myself over to you, sir. Though I was wondering if I might keep my truck here."

"We'll take care of the truck." He pointed to the insignia on Oskar's uniform. "I'm going to ask you again, what exactly are you doing here? Don't tell me you're with them."

"I was retreating in that plane." He pointed to the little transport.

The American, who had apparently not yet noticed the plane, was suddenly interested. "You're a pilot? You landed that plane on this hill?"

Oskar nodded. "You want to go for a ride, see the countryside?" He looked skyward, hoping a joyride might preclude an interrogation. "Why don't I prove to you I can fly, show you some acrobatics?" He took a step towards the plane, with visions of Forchheim in his mind.

"Maybe we'll go together."

Oskar's spirits lifted; perhaps flying with this American might provide him with protection against being shot down. "I'm nearly out of fuel, so with your permission I'll siphon some benzene from one of the trucks in the convoy." What he didn't say was that benzene was not the right type of fuel for his plane.

He followed the American into the plane and, with some difficulty, managed to start the engine. The only direction in which takeoff was possible was up the hill, which would not be easy. The plane began to roll forward. The American officer was watching him carefully as they rolled faster, nearing takeoff speed, but the nose refused to lift off the ground. The upward sloping meadow, the benzene, and the weight of the huge American all conspired against the struggling little plane's takeoff.

Oskar's eyes were on the ground, waiting for it to drop away, when he noticed a gully cutting across their path. He struggled with the controls, trying to lift the plane's nose enough to clear its other side. The plane slammed into the far side of the ditch, and Oskar and the American officer were thrown forward. Oskar switched off the plane's power to avoid a fire. The American was enraged.

"Enough acrobatics for today. Get out."

"There's another plane," Oskar began. "Right over there. We can get enough fuel by . . ."

"Forget it. You're going to an internment camp where they'll check you out and get word on anything you might have done." The American led Oskar to a transport truck that was filling up with interned German soldiers from the convoy. He climbed in and took his place among them.

They passed open fields, gentle hills, and dark pine forests. Here in the countryside the war's damage was centered on populated areas. Villages and farms. Hanging from a tree on the remnants of one farm were three decaying corpses, a woman and two young girls. The truck slowed as it went by and Oskar was able to read cards hung around their necks that read "we were hung for stealing eggs."

The Americans at the internment camp checked everyone's insignias against their own information, which to Oskar appeared considerable and accurate. Occasionally a prisoner found to be a war criminal or member of the SS was removed. Oskar was examined, asked some questions, and told to wait.

During the first week of June 1945, he was put on a truck bound for Bamberg, north of Forchheim.

He was going home.

10

He arrived exhausted. On the ride back from Austria he had silently viewed a passing panorama of devastation. Cities had been bombed to powder, urban landscapes reduced to bits of rock and bent metal. Forchheim and nearby Erlangen, fortunately, had escaped air raids and, unlike Nuremberg, were relatively undamaged.

Within days of Oskar's arrival, Sophie's joy at seeing her only son safely returned dissipated enough for her to gather her children in the salon and offer a grave description of the war's local tolls. "Your grandfather's house was hit and burned out. Anton and Nikki live on the first floor now, which is all that's livable."

"At least they're all right." He looked at his sister, now a young woman.

"We were lucky," Hilde said. "Bavaria has been occupied by Americans rather than Russians and French, who are enraged at what Germany did to their countries."

"The Americans treated me well." He looked at his mother, and didn't have to ask the question.

Sophie's eyes filled with tears, which she angrily brushed away. "I haven't heard from your father." She brightened. "You ought to thank me, Oggie. Before and after you were drafted, letters arrived ordering you to show up at the SS office."

"I never saw any letters."

"I wouldn't let you see them!" she said proudly. "I burned them all, except one, which I'll find in a minute. I saved it to prove to you that they came. You were so enthusiastic and patriotic, such a boy. I knew if you saw one of the letters, you would have shown up at their office, and probably joined, and where would you be today?" She gave him a satisfied smile. "So? I'm waiting for a 'thank you.'"

The quick anger he felt that his mother had violated his trust by taking his mail disappeared as he realized she was right. He pulled her to him, thanking her in a voice muffled by the folds of her blouse, while noticing how little of her was left.

She pulled away. "I'll be back with something for you to eat."

Sister and brother looked at one another. "She's been ill," Hilde said quietly. "Terrible gall bladder pains at night."

"She's lost most of her teeth," Oskar said.

"Here we are!" Sophie had returned with a plate of bread crusts. "I eat only the insides," she said. "I've been saving the crusts for you, Oggie."

"She says throwing them away would be a sin," Hilde said.

"You always loved crusts, Oggie! You once asked me to make you a cake of nothing but crusts! These are my welcome-home gift!"

Oskar forced a laugh. "So now I suppose I've got my wish!" He took the crusts, which had hardened and were now like small, oddly shaped stones.

"I soak them in a linen sack to soften them up before eating them," Sophie boasted.

Bread crusts were the most plentiful food in Forchheim in 1945, a supplement to the tiny rations allotted by the authorities. He learned to be grateful for them. Later he would credit the crusts with saving his health.

Bread crusts were not Oskar's only unlikely source of luck. He found his way into what small pockets of labor existed to a job repairing electrical wires and restoring the railroad, work well suited to the son of an engineer. While a laborer's wages were meager and the food he could find for himself and his family scarce, Oskar knew that even such an unattractive job was a stroke of luck. With the rations he earned and the bread and crusts his mother and sister saved, the Eder family managed to survive the most difficult months of scarcity in the immediate aftermath of Germany's surrender.

One cloudy September afternoon, Oskar ran to answer the doorbell to find a broken old man in a tattered German army uniform. The two looked at one another.

"You want some bread or something to drink?"

The man recoiled as if he had been pushed. "You don't recognize your own father!"

Oskar ran forward and pulled his father to him. "We didn't know what happened, where you were, if you were a prisoner or had been killed."

His father pulled back. "My grandfather fought in two wars; my father in two; I myself fought in two wars. Ours is a country of wars. Some advice for you, son, you'd better get out of here as soon as you can."

Once the family had calmed down and dried their eyes, and once Wilhelm had been washed and fed and given a chance to rest, the family listened while he told them of life in the engineer corps of the

German army. His primary weapon had been his age. A soldier in the First World War, initially he had been too old for combat, though during the desperate days towards the war's end, his age would not have protected him.

He did what he knew, happy to be away from the politics, the Nazi arm-twisting that had been part of civilian life. Ironically, it was in the army that he found freedom from the Nazis. Forced to enlist, he went about what he did best, running power stations, without looking past the day's rations or his own survival and comfort.

Happy to have him back, neither Oskar, his sister, nor his mother dwelt on any moral questions surrounding Wilhelm's involvement in the war or his understanding of its place in history.

He had been in Czechoslovakia and Russia and, later, had fallen into French hands and was kept for six months as a prisoner of war. He did not describe his life as a French prisoner, except to say that the French were eager to exact revenge for what the Nazis had done to France.

Sophie threw herself into the task of restoring Wilhelm to good health, and after a few months of healthy if meager rations and bed rest, Wilhelm began to resemble his former self.

The American reeducation program would take time, Wilhelm was told, and he would not be able to return to engineering or running power stations before he was through the de-Nazification process, so he found a new use for an old hobby and opened a stamp-collecting shop in Fuerth, Nuremberg's sister city.

Americans enjoyed buying stamps as souvenirs, often paying as much as half their price in powdered eggs and milk, which Wilhelm was more than happy to accept. While he spoke no English, Wilhelm was able to pantomime his sales. The system worked well, since the Americans procured food much more cheaply than he could, so when he was paid, his take in food was higher than it normally would have been in currency had he used the money to purchase food. Wilhelm occasionally requested payment in cigarettes, which were scarce and in demand, and which he then traded to local tobacco-starved farmers for bread, eggs, and cheese.

The material goal of de-Nazification was a certificate which allowed one to get a job. In local German slang, the certificate was called a Persil-Schein, the brand name of a common powder used for washing surfaces. Earning a Persil-Schein certificate implied that one's Nazi "stains" had been scrubbed away. The reality, Oskar found, was that, like the product it was named for, the cleansing was often only on the surface.

"So, the railroad's finished?" Wilhelm looked at Oskar, who was reading in a chair in the corner.

Oskar looked up. "The part I was working on in the shop is finished." He went back to his book.

"So what now?"

"Those who want to keep working will be transferred to wherever the work is. They're putting workers up in railcars."

"I don't think that's what your father meant," Sophie said, and Oskar saw his mother and sister watching him as though waiting to hear something important. Even now, after coming home and seeing his father nursed and fed back to health, Oskar felt apart, different. It did not occur to him that the war might have changed him, that watching the foundation of his world crumble away and having his own moral center spin out of control might have distanced him from those who had provided his emotional foundation.

"He meant what now . . . for Oggie?"

"I'm not interested in sleeping in railcars."

"Oggie." His father sounded impatient. "What are your plans?"

His sister started to say something, but Oskar shifted his glance to her and she seemed to change her mind.

His father did not wait for his answer. "The university at Erlangen will reopen in January. You have the background in technology and physics, perhaps . . ."

"All well and good," his mother countered, "if Germany is to be turned into a potato field, as that American, the treasury secretary . . ."

"Morgenthau," Hilde offered.

"Didn't he suggest such a thing to Roosevelt?"

"Well," Sophie said kindly. "That's what they say. Maybe you could become a physician," she continued, her tone indicating she expected her son to agree.

"Where would the money come from?"

"Never mind that," said Wilhelm.

"Your father saved his salary, even during the war," said Sophie. "The stamps sell well and he can return to his former position after the de-Nazification program."

"Which won't take very long," Wilhelm promised. "The head of the *Spruchkammer* where they make these decisions knows me for years, and he knows I'm no Nazi."

Oskar went back to his book.

"What's that you're reading?"

"You wouldn't be interested."

"I wouldn't have asked if I wasn't interested."

"It's called *Life of Ramakrishna*."

"What is it?"

"It's about a man who lived in India a hundred years ago. He sought God, and he believed that no particular country or religion or age could say they were the ones who spoke for God."

"Why are you reading it?"

"I was in the American library at Erlangen, and a very helpful librarian suggested I might find it interesting."

His father shook his head. "That's not what I—"

"A German wrote this book?" Sophie interrupted.

"A Frenchman," Oskar said. "Romain Rolland was his name. He was a soldier in the First World War and had been a German prisoner. He knew that many of the French pray to Jesus, Mary, and Joseph for victory before going to battle. As a POW, he noticed that the Germans did the same thing. So he saw both sides praying to Jesus, Mary, and Joseph and wondered how God decides which prayers to answer. He was confused and wanted to understand religion better, and he came across the writings of this man, Ramakrishna."

His father was shaking his head, turning to his wife. "Is there something else I can have to eat?"

"It sounds interesting, Oggie," his mother said. Her words were a pat on a little boy's head, telling him to run along and play.

Oskar was happy to play . . . on the bright white field of the printed page. He played voraciously and constantly. The book about Ramakrishna attracted him as though he were a flying insect and the long dead spiritual seeker a bright light.

He read that during years when faith and genuine spirituality were fading and giving way to materialism and cynicism, huge numbers of followers were drawn to Sri Ramakrishna and his shining proofs of the existence of God, attracted by his personal magnetism and apparent lack of ego. These followers were from all religions, all backgrounds and walks of life. Far from insisting that his own particular interpretations be followed, Ramakrishna preached the harmony of religions. Those who flocked to him found paths to enlightenment and spirituality as diverse as their own backgrounds.

Oskar devoured the book as though it were a banquet and he a starving man. He would soon go back to the library, to his kind American benefactor, seeking a second helping, and a third.

One night, after hours of quiet study, there was a soft knock on his door.

"Come in," Oskar whispered, and was surprised to see his sister peeking tentatively at him, eyebrows raised.

"Come in."

"I'd like to hear more about what you're reading."

Oskar launched into an earnest description.

"I was wondering . . . if I might borrow one of these books—when you're finished, of course." She gave a half-embarrassed shrug.

When he had finished reading about Ramakrishna, he moved on to Vivekananda, an influential and prolific young swami and disciple of Ramakrishna's who wrote and lectured in America and Britain before returning to India and founding a mission. His appetite for knowledge and search for meaning whetted, Oskar continued to satiate both, devouring the works of European philosophers and literati including Kant, Schopenhauer, Tolstoi, Ortega y Gasset, Thomas à Kempis, Pascal, and Descartes.

Wanting to learn the genesis of Germany's mistakes, he scoured the history of Bismarck's Second Reich, noting the parliamentary claim of one Reichstag member and academician who claimed to have dissected hundreds of human corpses over many years, but never found a soul.

When a person lacks a particular vitamin or nutrient, he may find himself craving a food or beverage containing it, and may find its taste especially delicious. Oskar's mind, reeling, wounded by the amputation of its core beliefs, was salved and nurtured by his reading. That there might be some universal meaning became a flickering glimmer of possibility. The stem of the baby sapling of Oskar's hope grew a tiny bit stronger, tentatively pushing in the direction of that flickering light.

The words of what he had read the night before resonated in his mind, fitting themselves to the motion of the train, jostling comfortably along with the metallic grunts and rattles. He caught the eye of the boy standing just down the crowded aisle. Oskar looked away, scanning the rows of seats for an empty place, but found none and returned his gaze to the passing greenery and his thoughts to the mysteries of eastern spirituality.

The boy was edging toward him. "You're Wilhelm Eder's son, right?"

Oskar didn't answer right away, but searched his memory, found what he was looking for. "Ah. Fritz. Your father's . . ."

"The district governor, yes. But don't let that stop you from talking to me! Our fathers were good friends, so no need to be intimidated."

Oskar nodded.

"Going to the university?" Fritz asked. "What are you studying?"

"I'm not sure yet. I was considering medicine."

"What about law?"

"I'm not really interested in law."

"So? Once you have a law degree you can do anything. It opens doors. Take my word."

Oskar remembered Fritz's father and respected him. Like his own father, he had been forced to join the Nazis but was not a true believer. During the day Fritz's suggestion resonated in his thoughts, and that night, instead of reading, he lay thinking, one hand over the other on his chest.

The following semester, in unheated classrooms, shuddering in his thin coat, writing with half-frozen fingers, Oskar began to study law. He appreciated the structure and order of law because, unlike the political order he had once so mistakenly trusted, he believed he could trust its underpinnings.

During the last few months he had come to feel at home on the train; its motions and sounds had grown familiar, were comfortable and conducive to thought. This was part of his new, character-building life as a law student at the university at Erlangen.

The train was crowded with laborers, farmers, women, and students who had become the backdrop of his new life, his new sensibility. To his right was Georg, who had been a captain in the infantry during the war and was now making something more substantial of himself. And here, moving toward him, was Baldur, whose father was the director of a school in Forchheim and who himself had been a second lieutenant in the artillery corps. Each had been seriously wounded, yet, Oskar noted, each was now putting his past in its place and struggling to move forward.

Baldur continued to move closer, limping on a prosthetic leg, and when he reached Georg, Oskar watched him go out of his way to slam his prosthesis down on Georg's foot, which had been frozen at the Russian front and his toes amputated.

Georg screamed and Baldur grinned. "A nice experience for an infantryman's stump, eh?"

Oskar recoiled, then regained his composure. "Are you crazy, Baldur?"

But Baldur laughed. "For an infantryman like him, it's heaven. You know how they are." He limped away, giggling, and Oskar saw that Georg was openmouthed in pain.

Several years later, Baldur would become a judge.

Oskar studied subjects including physics, medicine, and philosophy. He particularly liked his philosophy professor, who encouraged his charges to read Kant, which led Oskar to appreciate the idea that inner laws govern humanity's outer existence. With such thinking, he postulated, hostility and war might someday be overcome.

He searched without knowing he was searching. He wondered whether study at a university builds character. He returned to church but found the sermons unconvincing and remote. He took long bike rides in the green Franconian Suisse hills east of Forchheim, finding more spirituality on his rides than in listening to sermons on Sunday mornings.

He formed a friendship with the son of a forester. Heinz Brunner's father was a government official whose responsibility was to see to the health of great green expanses of forest by preventing disease, keeping out poachers, and maintaining the habitat's balance.

"I think sunset is my favorite time of day," Oskar said, as he and Heinz walked in the red glow of the day's waning sunlight.

Heinz lifted his eyes skyward.

Oskar went on. "Half of nature goes to sleep, half wakes up. You can hear the change."

"I can sort out what I think at this time of day," Heinz agreed. "If I'm confused, I can come out here for a few hours and pretty soon I'll know what to do."

Oskar picked up a pinecone and examined it as he walked. "Is hunting part of your father's job?"

"He's a conservationist, and sometimes he has to prevent a particular animal population from taking over." They approached Heinz's cabin.

"By shooting them?"

Heinz opened the door and Oskar was surprised to see heads and horns of animals mounted on the walls. In the center was a person's picture adorned with two deer horns over a cross.

"Who's that? Your father?"

Heinz laughed. "The foresters' patron saint. Legend says that there was a well-known hunter named Hubertus, between the sixth and eighth centuries. As he was about to kill a deer one day, he saw a golden cross between its horns, so he refrained from killing it. Now he's St. Hubertus."

"So sometimes he has to shoot the animals to protect them."

Heinz nodded. "The animals of prey that once kept nature in balance are gone. Now he does the job. Nature can be cruel. Survival of the fittest."

They began walking back the way they had come. Oskar shook his head. "You're lucky, being able to do this for a living. Maybe I'll change my major to forestry."

Heinz laughed. "The classes are full. You'd never get in. But you can always come out here and enjoy this, whatever your major is."

"Then again, if it becames my major, I might not like it quite so much."

That night he sat outside watching the stars with his mother and sister. The door opened and his father brushed a space clean on the steps and sat down. "The engineering I've been hearing about, the new technologies . . ." He shook his head. "I wish I were twenty years younger. Radar, ultra shortwaves, superconductors, rockets developed during the war, and of course the new American bombs . . ."

"Please don't talk about bombs." Oskar kept his eyes on the sky.

"Well," Wilhelm mused, "the Big Silent One finally speaks to his parents! Don't blame me for your nightmares, Oggie. Besides, it's really technology I'm talking about, not bombs."

"When you mention bombs, it's not technology that comes to mind." Oskar finally forced his eyes from the cascade of stars.

"Did you read that bit in the newspaper about those girls in Heroldsbach who had a religious vision?" Hilde looked at her mother, knowing she had to have taken note of the article.

But it was Wilhelm who nodded. "Like the girls in Fatima, years ago, who said they saw a vision of Mary."

"This time just a few kilometers from Forchheim," Hilde said, looking at the sky.

"And always at the ends of wars," said Oskar.

"What do you mean?" asked Sophie.

"Fatima was at the end of the first war, and now Heroldsbach."

"Anyone who goes there to try to worship will be excommunicated," Wilhelm warned.

"I don't think our children are planning on going," Sophie mused. "Interesting, though, that the church would excommunicate those worshipers on the one hand, but not Nazis—murderers who are registered Catholics—on the other!"

"I suppose," Hilde concluded, "Heroldsbach must be the bigger sin."

"Oskar," Sophie said quickly. "I think it's time you joined some extracurricular activities at school, don't you?"

"I hadn't thought of it."

". . . instead of wandering around the forest with that boy all the time. That can't be healthy."

"I'm not really interested in activities, Mother. I have plenty of work."

"Why not ask about it tomorrow?" She waited a moment. "I'm glad that's settled." She sat back on the steps, allowed her head to loll back, and gazed at the parade of light above them. "I remember what fun it was before the first war, finding things to do with the other children. I remember the boys in the glee clubs and the fencing clubs—Oggie, didn't I suggest you look into one of them a few weeks ago?"

"Yes, and I did. In fact one of my friends also recommended it. One of the great fencing goals around here, apparently, is to get one's face slashed. And if the scar isn't that noticeable, you rub it with black pepper to make sure everyone can see it. Evidence of one's swordsmanship."

"I'd have thought a great swordsman would be unmarked," Hilde commented. "It seems that their goal is not to be great swordsmen, but to *appear to be* mediocre ones."

Oskar laughed. "Touché."

He found Fritz on the train the next morning and put his mother's question to him.

"Not that I'll necessarily join anything, mind you. It was my mother's idea, really," he added, as an afterthought.

"I know something you'd like. An evening club."

"What's an evening club?"

"A sort of a glee club."

Oskar made a face. "A glee club? You mean we . . . sing?"

"We drink. And then we sing a little. And then if there's time we do something else, now and then. Singing or going out together, we have a good time."

"So it's a drinking club."

Fritz leaned close to him and gave him a playful shove. "Did you want to have a semantical discussion about it?"

The students played hard at night, but during the day the schoolwork and the afternoon's and evening's homework were challenging.

Oskar's state law professor, in particular, seemed arbitrary and dogmatic in his teaching. The man used his force of intellect rather than clean logic and dialectical process to force his ideas on the class.

Once in state service, the professor suggested, the way to win your case is to appeal it until the opposition runs out of money or nerve—a concept, Oskar noticed, not unlike this very professor's teaching method. He struggled to absorb the material, reminding himself of the degree he would receive and the doors it would open. The class challenged him, not in the academic and legalistic ways he had expected, but morally and ethically.

Bureaucratic solutions, red tape as a means to one's end, were perfectly legal, and might be used to great effect, the professor explained. With effort, Oskar forced himself to swallow the idea, much like eating the pig his father had once put before him.

He found a home in trustee taxes, a new area that straddled civil and tax law. As the final exam drew near, Oskar tried, by observing the schedule, to determine which professor would be testing him. The test would be skewed in favor of that professor's specialty. It appeared that his civil law professor would be in charge on that day.

When he reported for the oral portion of his final exam, Oskar found that there had been a change in schedule, one which realized his worst fears. He found himself seated before his state law professor—all that stood between Oskar and a law degree, between Oskar and a lifetime of opportunity.

After the test, the professor smiled faintly through his thin moustache. "I can dismiss you now and you'll have to take my course all over again." He didn't wait for an answer. "I saw your written exam, you know. It was excellent. Except for a few typographical mistakes, it's perhaps the best in the class." They looked at one another. Finally, the state law professor slapped the top of the desk. "So! You have a choice. I can pass you with the lowest grade or, for a chance for a higher degree, you will have to repeat my class."

Oskar dipped his head, then raised it, chin forward. "I will have my doctorate of law either way?"

"Well . . ."

"I don't suppose anyone would go around calling me Doctor Summa Cum Laude anyway, would they?"

The professor said nothing.

"I will accept my degree then, regardless of the grade. Thank you, sir."

He strode from the building, trying to keep from running, yelling to the sun that he would never have to study state law with that man again.

The glee club was, Oskar suspected, not quite what his mother had in mind when she had suggested he find a diversion. Drinking, dancing, excursions with daughters of club members were all diverting, and he enjoyed the company as often as not, laughing and joking about unimportant nonsense.

Tonight, with the help of an instructor and his delightful wife, the dancing had been wonderful. Everyone had paired up so quickly and, finding himself alone at the edge of the shining floor, the music floating over him, Oskar invited the dance teacher's wife to be his partner. She was petite and soft and light on her feet, and they went round and round together so perfectly that the class stopped to watch. Ignoring the other students, Oskar and the dance teacher's wife whirled in perfect balance over every inch of the floor, her eyes looking up at him while her breath tickled his neck.

The teacher had ordered the music stopped, and for a brief moment they danced on. Finally, the instructor's wife held Oskar away from her. "Good thing you stopped the music when you did," she said to her husband. "The boy's head might have been turned!"

Several hours later, Oskar stumbled off a late train from Erlangen, the night bubbling around him as he tried to figure out the time by looking at the sky. Two in the morning, perhaps, possibly three. The street lamps seemed to glow, or perhaps it was he that was glowing. Something appeared to be swimming around one of the street lamps, and Oskar staggered closer, straining his eyes.

A small swarm of insects circled the light, like atomic particles around a nucleus. The effect of the alcohol melted away and he was suddenly cold sober. He was much like them, he realized, drawn to false lights, wings apt at any moment to be burned, his downfall assured. He walked purposefully home, and crawled into bed, determined to change.

He found himself in the countryside, at the edge of a healthy forest bursting with noisy animals and fragrant flora. The hillside behind him was alive with trees and cows and bustling villages.

A sudden whistle and a deafening explosion blotted out everything. He was instantaneously paralyzed, surrounded by green light. He struggled vainly to move. When finally he managed to budge a finger, he forced his hand to crawl over his thigh, and found it icy cold. His whole body was frozen and Oskar wondered if he were dead or alive. He struggled to open his eyes, and for a moment could not, but then he managed to force them open and saw only more of the same green hue, this time all around his bedroom.

The glow was from the moon, reflected in the green glass face of the radio next to his bed. He sat up, breathed a welcome lungful of air, and lay down again. It was some time before he was able to relax enough to sleep.

The next morning he skipped breakfast and went out without saying a word to his parents or Hilde. He wandered the woods, the dream playing over and over in his mind. He thought of the times his parents had mentioned the atomic bomb.

He spent less and less time at the glee club, stopped drinking entirely and shied away from his old friends. It was time to apply himself, and find a legal apprenticeship.

II

The voices around him grew faint, and the wood panelling disappeared.

The information he had been reviewing vanished and he was faced with Schopenhauer's idea that we cannot directly perceive or experience what is truly real. An evasive nonanswer, Oskar decided; he was searching for bedrock, some kind of philosophical foundation to replace the crumbled ruins he had been left with. A serious applicant for that position must be universal, unshakable, permanent. Individual experience, Schopenhauer claimed, was deceptive, not at all what it appeared. The nature of reality is Will, and, unfortunately for all of us, it is ultimately unfulfillable, inevitably leading to unhappiness.

Unsatisfactory, to say the least, was Oskar's disappointed conclusion. He was looking for building blocks, not wrecking balls. While Schopenhauer built on Kant, he did so in a negative way. Oskar had been excited and motivated by the possibility of universality, but Schopenhauer's view of universality, while impressive, was a mere theoretical possibility rather than a workable solution. He wanted to move forward and Schopenhauer was a lateral step at best.

So he ignored the tugging at his consciousness, and tried a different tack, putting aside abstract philosophy and instead attempting to make sense of something more concrete. He tried to understand what had happened to his country, his heritage, to comprehend what had been so seductive, by reading *Mein Kampf*, but the book, written in low street German, offered no insights or answers. It was nothing more than a monstrous pamphlet. And worse, it made no sense. To Oskar, it was barely more than gibberish.

He struggled to understand anti-Semitism, as though somehow following Hitler's logic could account for the disintegration of his own reality. To raise Germany from the destitution of World War I, it had supposedly been important to have the country focus on its enemies, which would motivate and unite the populace. In terms of pure nationalistic motivation, the strategy had worked. But blaming many enemies, a world of enemies, would have left the Nazis without focus and its people discouraged. Better to distill the list to one.

History had already laid a foundation for vilifying Jewry. Oskar had witnessed it in his early experiences at school, and not all at the behest of the Nazis; Hitler had picked up on a widespread, yet half-formed, rather vague dislike and distrust of everything Jewish and molded it into the centerpiece of a national movement.

He understood why critical Germans had derisively referred to the book as *Mein Krampf*, the latter word meaning spasm, the connotation being that it was a spew of nonsense. But to belittle the book and its philosophy was not enough, not now, so close on the heels of all it had wrought.

Someone was calling his name.

"Mr. Eder!" The judge was shouting. Oskar looked around, shaking the philosophies and debates from his mind, remembering where he was: the ancient stone courthouse in Forchheim. When he had first entered, he had wanted to run his fingers over stone that had seen the days of Charlemagne. The building had an attractive air of permanence. The *Kaiserpfalz* had been one of Charlemagne's administrative offices, as well as a residence when he was in the area. It had been damaged in the Middle Ages and later repaired.

The arguments were finished, the verdict determined, and the burglar was ready for sentencing.

Seeing Oskar's eyes focused on the proceedings, the judge returned to his business, sentencing the man to several months in jail. Oskar glanced at the perpetrator. A shapeless man with a flattened nose and crooked smile. He had gotten what he had wanted, a few months in a heated cell, all accommodations provided. It was why he had committed the burglary in the first place! The winter was cold, the snow drifts deep . . . the jail warm and safe.

A different court, another day, but his thoughts had not changed, only moved further along what had become a natural estuary created by a gasping need for reason. But as an estuary might run into an ocean's tides, Oskar's need for reason ran into an opposing current.

He was in the regional district court of Bamberg, representing the state prosecutor's office, assigned to prepare an indictment. He struggled to focus on the case's facts. A traveling salesman had turned himself in to the police, claiming he had killed a prostitute. He had taken her by mutual agreement into some bushes and, during their intimacy, had felt his wallet, stuffed with weeks' worth of earnings, being slipped from his pants pocket. When he tried to retrieve his money, she had resisted, and to subdue her, he applied pressure to a point in her neck, a Japanese fighting technique he had learned years earlier.

But in his excitement he had pressed too hard and the prostitute had died.

Oskar's mind drifted into a discourse he had read recently about life after death. Of course, there was no proof either way, but the question of what happened after one died was intriguing. He had found particularly interesting the question posed by a Chinese philosopher: might souls who pass away later regret their clinging so desperately to life?

"What is your recommendation?" The prosecutor, Oskar's superior, a rangy, loose-jointed man with a furtive, squirrely expression, was wrinkling his nose, as though smelling an approaching predator. "So, assistant prosecutor?"

"This is manslaughter," Oskar said confidently.

"I disagree," his superior said. "It is a murder of passion and belongs in a higher court; the suspect will remain in custody until the proceedings are complete."

Oskar shook his head, feeling himself edging out along a figurative limb. "But there's no evidence passion was directly involved."

The prosecutor stared. "But they were, they were, intimately engaged during the commission of the crime! How can you say—"

"While they might have indulged in sex," Oskar said, "the murder, if that's what it was, did not result from it. The man only intended to prevent a robbery. Look at the records; he has no previous criminal history, a good reputation. He deserves the manslaughter charge, which will allow him bail."

The prosecutor's eyelids fluttered, as though he were leaning into a strong wind. "It has already been determined from on high."

"But you can't just order this, . . . sir. Accusing a pickpocket of armed robbery is itself a crime!" He felt the limb he was on crack.

The prosecutor sat for a long time, offering no visible reaction. Finally he leaned back, and clasped his hands in front of his chest. "Now that I think of it, you are right. I will recommend the charge of manslaughter when I submit the case to my superiors for final review."

Oskar's upbringing had been disciplined and tinged with religion, although not so much religion as to discourage interest in the opposite sex; however, considering the turmoil of postwar Germany and his own inner struggle, his reluctance to get married is easily understood. What might have otherwise been a healthy and natural interest in women became instead a drive for understanding and a place in the universe.

It was a confusing time in Germany, whose future now lay in the hands of others, a period of reform and of amorphous, bubbling uncertainty, and Oskar wondered what would rise to the surface to bring about the order he had been taught to revere. Would an economic collapse occur again, from which another demagogue might rise? Whatever happened, he vowed never again to be caught on the wrong side.

And so he continued to read, struggling to understand, to find an inherent nature or order in the universe that would unfailingly point him in the right direction.

For the moment, Germany's future was out of control. The Fatherland had been divided, like a pie, into four pieces. Squabbles between the Soviets and the western Allies led to the Berlin blockade in June of 1948, which cut West Berlin off from the West. The Berlin airlift carried out by the United States bypassed the Soviet blockade for nearly a year, all of which led to the seemingly permanent partition of Germany into east and west, neither particularly recognizable as being descended from the Bavaria of Sophie's sweet, dignified bedtime stories.

Political divisions and de-Nazification did little to confront social problems, including anti-Semitism. Contempt for the Jews, cultivated over centuries and now so cunningly reconstructed, lingered untouched by domestic efforts or foreign intervention. State laws and programs can perhaps slow the effects of bigotry but the ideas cannot be legislated out of existence.

His experience with the Czech underground demonstrated to Oskar that he had been led astray in his thinking about Jews. But he had no countermodel except for the lone Jewish refugee he had met and pitied so briefly. He was still unaware of the enormity of the Holocaust, not because the facts had never been presented, but because he had no means by which to absorb them.

He had been prepared for the reality of death, even before joining the Nazi army. That there might have been a policy of genocide, the murder of millions, was a concept he could not and would not grasp. His conscious mind ran for cover, seeking a salving concept and finding one in the Latin phrase *vae victis*, according to which the defeated are blamed for their defeat with no mention of the transgressions that occurred along the way.

His interest in the East persisted and grew with political developments in Africa and Asia. New nations, like Israel, came into existence, but it was India and Gandhi which stimulated Oskar's interest.

Strangely, he did not connect Israel's independence with the Jews he knew were victims of Germany's aggression. In a book review, he had read that, since the discovery of America by Columbus, more than 85 percent of the world's wars had been fought by Christians, either among themselves or against others. He had no idea whether the author counted local battles or blood feuds such as the suppression of the Waldenses and the Huguenots, or those between African or Indian tribes, but, even allowing for such inaccuracies, the report was shocking. Europeans had fought Europeans, Europeans had fought Asians in the name of Oskar's own religion of birth, in the name of gentle loving-kindness. The fact that Christian Europe may have been better equipped to wage war than other parts of the world seemed less relevant than the intent.

Whereas the West had turned out political leaders such as Hitler and Stalin, the East had produced Gandhi. Oskar was as enthralled and attracted by Gandhi's nonviolent success, despite the bloodshed of India's civil war and separation from Pakistan, as he was repelled by recent western history.

Far from being triumphant in these discoveries, Oskar was dismayed and confused. After all, his own civilization was supposedly based on all he had thought good and spiritual, whereas Gandhi was, from the Christian West's point of view, a pagan.

The prosecutor's superiors had recommended that the case be tried as a murder of passion, rebuking the prosecutor, Oskar's immediate superior. In a rare display of candor, the prosecutor communicated to Oskar his dismay at this reprimand, which implied the postponement of his promotion, but said that he was confident he had taken the right action; his conscience was clear.

The district, on the other hand, decided not to hear the case of the salesman who had killed the prostitute. They agreed with Oskar that there had been no murder of passion, but rather simple manslaughter, and had remanded the case back to the local prosecutor, Oskar's boss, to prepare the indictment.

While the prosecutor stayed on sans promotion, the convicted man was less fortunate. His retrial resulted in a sentence of time served and he was allowed to go free, but through official medical reports Oskar learned that the man suffered a breakdown while in custody and had gone back a broken man to what was left of his family, which had fallen apart during the ordeal.

The experience added fuel to Oskar's search for permanence, universality, and spirituality. The obstinate application of the law, assumed to be a constant force for coherence if not good, had let this man down, and in doing so it had let Oskar down.

He was stepping across a busy street, finding a clear path between workers hurrying home from work on a chilly afternoon, when he thought he saw a familiar face.

"Heinz, over here!" he called. The man turned, and Oskar saw that it was indeed his old friend Heinz Brunner, son of the forester. Heinz gave him a confused look, then recognized him.

"What are you doing in a city?"

"Well, I've gotten married," Heinz said proudly.

"Married? I never thought you'd be the first of all the guys to get married."

"Well, you never know. What about you?"

Oskar looked in another direction. "I haven't even settled down myself. I've gotten my doctorate in law, though. The exam was just a few weeks ago, in Munich."

"Congratulations!" Heinz clasped Oskar's shoulder. "So, have you found a job yet?"

"I've spoken with a big commercial bank in Frankfurt. I'm waiting to hear."

"How is your family, your sister?"

"She's a bacteriologist at the university in Erlangen, but she's dissatisfied, and lately she's been job hunting also. She saw an ad in the paper for a group connected with Albert Schweitzer in Lambaréné, which is in French Equatorial Africa, and applied with them for a job."

"In Africa? Doing what?"

"As a nurse."

"Well, I wish her luck. I'm surprised you're going into banking, Oskar. With your idealism, and a law degree, I'd have assumed you'd be defending the oppressed."

Oskar's voice grew serious. "Maybe once I would have, but the legal system really crushes people." He looked his old friend in the eyes until Heinz had to look away.

"So law school has taken all that idealism away?"

Oskar shrugged. "I don't know about that. You know how it is, work and the job hunt keep me busy. Listen, I've got to go." He turned and walked away before Heinz could say another word.

His mind had rushed off, as though someone on a spinning merry-go-round had plucked it like a brass ring, and he was suddenly preoccupied with the war and the reeducation program, as though he had been for hours. The words of his childhood teachers came back to him, explaining that the Jews had to suffer for crucifying our Lord. The question rang in his ears about what Semites had to do with Jews. Why was it not called anti-Judaism? His mind wrestled with the slippery question as though it were covered with wet mud.

A message was waiting when he returned home. He was to report to the Commerzbank in Frankfurt in two days.

He watched his mother dip clothing into the heavy iron pot, scrubbing fabric against fabric. He had avoided state service successfully. The wheels of the train heading into his future were firmly on track; his destination was in sight, and for a change it was one he had sought.

He was interested in the business world, in the interwoven relationships of the economy and how money traveled and grew, like a plant's tendrils. For the first month in Frankfurt, he was assigned to the bank's chief lawyer, who helped him learn about the different divisions: savings, trade, and loan.

Because his background was not in business, he was taken in by the loan department, where legal complications and challenges often arose in the confusing, somewhat anarchic postwar environment. Slowly Oskar came to understand the workings of the bank's departments and how international currencies functioned. He moved to Frankfurt, and, in time, settled into his new life.

In 1948, the German government had begun a loan program to help individuals and businesses which had suffered during the war get back on their feet. Banks were encouraged to spur business growth by giving low-interest loans guaranteed by the state. Oskar became involved in setting up these loans, taking information, helping to determine rates of interest, and working out repayment scenarios. Seeing refugees given an opportunity to regain productivity was an unexpected reward, a bonus beyond the expected lessons in trade, industry, and finance.

The German government's low-interest loan department gave rise to another department, which handled loans with legal difficulties, and Oskar became the head of this department. After a year, along with a colleague, he was given cosignatory rights on the bank's behalf.

Oskar shared what he learned, writing a newspaper article designed to help readers better understand insurance law. Months later, the bank's chief legal advisor showed him a document from the nation's highest court, a decision which cited his article. The advisor congratulated him, but warned him not to write articles for publication without notifying the bank's authorities, a suggestion he did not take seriously. He continued to write articles and papers, focusing on guaranteeing trade loans and rebuilding homes.

All went well for a year and a half.

Hilde had not received a response from the Schweitzer institute, so she found a similar job in the Bahamas, which had the requirement, in addition to her degree, that she be "willing to work with negroes."

When he said good-bye to his sister, Oskar realized how much he had come to admire her and how much each of them had changed. A year or two earlier, she had given him a bookmark with an image of two people squeezed into a paragraph symbol, and told him that to her it represented what the legal system did: it squeezed and crushed people. After his experience as assistant prosecutor, he had to agree, and now that he was saying good-bye to her, he made a point of keeping the bookmark safe, as a reminder of the values he and Hilde shared, a bond they had only recently discovered.

A new, ambitious bank director arrived from Berlin, a man less interested in giving out low-interest loans than in making ever-greater profits. Oskar's view was that the bank's business responsibilities should not prevent it from helping common people, so he continued to recommend and approve loans to those in need.

One morning, after approving a loan, Oskar was summoned before the new director. "I gave the order to refuse such loans, so I expect our employees to find a way to refuse them. We want big business here. Send this fellow somewhere else."

Expressionless, Oskar stared at the new director.

"Do you understand me?" asked the director.

"I will take what you said into consideration."

A week later, a dentist who had been a refugee from East Germany, a man with fine references, applied for a loan for a few thousand marks so that he could purchase a dentist's chair.

Oskar advised the director to approve the loan and argued that refusing it would give the bank a bad name.

"I don't care. I don't want this kind of business," said the director.

"Refuse the loan."

"You know, sir," Oskar began, "it's not only the East Germans who lost the war. It's all of us." He gave the director a conciliatory smile. "It's only a matter of filling out a form. There's really no risk in it."

The director could not believe what he was hearing. With difficulty, he managed to control his anger. "The bank wishes to grow, and loans like this are not the way to do it. Just send the man somewhere else and say no more about it."

As Oskar was walking out he heard the director's voice. "And don't ever, ever come in here with such a request again."

At home, in his spare time, he read and considered what Marx suggested, that many of the world's struggles stemmed from economic inequality and the relationship of the worker to the means of production. Oppressed versus oppressors.

His sister, meanwhile, had sent photographs from her new life, and, as the Eders' neighbors were curious about her, the family invited friends and neighbors, including people Wilhelm had known from his government job, to the house to see the slides.

The group sat in silence, as Wilhelm showed the pictures proudly. Towards the end, the mayor's wife exclaimed, "Jesus, Mary, and Joseph, she's among blacks!"

To which Wilhelm could not refrain from responding, "She would rather work with blacks than with you black Catholics!"

Eventually, Hilde would marry a French widower and move permanently to the Bahamas.

Making sense of what had happened during the war remained a constant motivation. When Oskar asked his father about the war and the atrocities he was only beginning to learn about, Wilhelm responded with a story about one of the heads of the local Social Democratic Party. In the 1930s the man had been sent to a concentration camp with Communists and other political malcontents. A year later, he showed up in Lauf, and when Wilhelm asked about his imprisonment, the man explained that he had merely been detained as insurance that he and others would not be a threat to the new Nazi government.

After the war, Wilhelm saw the man again, and now his story was different. He claimed that his years of imprisonment were a horrific time. When asked why he had never said so, the man explained that he had been told that he would be killed and his family imprisoned if he spoke a word.

"But you told me lies," Wilhelm had said. "If you told the truth maybe something could have been done."

"Easy for you to say," the man responded. "I love my family and didn't want to put them at risk."

Wilhelm finished the story with a sad smile for his grown son. "And this was the end of my friendship with the man, once a political leader whom I looked up to."

Oskar had visited churches in Forchheim and now he did so in Frankfurt, spurred by interest in what the priests had to say about what had happened during the war.

Each religious group he encountered claimed theirs were the only answers. While the individuals were often friendly, genuine people whom Oskar came to like, they tended to set themselves apart and above others, which repulsed him. His secretary at the bank was a Jehovah's Witness, then referred to as Watchtower people, a name derived from their print publication.

Oskar, sensing his secretary's strong convictions, visited the man's home and listened to him air the only views, philosophy, and theology worth holding.

12

Memories and ghosts of the war haunted him in the yellow, distorted twilight hours between waking and sleeping, when reality is experienced through the prism of the subconscious mind. Fifty million killed was beyond his comprehension—multitudes of innocent civilians sent coldly to their deaths by his own country, by Bavarians descended from the same noble Ludwig of his mother's whispered stories. In his mind, Oskar continued to search for escape, for validation, for identity. The atomic bomb compounded the shame and horror he felt with a new fear, the spectre of another unimaginable horror; if fifty million could be killed before the invention of this new weapon, what might be possible now?

He began taking vacations, bicycling into the Alps. If the war he feared did break out, perhaps these scenic mountains might provide some natural refuge.

His first ride was to a sparkling lake on a beautiful day. He rode easily, absorbing the countryside and feeling the wide alpine sky above him; he was in the moment, his fears forgotten. The lake added to his relaxation; it was just what he needed, and he rode home in the late afternoon exhilarated, flying downhill, leaning forward over the handlebars and into the wind, remembering the feeling if not the details of his years as a pilot.

He let go of the handlebars and leaned back, the sun warming his face, arms out at either side like wings. The road banked sharply and he managed the turn by leaning his weight to one side, but as he navigated the bend he drew a sharp breath and threw himself forward. On the other side of the turn, in his path, loomed a toll booth.

With only a moment to act and none to think, he slammed on his brakes, which stopped the bike but not his own momentum. He hurtled over the handlebars, flipping over and slamming his head on the gravel road.

He woke up in a hospital, and was told he had a concussion. He remembered little of the incident. Some passersby had lifted him into their car and driven him down the mountain. His bike was still at the toll booth, where he could retrieve it when he was able. While a doctor advised him to stay a week, Oskar ignored his headache and bruises and convinced someone to take him back to the toll booth for his bike.

The toll operator recognized him and brought him his bicycle, which was in workable condition, and he and Oskar sat down in the booth. Oskar watched the cars while the man told him what happened.

"I watched you coast in really fast, saw you crash, and brought you inside. I kept the barrier shut across the road, hoping a car would take you to the hospital. Six cars passed and no one offered you a ride. You were bleeding and hardly breathing. Some of the drivers thought you would stain their upholstery, others said they weren't going near the hospital. The seventh car took you."

"Those six who went by," Oskar said, "committed crimes, didn't they? It's illegal to pass an accident without offering to help, isn't it? I'm lucky you were here. I can't thank you enough."

As he carefully pedaled home, he wondered about human nature.

Perhaps humans are just another animal, with higher brain function and ability, but little more. He realized and regretted that he had not taken the man's name so he might properly thank him after returning home.

It was the summer of 1954. Oskar read about a seminar being given at the Albert Schweitzer College, in Churwalden, in eastern Switzerland. Remembering Hilde's fascination with Dr. Schweitzer and feeling his own admiration for the theologian, scientist, concert musician, and philosopher (whose doctoral dissertation subject had been Kant), he decided that a vacation, particularly one with some intellectual, philosophical stimulation, would be a good idea.

He rode his bicycle all day under a burning sun, the asphalt melting under his tires, his legs battling the mountains on the climb from Frankfurt to Zürich. The ride was several hundred miles, but Oskar had been an avid and consistent cyclist for years and felt up to it. Besides, how could this ride through the Alps have any worse an ending than his last one, only a few years earlier?

At nine-thirty that first evening, he arrived in Zürich, sweating and exhausted, and, without any forethought, he bought and ate a huge tub of ice cream.

The next morning he awoke dizzy, dehydrated, and hung over from the sugar. He started on his way again, but quickly collapsed; finding his way to a field, he tried to collect himself. The mountains of Graubünden were thick with forests which opened where gravity and the upper Rhein had carved meandering gullies. Churwalden was a long, narrow village in which a college was built into the side of the mountain, as though Dr. Schweitzer himself had been a force of nature stamping it there.

Oskar was surprised and delighted with the quality of the programs, particularly one in which Neville Chamberlain's adviser in

1938, Lord Runciman, lectured. Afterwards, during the question and answer period, Oskar's hand went up. "How do you feel, after so many years, about the decisions you made in 1938 regarding the future of Czechoslovakia?"

Students and participants turned around to see who had asked such a direct question. Oskar noticed one young woman, all dark eyes and shy smile, catch his eye, then look away.

Runciman did not avoid the question. "We did the best we could at that time to save Europe, to save the Czechs. Hindsight, of course, changes our perspective."

Oskar quickly followed up. "How does Christian teaching translate into politics? What I mean is, how does 'my country, right or wrong' square with Christian doctrine?"

Now the girl was staring at him. He was sure of it. He tried to look at her without staring. He only half heard Runciman's answer.

"Well, it is certainly difficult, at times, to square politics with loving your neighbor and enemy equally, that is"—he cleared his throat—"if you take the church literally. Sometimes you have to follow a doctrine of might makes right. Right without might, you know, is a farce; might without right is just brutality. It's when you have a balanced combination that we've really achieved something. I'll admit we could yet be fooled by another Hitler. We tend to be idealistic, and so we listen to anyone who brings us hope."

Oskar's disappointment in the answer was somewhat muted by his infatuation with the dark-eyed girl, but when he tried to speak with her, he found her distant, laconic. Though she told him her name and politely answered his questions, her responses were indirect, and he could not tell if she was shy or uninterested. Her smile followed by her restrained manner confused Oskar, and he began to ask around about her.

She was a Jewess, he was told, and unlikely to be interested in a

German boy. The news caused him to remember Czechoslovakia and the coughing Jewish refugee. The man had been normal, if under-nourished, certainly no monster. And this young woman was deli-cate, attractive, interesting and . . . unlikely to be attracted to a Ger-man such as himself.

A week after returning home, he awoke in the middle of the night with cramps deep in his abdomen, and then he began to experience persistent constipation. He tried the usual home remedies, followed by a visit to his doctor, but the symptoms continued. He went to a sec-ond doctor, then to a homeopath, but nothing worked.

Meanwhile, he struggled to make his way to work each day and muddle through his job. Oskar's secretary noticed his discomfort and when told what the problem was, recommended his own doctor, a practitioner of some kind of natural medicine in Offenbach, about sixty kilometers away.

Oskar took a train to see the doctor and began describing his con-dition, but the doctor waved away his explanation. "I need to look into your eye," the doctor said, "to learn what's wrong and what needs to be done." True to his word, the doctor examined Oskar's eye, diag-nosed gastritis, and prescribed a natural remedy, claiming that Oskar would find relief within a few days, and would be entirely comfortable within a week.

"It's hard to believe," Oskar said. "Normally I can eat rusty nails and I'm fine."

"Or so you thought."

"How did I get this way? Where did it come from?"

"Let me look in your other eye, and I'll tell you. Yes, from what I can see, you appear to have inherited a weak stomach from your mother. If you stop doing silly things to your stomach, you'll be healthy."

"I did have a big bowl of ice cream after a long bike ride recently in Zürich."

"And I notice that ten or twelve years ago your mother developed painful gall bladder trouble."

"She did!" Oskar exclaimed. "Just before I went into the army she spent a week crying in pain at night from gall bladder attacks."

After leaving the doctor's office, Oskar began to reconsider the way his diet affected the quality of his life; he stopped eating meat and eggs, though he continued eating fish for a time. He would remain a vegetarian for the rest of his life.

While Oskar had found a way of life that suited his body, he continued to search with his mind and soul.

Through acquaintances at work, he came across a Sufi group located not far from Frankfurt and led by Pir Vilayat Khan, a young Pakistani, the son of a world-famous Sufi teacher, author, and musician in Versailles, France. Oskar listened to the man and members of his group with increasing interest and excitement. He had also read and been influenced by a booklet containing concepts popularized by Raja of Aundh, called *Surya Namaskar*, which loosely translates as *A Greeting to the Sun*, or *Sun Salutation*, as the physical yoga exercise is known today.

The Sufis were self-styled pilgrims on a journey requiring repentance, a modest lifestyle, patience, trust and joy in God, and acquiescence to God's will—all resulting, they believed, in a higher consciousness, a oneness with the Supreme Being.

The promise of spirituality, along with their rejection of opulence and materialism, appealed to Oskar, who identified with their spiritual search, their sincerity and honesty. His personal experience, as well as a sensitivity inherited from and taught by his mother, contributed to a fascination with Sufism in general and the charisma of Pir Vilayat Khan in particular.

Reading about Ramakrishna and Vivekananda and sharing his enthusiasm with his sister, then having these new outlooks become part of a bond between them was a foundation naturally built upon by the Sufis, who practiced daily meditation and certain physical exercises and devotions. Oskar had already tried to turn to his religion of birth by examining local Christian groups, but found that each claimed it was the only true way and rejected the beliefs and practices of other seemingly worthwhile sects, factions, and religions.

The Sufis did not; their inclusiveness attracted Oskar and spoke of a sincerity he had sought but not yet found in the West. His Indian readings had contained the same quality, and Gandhi's astonishing, unprecedented success appeared to Oskar to be conclusive evidence of the worth of the man and of an eastern way, whereas the unprecedented crimes of the Nazis and Stalin's Bolsheviks and the development of the atomic bomb seemed to be convincing indictments of the West.

The prayers, exercises, and meditations seemed pragmatic and sensible, not tied to dogma. He began attending Sufi meetings regularly.

Vilayat, as he was called, warned Oskar that one day he would encounter physical problems and find himself unable to continue his practice, but he enjoyed the daily regimen and agreed with the group's teaching and so ignored or minimized the warning. Just as Vilayat had predicted, he did one day find himself unable to practice, and, not knowing what else to do, he tried performing his exercises while visualizing a cross, but without success.

As he became more frantic, he had what he would later call a vision, of his grandmother, Pauline, who had passed away several years earlier. She had been a devout Catholic and had hoped for a time that he would become a priest. She was praying for him, he saw, and she was smiling, radiant and beautiful, assuring him that he was on his own journey now, and could proceed safely. He accepted the experience at face value, and the idea of a more tangible journey began to form in his mind. What he had found so far could be merely its beginning.

The idea of his own search, not only of mind, heart, and soul, but his own physical journey, grafted onto his desire for answers and identity. Where there had been horrific emptiness, Oskar began to create his own joyful answer.

Traveling by plane would present him with too sudden a change in culture and climate, whereas a boat would be gradual and scenic, he decided. From Hamburg, he might travel around Africa and head for India. The idea percolated during late 1954, as his difficulties at the bank dissipated, perhaps because it had been nine years since the war's end and the sort of charitable loans he so favored had become less necessary. Oskar became a success at the bank, so much so that at year's end, when successful employees were receiving one or perhaps one and a half months' salary as a bonus, Oskar received a bonus of three months' salary.

He booked passage on a ship for June and, at the suggestion of a coworker, placed an ad in the newspaper describing his trip and offering to conduct business on behalf of anyone who might have such interests in India. When he told his friends in the Sufi group about the trip, he learned that the group's leader, Vilayat, was himself traveling to Karachi, Pakistan, by car to visit family. Why not, it was suggested, ask to go along?

At the next meeting at which Vilayat was present, Oskar did ask and was told he would be welcome, so he cancelled his ship tickets but asked if his suitcase might be sent without him. The suitcase was packed with tropical clothes to be worn once he arrived in Bombay, and would only take up unnecessary room in Vilayat's car.

Meanwhile, two business opportunities had presented themselves. An Austrian hoped to sell an antimosquito pesticide and a leather dealer hoped to find cheap hides in India.

When he handed in his resignation, his superiors at the bank in Frankfurt were astonished, unaccustomed as they were to seeing rising, successful employees walk off the job in favor of spiritual quests. When he returned in a month or two, his job would be waiting, Oskar was assured. In fact, why not simply arrange for a few months of leave? Thanking his colleagues and superiors, Oskar politely declined and instead accepted a gracious letter of recommendation.

His parents were supportive, if surprised. He was a grown man now, his father told him, and responsible for his own decisions. They had accepted that Hilde had had to find her own way in the world, and were satisfied that she had done so in the Bahamas; perhaps Hilde's experience softened them for Oskar's decision.

"Keep good and straight . . . and stay in touch," Wilhelm said, as they said good-bye.

"And mind your health," Sophie reminded him.

Vilayat met him with a Volkswagen Caravan one balmy, windy day in mid-June. Clouds hurried overhead as though they too were straining to get away. With Vilayat were his wife, sister-in-law, and sister-in-law's friend.

The first day was spent riding towards Yugoslavia, through gentle, green European hills and a cool spring wind. Because Oskar was young and single and the only man besides Vilayat, it was agreed that he would sleep on an air mattress on the luggage rack on the car's roof.

He had trouble sleeping that first night, not so much because the mattress was uncomfortable; he didn't notice that at all. The journey—now that it was real, it had become more of an adventure—

spread out before him, every bit as unknown as his plans for the rest of his life. All were up to this chilly European wind.

His eyes wandered the diamond sky, the car stuffed with people and luggage and blankets beneath him. Now and then someone moved and the car rocked a little. He dozed lightly, and awoke at one point to see one star shining more brightly than the others, and for a while he did not take his eyes from that star. When he did, it was only to close them.

The next day the crowded Caravan wove through the mountains of Greek Macedonia, through the Halkidiki peninsula, passing by Mount Athos, named in mythology for the massive stone which the giant Athos was said to have hurled at the sea god Poseidon in an epic battle. The mountain's evergreen-laden sides rose to a bare apex, and it was easy for the travelers to see why so many religious orders found the mountain the perfect place for worship. Oskar would return years later for a longer stay in a very different context.

The hills and occasional plains brought them to Turkey, and the city of Adrianople. Vilayat hoped to reach Karachi with little delay, so the Sufi travelers did not stop to take in the sights or educate themselves about local history, color, or culture. They drove during the day through Europe and countries which bordered on the Middle East, but that would change as the daytime heat rose, until, by the time they reached Syria, Vilayat and Oskar shared the driving and did nearly all of it before or after midday. Meals were cooked outdoors, camping style, next to the van. After supper and into the evening Vilayat taught Oskar and the women Sufi thought and literature. Oskar paid attention to Vilayat's demeanor, which was relaxed and easy, even when difficulties arose. He had a genuine smile and a way of looking at a person that convinced one with only a glance that he understood completely.

The Turkish cities, Adrianople and, a day to the southeast, Constantinople, began to look Middle Eastern, their traffic consisting of donkey carts, trucks, cars, and hordes of people, all of which Vilayat maneuvered through with consummate skill. English road signs had grown scarce, and dwellings and stores were now of simple wood. More adorned were the mosques, their tall minarets reaching skyward.

They passed through Konya, the famous Town of the Dervish, and while Vilayat visited an acquaintance, Oskar strolled the streets, hoping for a glimpse of the whirling dancers, but learned that they did not perform during the summer. Greece and Turkey were less green than Yugoslavia, more mauve and brown as the southeast European air mixed with desert dust.

The heat and sun, which seemed somehow to have moved closer to the earth, dominated the drive through Syria, through Haleb toward Damascus. The desert was unlike any Oskar had seen, made not of grains of sand but of solidified lava. The heat was dizzying and he paid little attention to his surroundings until Vilayat encouraged him to keep up with his Sufi exercises and modify them to the driving schedule. When he did, Oskar's head cleared and he noticed that Vilayat appeared especially alert, nervous. The others had become quiet, less animated, more watchful.

"Sufis are not considered typical Muslims," Vilayat explained. "We're seen as having strayed, and we might not be very popular. We'd do best to just pass through. We'll have to stock up on food and gas, since we'll be in the desert for quite a while from here on in."

They passed through Amman, which had the look of an enormous desert village. As the sun seemed closer in the daytime, so did the sunsets, which were pastel panoramas, and the stars appeared to be so near that Oskar felt he was among them. He had been impressed by the way his friend Heinz had found a place in nature, and this experience reminded him of that, but this feeling was more stark and raw and powerful. He remembered the descriptions in his old Karl May books and smiled at the accuracy with which their author, who had never left Germany, had written of Arabia.

They crawled the Great Syrian Desert, unpassable by ancient caravans, which instead had taken the *via maris* route connecting the Egyptian Mediterranean in the west with Babylonia and parts east. The quality of the road's pavement varied, until the scenery began to change from endless desert to Iraq's tall, green date orchards.

Oskar's exercises allowed him to view the sun with the same indifference as he did the moon. The heat was now barely an irritant. Within two days of passing the Iraqi border, they arrived in Baghdad. He slept on the Caravan's roof that first night, his face open to the stars, but awoke in mid-dream to shouting and sudden lurching as the car began to pull away beneath him. Vilayat and his sister-in-law's friend were yelling, and Oskar pressed himself against the car's roof until all noise stopped, and he climbed down.

"Thieves," Vilayat said. "They broke into the car. I was trying to tell you to hold on while we tried to get away."

"Which we did, if barely," said his sister-in-law, while she sifted through her bags.

Oskar did the same and found that his wallet, money, and traveler's checks had been stolen. "I can't go to Karachi without money. What am I going to do?"

He marveled at Vilayat's calm. "In the morning we'll go to the police. We'll work something out. In the meantime, we need our rest, particularly after all this stress."

13

The Baghdad police were friendly, even jovial. While his lieutenants stood by, the chief asked where they were going, and, when Vilayat explained that their next stop would be Teheran, the swarthy official leaned back, hands folded across his chest, appraising the five young Europeans. He seemed to come to a decision and leaned forward, as though telling them a secret.

"You've heard of the Thief of Baghdad? I'll tell you a story. There's also a Thief of Teheran." He leaned back in his chair. "The Thief of Baghdad thought life here was becoming too risky, so, you see, he went to Teheran. Meanwhile, the Thief of Teheran thought his life there was also too risky and he decided to come to Baghdad. Well, they met halfway and had a little chat, each telling the other how difficult it was to work in his city. The Thief of Teheran said, 'I'm sure I can handle working in your city.' His counterpart from Baghdad said, 'We'll see.' At that moment they looked up and saw a bird's nest at the top of a telegraph pole, and the Thief of Baghdad pointed to it and said, 'If you can steal the eggs from under that bird you'll be worthy of being a thief in Baghdad.' The Thief of Teheran said, 'It's nothing,' so he climbed the pole and stole the eggs and the bird didn't notice a thing. He came down but the Thief of Baghdad was gone and so were all of the Thief of Teheran's possessions." The police chief smiled and straightened his back, his fingers interlocked across the top of his stomach. "All he had left were the two eggs."

Vilayat nodded. "I see."

"So, what's the point?" Oskar asked.

"The point is to be very careful, wherever you go. There are all kinds of thieves, everywhere. No sleeping in cars with open windows. Lock your belongings up."

"They'll be all right, these Germans," one of the lieutenants said. "It's the English who ought to worry." The man, who was thin with tight shining cheekbones and hair that looked wet, laughed suddenly. "King Faisal, like Farouk in Egypt, deals with the British, but everyone knows the people favor the Germans. Just look at Premier Ali's revolt in 1941. You know where you stand with the Germans. None of this colonial—"

The chief cleared his throat and the lieutenant went silent.

Oskar looked at Vilayat. "I don't suppose we're going to get our money back. Maybe you ought to take their suggestion"—he nodded towards Vilayat's sister-in-law and her friend—"and put me on a boat, or leave me here."

"No, no, Lilly White." Vilayat shook his head, using a nickname Oskar was unable to get used to. "Continue on with us." He gave a charming smile, as if such a decision were as easy as choosing one's breakfast. "We've done what we can here. You'll pay us back later."

After a night in a caravansary, an inn for caravans, Oskar slept during a day of driving through Iran. In his sleep he heard an argument, which became confused with his dreams so that he woke disoriented. The van had stopped and Vilayat was taking small steps in an irregular pattern a few feet away. He bent and picked something up from the ground every now and then. Oskar got out of the van to see if he could help.

"No, thank you, Lilly White, I'll manage." Vilayat went back to what he was doing.

Oskar looked closer. "Why are you picking noodles up from the ground?"

Vilayat answered without stopping what he was doing. "Because this is where my wife threw them."

Oskar looked over at the women, who were sitting on a blanket behind the van. Vilayat's sister-in-law and her friend were chatting easily, but his wife sat alone, looking into the sunset, her expression unhappy.

"Better to pick up noodles than to make arguments," he heard Vilayat say.

They passed through sinister Qum, picturesque Isfahan, and artless Kerman. Soon they were driving east, towards Zahedan, a town near the Pakistani border, Oskar at the wheel.

"Have you noticed that people in each country look alike, but with individual differences?"

"How so?" asked Vilayat's sister-in-law; his wife was still sulking at one of the windows.

Oskar explained. "In Greece you can tell you're looking at Greeks, in Turkey Turks, even allowing for differences. There's a sameness." He glanced at her. "And you know what else is the same? The affection mothers show their children."

The sister-in-law's friend spoke up. "That's not the culture, that's human nature."

Oskar agreed. "Still, it's impressive. Irrespective of hair or skin color, nationality, historical background, all the mothers love their babies. What a great influence they are." He stared, mesmerized by the dust swirling over the road, which faded and seemed to vanish in spots. "I wonder if my mother, who is so loving, were Persian or Turkish, what would be important to me today? How would my values, not only cultural specifics but the underlying values, be different? Seeing so many different cultures broadens my thinking." He started to turn towards the back seat, to look at the sister-in-law's friend, who had last spoken, but the van slowed and Oskar gripped the wheel. They came to a stop and Oskar craned his chin over the steering wheel, which was pressed nearly to his chest, trying to see the road, but it had disappeared in the dust storm.

He pressed the accelerater but the wheels spun and the car sank into the sand. Oskar got out and tried to sweep the sand away from the tires, digging to find asphalt, but there was only more sand. By now the wind had blown deep drifts around the car.

He heard what sounded like a cry. "Did you say something?" he called out, but no one answered. A moment later and from all directions a weird, echoing noise arose. Oskar cupped both hands around his eyes and tried to see into the distance, but could make out only man-sized mounds of strangely shaped rock. The wind and sand playing through and around the rocks, he realized, was causing the howling. When the wind blew harder, the sound went up in pitch, and as it dissipated, the tones lowered. Later they would learn that this was known as the Singing Desert.

The car was being buried by the sand, so Oskar got back in and tried again to drive away, but the wheels still spun and the car sank.

"Come out and help me push," he yelled, banging on the windows. Everyone got out, but even with five people pushing, the car wouldn't budge.

"So, what now?" Oskar wondered, leaning against the car, exhausted. He looked to Vilayat for an answer.

Vilayat looked around. There were no buildings, trees, or people in sight, only mounds of howling rock. "It's getting late. Nearly four o'clock already."

Vilayat's wife had forgotten whatever had made her throw the noodles out the window. Oskar saw fear mirroring his own on the women's faces. Only Vilayat remained entirely calm. "We'll just have to try to get the car free and if we can't we'll sleep inside and try again in the morning. Someone will eventually pass by and help us."

"I'm going to walk back a bit and try to find the road," Oskar volunteered, and started jogging through the fine-grained sand. After running a short way, he turned around. The van was gone. He ran a while longer, saw a truck ahead, sprinted to catch it, then realized it was stationary. He slowed, a little out of breath, and approached the driver's side door.

He looked at the driver, then staggered back. The driver was dead, mummified. He turned and sprinted back the way he had come, but the van was not where he thought it should be. He spun in all directions, but there was only darkening sand and howling wind.

He looked down and was able to make out faint tire tracks. Somehow his friends had gotten the van moving. He followed them as quickly as he could, but after ten or fifteen minutes he slowed. He was tiring and the swirling sand made breathing difficult.

He tried walking quickly, and after another five minutes the van appeared. His friends were waiting for him.

"A Bedouin with camels passed by," Vilayat explained. "We shouted to him and his camels pulled us out. We followed him for a way, then decided to stop and wait for you."

The traveling party would need its sleep. The desert in Balochistan,

Pakistan's northwest province, bordering Iran, was known for its extreme heat. When they crossed the border, leaving Zahedan, they were warned that driving during the daytime was forbidden. This desert, the border patrol claimed, was the hottest place on earth. The car's tires would explode.

They began driving at ten P.M., when the temperature dropped a fraction, to 50 or 60 degrees centigrade, or 120 to 135 Fahrenheit.

They traveled southeast through the Indus Valley, from which the English word "India" derives, to Karachi, which is on the southern point of Pakistan. Karachi was equally hot and its streets teemed with pedestrians wearing loose-fitting clothing.

Oskar ignored the scenery. "Before we go any further, I want to make sure we get to a bank, so I can repay you."

Vilayat asked someone for directions and they found a bank, where Oskar explained to a clerk that his traveler's checks had been stolen and he needed to have them replaced.

"I'm very grateful for all you've done, especially after what happened in Baghdad," Oskar explained to Vilayat, as they waited for the clerk to shuffle through their paperwork.

"It's not often," the clerk said, "that one sees Europeans traveling through here. Where are you from?"

"We're from Germany," Vilayat answered.

A black eyebrow went up. "Oh? What did you do in Germany?"

Oskar met the clerk's curious eyes. "I worked in a bank."

"Really. In what capacity?"

"I was a lawyer and arranged for loans."

"Well, then, you must have had the right of signature."

"Certainly," Oskar said proudly.

"That might be useful. What bank were you with?"

Oskar explained where he had worked and the clerk disappeared for a few minutes; when he returned, he carried a large, open note-book. "Please sign here, Mr. Eder."

Oskar signed and the clerk turned the notebook around and examined the signature. "Well, this does match, so it seems everything is in order. We can refund much of what was lost."

"Why not all?"

"Regulations. But you may be able to get the rest back in India if that's where you're going. We can give you a few hundred dollars."

"A fortune here," Vilayat pointed out.

"Bombay would give you the best chance to get the rest of your money," the clerk explained.

Delighted with the settlement, Oskar took what was offered, gave much of the money to Vilayat and said a grateful good-bye to his teacher, along with Vilayat's wife, sister-in-law, and her friend. Still taking little notice of the city, he found a hostel and settled in for a long, dreamless sleep.

The following morning Oskar made his way to the airport and took the first plane he could to Bombay, a city at least as hot and crowded as Karachi, and even more humid. He found a room in a hostel, then set about trying to find his suitcase, which had been en route from Hamburg. He presented his documents to a port official, but the suitcase was nowhere to be found. The official offered to give him a document he might present to his insurance company, proving his bag's disappearance, an arrangement which pleased Oskar, since money from an insurance settlement would be better than the fancy, tailored clothes he had mistakenly packed before leaving home.

Oskar wandered around Bombay for the remainder of the day, sampling foods sold by street vendors, which proved too hot for both his tongue and stomach. Alongside British-influenced opulence, he saw stark poverty. Girls in their teens and younger sold their bodies in the red-light district; their slack, beautiful faces showed that they were resigned to lives which had never been their choice.

With each meal, Oskar learned to ask for less and less spice, but the fiery cuisine was still beyond his capacity, and would remain so for weeks.

The street traffic appeared to defy the laws of nature. Cars, cyclists, rickshaws, bull carts, pedestrians, and porters all seemed to float in arbitrary directions and at their own speeds rather than following any cut-and-dried rules. It seemed that the city, rather than being built on a conventional infrastructure, was itself an organic vital being with quirks and idiosyncracies that defied hard-and-fast laws.

He returned to his room and went to sleep dreaming of wet, sweet fruit, and woke up instead with the smooth bread of flour and water, chapati, on his dry lips. He looked at his sun-browned face in the mirror and gave a half smile. "No more Lilly White, eh?"

He went out into the already steaming street and hunted down a vendor, bought a few bananas and turned towards the side of the road to eat. A poor elderly woman was begging a few feet away, and her hungry eyes told him what she felt. He had never seen the poverty of street beggars and was shocked by the woman's condition. He saw a woman who might have been Mamushka, the Czech grandmother, and because he could, he had to help. He had been told he would see many beggars who looked poor but stowed away what they begged. His money was in the hostel's safe, so without another thought he handed her a banana.

The old brown woman looked at the banana as though she had never before seen one, and then looked at Oskar; a smile broke over her face. Oskar turned to the vendor to buy another with the few pennies he had been given as change. The vendor handed him a banana and waved away the money, though it was only a few cents.

"White man, good man," he said.

Oskar thought about leaving the money on the countertop, but decided that the vendor might be offended, so he smiled and went on his way, peeling and eating the banana, satisfied both in appetite and with the feeling of humanity he sensed from people his former acquaintances would have labelled primitive.

Energized by the experience or perhaps by the healthy fruit, Oskar decided to visit the German consulate, so that someone would know where he was in case of emergency.

The consul, a middle-aged, nondescript man with small eyes, listened while Oskar explained who he was.

"Why are you visiting India?" the consul asked.

"I'm interested in the culture."

"I see. Well, don't mingle too much with them. By the way, what's your next stop?"

"The capital. Delhi."

"We have two planes going there every day."

"I prefer to take a train, so I can get to know the people."

The consul was horrified. "Take the plane. We white men have to preserve what little prestige we have in these countries."

Oskar thought about asking the man why he, a German, whose country was so recently defeated, would wish to preserve the prestige of the white man. But he only commented, "Well, that's not my view."

The consul shrugged. "Take the train at your own risk."

On the train ride to Delhi, Oskar was intrigued, as he had been during the drive with Pir Vilayat Khan. The Indian people were uniquely . . . Indian. They were themselves. Their most describable characteristic was that they were friendly, but of course it was much more than that. Everyone he came across was warm and welcoming. When he stepped onto the train platform in Delhi, Oskar was happily looking forward to getting to know the city.

One of the waiters on the train explained the difference between Old Delhi and New Delhi in terms of hotel rates: the very best fancy hotels in Old Delhi would cost perhaps fifteen to twenty rupees per day, whereas the most run-down rooms in New Delhi would be much more—at least eight dollars per day, and the cheapest European-style hotel would be at least forty to fifty dollars. Remembering the consul's words, he took the opposite tack, determining not to surround himself with Europeans, and so set off for Old Delhi.

The first days in Old Delhi went by in the rush of immersing himself in a new culture, looking for business, and meeting more people than he had in the entire last year. He found buses and day trips to palaces, the Lokh Saba, or Parliament, and the Red Fort, so called because it was constructed of red stone.

He tried to use the little bit of Hindi he had learned in a very short class he had taken on a whim in Frankfurt, but whatever was spoken in this part of India bore little resemblance to what he had learned. Likewise, he mused, a person who spoke only High German would not easily understand Bavarian or the Low German dialects.

The hotel was clean and offered all the fruit he could want in addition to delicious, substantial meals. The guests and staff were friendly and easy to talk to, and Oskar made the acquaintence of a lean young man who agreed to show him around the city. Now and then as he sat and walked with his new friend, he thought of the consul, and it occurred to him that such feelings of superiority were what gave birth to the Nazi idea of a superrace.

New Delhi was modern, clean, and up to date, while Old Delhi was a mixture of ancient dirty bricks and even older ornate temples, women wrapped in exotically patterned saris, shouting bony boys with wiry legs and bare feet, gaunt brown men with white beards hawking broken-down wares. And the smells were deeper and stronger than those a German nose was accustomed to. The novelty of such strange sights quickly wore off as Oskar was struck by the poverty: whole families living under a blanket or umbrella, school-age children purposely mutilated and deformed to arouse pity and spontaneous generosity on the part of passersby.

Yet cows wandered freely. At any time a cow might approach a vendor's cart and eat as it pleased, leaving the vendor feeling blessed. Oskar asked his new guide why the cow was considered holy in India.

"I don't think the cow itself is holy," the young man answered. "It's a symbol. The cow has admirable features. The cow eats grass, but not down to the nub so it cannot grow again, the way a goat does. The cow is not a coward. If its calf is attacked by lions, the cows will form a circle around the calf, defending it. Yet a cow will never attack others. Men can learn from this. A cow gives us useful things: milk, of course, and dung, which we use for fertilizer."

His guide took him to see temples and historical icons. He saw an iron column said to be more than two thousand years old, inscribed in Sanskrit, unaffected by rust or degradation of any kind. A kind of miracle, Oskar thought. He saw another tower that was said to date back to the early Muslim period, approximately the eighth century.

"How old would you say this is?" Oskar asked.

"Very, very old," replied his guide.

"How old?"

"Ninety or nine hundred years. As you please."

Oskar looked at the young man but his answer had been entirely serious. "The time itself is not so important, is it?"

The guide looked at Oskar as though *he* were the cultural icon.

"Our words for yesterday and tomorrow are the same." Oskar realized that in German and English the words "*einst*" and "once" can refer to the past or future.

During the first weeks in Old Delhi, Oskar met people and visited places which made a profound impression on him. He became acquainted with a young Indian struggling with a desire to follow Jesus. He was a Hindu but had read and was attracted to the New Testament. His conflict was over which of the many Christian roads to follow—the Baptists, Catholics, and Pentecostals each appeared to lay claim to the true way.

He asked Oskar's opinion, but Oskar was embarrassed and claimed he did not know the answer. "If you really intend to become a Christian, perhaps you should look at the way each group lives, their communities, their people. See who you would be most comfortable with, who's the most honest and straightforward."

He met three very angry black South Africans recently arrived from Capetown. They had been raised by missionaries to believe that the black race was meant to be slaves. In the Bible, they had been told, the story of the sons of Ham in the ninth and tenth chapters of the Book of Genesis proved this and justified their slavery. Recently the three had read English translations of the Bible but could find nothing of the sort in the text. Their Dutch text had been manipulated, they learned, to demonstrate that descendents of Ham, one of Noah's sons, had been ordered to serve whites.

He saw wonderfully crafted statues of four lions, carved in smooth, shining sandstone, dating back more than two thousand years, and was reminded of the western reverence for Greek and Roman art and architecture, which were held up as proof of the West's innate superiority and birthright of cultural leadership. Yet this ancient art was every bit its equal.

He noticed a local taxi, a cart pulled by a cow. Its driver spurred the cow to greater speed by vigorously and violently twisting the animal's tail, which had been broken from so much twisting and was now deformed. You cannot kill a cow, Oskar mused, but you can twist its tail.

While riding in a horse-pulled cart, Oskar noticed that the horse had a festering wound on its hindquarters. The driver used a long stick with a nail through one end to hit the horse on its wound. In trying to get away from the painful stick, the horse ran faster.

Oskar yelled at the man to stop, but the driver ignored him. He shouted again, using hand gestures and pantomime, but the driver went on hitting the horse with the nail. Finally Oskar jumped out of the cart and threw a coin at the driver, who stopped and stared with wide eyes and open mouth.

He met a young man who invited Oskar to his wedding, where he met the bride and the two families. The man explained that he had been studying in Edinburgh, Scotland, and had learned that his parents had chosen a bride for him, so he had returned for the wedding and would soon go back to Scotland while his new wife stayed home and learned how to run his household.

"How and why would your parents choose your bride? And why would they do so without consulting you?"

The man smiled. "This is the ancient system. They consult their spiritual adviser, who consults the stars and my horoscope and the birth dates of women until he finds someone compatible. When arrangements are made, they send for me and . . . here we are."

"But when you were in Scotland, didn't you notice the way people in the West choose brides?"

"That's exactly why I'm following my parents' way. In Europe, young people get caught up in quick romantic feelings and in two or three years the marriages end. I prefer a more reliable, time-tested system."

Oskar was impressed by the dignity of the bride on her wedding day, by the charming way she wore her sari, which, unlike western clothing, exposed little yet remained elegant and beautifully feminine.

Neither business he had hoped to conduct in India had materialized. The mosquito repellent he had thought to sell was no better than others on the market, and the leather business required knowledge of India's leather-related industries, which Oskar did not possess.

When Oskar mentioned these disappointments, his guide told him about another German who had come to Calcutta and would be returning to Germany by car. Perhaps Oskar might return with him, if that was what he wanted. So Oskar made the proper inquiries but found that the man had only recently taken on another passenger, and his car was now full.

He saw this as a sign that he should stay.

14

A woman in Germany had given him a written recommendation to a swami named Shivananda in an ashram at the foot of the Himalayas. Oskar dug through his belongings and was glad to find that the note had not been lost.

He packed what little he had into an English army knapsack he had bought in Delhi. Included was a Bible he had purchased at a British Bible shop. He had not yet decided whether to read it.

He took a train north to Dehra Dun, then spent a few hours on a bus to Rishikesh. The ashram was at the northern edge of a small town on the western shore of the Ganges River, not far from where the hills and plains meet.

On the main gate was a sign that read "Himalayan Forest University." Oskar wondered what it might mean. Inside he found small whitewashed stone buildings and narrow lanes. Monkeys scampered and screeched in trees and on rooftops. Orange-robed *sannyasis*, ashram devotees, were everywhere, walking in ease and silence. Occasionally Oskar saw half-naked, full-bearded hermits, their hair long and wild, their bodies smeared with ashes.

He was brought before the head of the ashram. Swami Shivananda was in his sixties, and was entirely clean shaven, a practice, he joked, which kept the gray from his hair. He asked why Oskar had come.

"I have a recommendation from an acquaintance of yours . . ."

"What do you hope to find here?"

"Clarity of mind. To find my purpose in life."

"What have you done so far in India?"

"I have been to Bombay and Delhi, had an opportunity to go back to Germany and decided to take it if there was a place in the car for me. Since there was not, I took it as a sign I should stay." He handed the letter from the German woman to the swami.

"Then you are welcome," Swami Shivananda said, without looking at the letter. "Why not stay a week or two, then see how you feel?"

The ashram's administrative buildings and classrooms were at the edge of the Ganges, whereas the bungalows and meditation hall for visitors—who were kept separate from permanent members—were on a hill. Oskar had been urged to rest for the remainder of the day, so he walked up the hill, past shops that sold religious articles and food, to a series of one-, two-, and three-room bungalows. His was a simple, single room with only a few shelves for books and clothing.

The heat and travel had exhausted him, so Oskar lay down and was soon sound asleep. A rustling woke him in the middle of the night, and in the dim moonlight he could make out a monkey throwing his books to the floor and rooting through his belongings. Oskar yelled at the monkey, which ran from the room. Falling asleep a second time took somewhat longer than the first.

The next morning, he was awakened and called to meditation. Most of the ashram's residents were Indian; no one spoke German. Meditation required that one sit, cross-legged, for long periods of time, which Oskar found difficult and painful. After class he was told to return to his room to be served breakfast.

"Why must I eat in my room? I'd like to be with the swamis, the Hindus."

"Foreigners are not allowed in the dining hall," someone told him. "It would make the dining hall impure. You will be brought a simple breakfast in your room. Afterwards you may attend the lecture and meditation classes."

He learned that the Hindus divided food into three groups: *sattvic* (from the Sanskrit *sat*, or truth), unspiced vegetarian fare considered the pure food of divine truth; *rajasic* (from *raja*, or king), royal food which stimulates passion and the senses; and *tamasic*, which is considered unclean.

The language barrier made lecture classes and even the meditations difficult to follow, so the swami suggested Oskar begin by helping in the office. Oskar agreed.

Daytime classes were supplemented by evening congregational lectures and music called *Satsang*, in which ancient Hindu scripture was explained, interspersed with yoga exercise and music played on a small piano or an eight-stringed sitar. While he did not understand the music, Oskar enjoyed listening to its subtly changing tones and rhythms.

He learned about karma yoga (karma, the effects of one's past actions; this was also referred to as the yoga of practical works) and about bhakti yoga, deeds of love for other human beings or the Almighty, jnana yoga, that of divine wisdom, and nada yoga, that of divine sound. These were only a few of the many types of yoga. Each came with its own practices and mental points of view. Unaccustomed to hatha yoga's stretching and breathing in such oppressive temperatures, Oskar struggled to follow the instructors and eventually found himself becoming more flexible as well as more able to stand the heat, which was now merely unpleasant rather than unbearable.

The food was simple: rice and lentils, the lentils often in a thin soup. Oskar began losing weight; he found he was hungry much of the time. After a few days he went into the village and found some alternatives to the ashram diet; while these were also composed of rice and lentils, they were in a more condensed form and were therefore more filling. Since he had become a vegetarian in Germany, he was not bothered by the lack of meat, fish, and eggs.

"The Indian view of karma is very severe," Swami Shivananda said. "One is rewarded or punished for past deeds. But I want to stress that you should not see this as unchangeable law. On the contrary, if one's actions caused bad karma in this life or the next, the outcome can be adjusted with present actions. Bad karma from one's previous life can be cancelled out by today's good deeds. If, for instance, a person is a beggar today, he might have been a rich but selfish person in the past, so he must learn to be needy today. Your job is not to pass such a man by and say, 'Oh, this guy must have been bad in a past life.' Your job is to help him, and so create your own good karma for the future. And the same goes for diseases and hardships that befall all of society."

Oskar listened, impressed, but wondered at the misery he had seen in Bombay and Delhi. The poor, diseased, and crippled had been left to themselves; the caste system was inviolate, even by Gandhi, whose nonviolent *ahimsa* approach advocated understanding and brotherhood, including an end to "untouchability," but not necessarily equality in wealth or material possessions. Oskar couldn't help thinking that the people he saw might be better cared for in the West.

He became friendly with another foreigner, a Greek woman named Avrilia, who had been married to a lawyer in Athens. When she learned of the German bombing of London, with her husband's assent she had traveled to England to help comfort victims. She worked as a masseuse.

Her travels allowed her to avoid the German occupation of Greece, during which her husband had died. Having returned to Athens after the war, she learned of the suffering in India, of disease, poverty, and of the trauma caused by the civil war, and knew she had to help. On her way to India she visited people she had met through mail correspondence in Jerusalem, Israel, a place that affected her deeply. For the moment, she had decided that she would try to help lepers, since they seemed to be the worst off of all. She was accepted at the ashram, whose purpose was also to help those in need, and she convinced the swami to found a branch of his ashram for helping lepers.

She was renamed Leela, which in Hindu is literally "divine play, amusement, or drama," and in her case was intended as "the divine song of Krishna." Oskar considered her the first true Christian, in every sense, he had encountered. They discussed Christianity and philosophy and the importance of service to humanity. In her selflessness and devotion she was a role model, and her stopover in Israel would eventually play a pivotal role in Oskar's life.

The meditation began as it did on any other day, with yoga poses and a long period of sitting. The teacher announced that today everyone would meditate on his or her own and contemplate the first thought that appeared. This was not the usual approach, but Oskar sat quietly, and watched his thoughts as one watches clouds on a breezy afternoon. His mind settled softly on the question of loving one's neighbor as thyself, a question he had asked his teachers about as a schoolboy, and he gave his mind permission to explore the question as a child might explore a quarry or cave, traveling over and around and through it, sniffing and touching, until he was satisfied and had come to some conclusions.

Swami Shivananda's teaching was based on knowing thyself; once you know yourself, you are prepared to know the other. We bow to the divine in one another. This is not a knowing the way one knows if one loves noodles, but a knowing of the inner self, the soul, or divine self. Once you know your divine origin or self, perhaps you might be in a position to know, and so to help, others. Perhaps this was what the Bible meant, Oskar thought. Practice yoga, meditate, and know yourself.

He felt that his understanding was enhanced, but he was still somewhat confused, so he sought out Leela after class. Her olive forehead wrinkled at his questions.

"High in the Himalayas," she said, gesturing towards the front gate of the ashram, "there is a famous hermit. People seek him out and ask him questions. Take a bus to Vashishta Goya, ask the driver about the hermit. He'll show you how to find him. Perhaps he can answer your questions."

Leaving the ashram was a good idea, Oskar was thinking as the driver downshifted and the bus jerked upwards, its engine revving in low gear.

"Don't forget to let me know when to get off," he called to the back of the driver's head. The driver seemed to nod towards his interior rearview mirror. An hour and a half later, the driver signalled to Oskar.

"Get off after the next stop," he said, "and walk up the mountain another four or five hundred meters. You'll know what to do when you get there."

A boy of barely twenty, seated a few rows behind the driver, caught Oskar's arm as he went back to his seat. "You're going to Purushottomanda?"

Oskar shook his head. "I don't know where that is."

"Purushottomanda is the hermit here on the mountain."

"Where're you from?" Oskar asked.

"Ceylon. You?"

"Germany, but I'm living at the Himalayan Forest University ashram at the moment. Why don't we walk up together?" Oskar suggested, relieved to have company with whom to approach the hermit.

They climbed the dirt and rock path silently, side by side when there was room, until they came to a small wooden door. As they approached the door, it was opened from the inside, and an orange-robed *sannyasi* welcomed them.

"Were you just leaving?" Oskar asked.

"Oh, no, no. I was just letting you in," said the *sannyasi*. As Oskar and the boy from Ceylon looked at one another, grinning with shocked pleasure and anticipation, the *sannyasi* walked a ways downhill and waited for them to catch up. He led them to a cave, and as they arrived, the hermit emerged. He was old, but spry, with a long white beard and shining black eyes. He invited Oskar into his cave and bid the boy from Ceylon to sit and wait on a large flat stone.

"Why have you come?" the hermit asked.

Still startled by their unlikely reception, Oskar stumbled over his story, describing his past, his experiences in Europe, and his fears as best he could. What would be the right path for him to follow, he wanted to know. How could he avoid falling into the trap of being seduced by another demagogue such as Hitler?

The hermit's gentle smile and sympathetic eyes put Oskar at ease. "You did not have to come all the way to India for your answer. Let's look at your own scriptures, the Book of Samuel, for instance, in which the people's own desires lead to their having a king, and so you have the stories of the kings Saul and David and Solomon."

Oskar listened to the hermit, heard his own heartbeat in his ears, and felt his breath quicken high in his chest. He had expected anything but biblical quotations from this half-naked old man.

"Go back outside, and send the boy to me," said the hermit.

Oskar stared at him for a long moment before getting up, and the hermit smiled with so little guile and so much understanding that Oskar had to look away and stumble from the cave. When he reached the boy from Ceylon, he could only point toward the cave's entrance, ignore the boy's questions, and sit down heavily on the flat stone.

When the boy emerged, he looked as dazed as Oskar felt.

"What happened?" Oskar asked.

The boy shook his head. "I'm not sure. He asked why I had come to India, listened to everything I had to say, all my questions, my problems, then he quoted from the Quran and told me to find my answers in my own religion."

"I thought he would try to convert us," Oskar said, "or at least point out some of the benefits of his religion. I've got to tell you I'm a little embarrassed that he's more familiar with the Bible than I am." After another moment, Oskar slapped his knees, stood up and went to the wooden door.

"I was wondering," he asked the *sannyasi* minding the door, "when we arrived and you opened the door for us, you couldn't have seen us. So how did you know we were there?"

"Well, Purushottomanda told me there are two boys with such and such an appearance coming; please open the door for them."

"But how did he know?"

"He knows," the *sannyasi* said. "You figure it out for yourself. Come on, let me take you back to the bus stop."

When he arrived back at the ashram, Oskar sought out Leela and told her what had happened.

She nodded, impressed but not surprised. "There's your answer. Delve into your scriptures." Her dark eyes were alive with encouragement.

A look of understanding broke across his face. "I have two versions of the Bible, English and German, and learning a foreign language won't hurt, in and of itself."

"You'll have plenty of food for thought," Leela agreed.

Oskar went on with his studies at the ashram, physical, mental, and spiritual, and in his spare time, he read the Bible. He began with the New Testament, with which he had familiarity from his academic studies. Some of the text he remembered and understood, other parts were mystifying, but he forced himself to read. He then moved on to the Five Books of Moses. Perhaps, he reasoned, if in his first reading he were to familiarize himself with the language and information, he might put aside the need for complete understanding. Later he could come back and fill in any gaps in his knowledge.

The trip to the hermit's cave had so impressed Oskar that he decided to go back again, though he had no specific questions to ask. Leela shrugged when he put the idea before her, and said that if he wanted to go back, she would not dissuade him.

He explained to the *sannyasi* at the door that he wanted to speak with Purushottomananda, but was told that the hermit was away, teaching and lecturing, so Oskar returned to the ashram, disappointed but with his mind alive with ideas for other spiritual and intellectual pilgrimages.

A week or two later, he took another trip high into the mountains to one of the four *tirthas*. A *tirtha* is a sacred place in the Hindu religion. The *tirtha* Oskar chose was Badrinath, not far from the Kashmir border, significant in that it is a northern directional *tirtha*.

The experience with the hermit had struck Oskar as evidence of something genuine, worth pursuing, and while he followed the hermit's advice, he sought more such encounters. It was as though his spirit had touched something true, recognized it, and hungrily sought to repeat the experience.

The bus ride to Badrinath was steeper than the one to the hermit's cave, the rocky slopes narrower and sharper, the curves more sudden and dangerous. The driver sang "Hare Krishna" before each turn, closing his eyes as he spun the wheel, and the bus somehow survived what appeared to be a series of near-death experiences.

Not far from the top, the bus's engine died. The driver sang "Hare Krishna," opened the hood and knocked on the engine, and they were once again on their way. Oskar would not have believed this if he had not seen it for himself.

Everyone was let off the bus and, since the bus had no toilet, passengers began relieving themselves nearby; Oskar turned away in disgust. They continued up the mountain on foot, joining another group heading toward the same place. Oskar walked with a wealthy Indian man and his servant, who carried the man's luggage.

The long walk in his thick-soled German shoes had left Oskar's feet swollen and throbbing. "How much further?" he asked the wealthy Indian.

"Perhaps half a kilometer."

After at least a whole kilometer, Oskar gave the man an annoyed look. "You're a spiritual man, or so you say. Why didn't you tell me the truth? I can hardly walk."

"If I had told you at the beginning how far it was, you would have been discouraged. Now you're well along, and it really isn't much further. I did you a favor."

"But you were dishonest. I expected the truth."

"Don't be so quick to measure truth from the abstract point of view, but instead by how much good, how much help one's words offer. Look, in my day-to-day life I'm a priest in the valley"—he pointed down the mountain, behind them—"and I have to help each person according to his ability to understand. I have to give the answer you can accept, but I still have to help you. My answer regarding the distance to our destination was appropriate for what you were able to hear."

Finally they arrived at the mouth of a cave. Inside was a figure, a statue of Krishna, the avatar, or human form, of the god Vishnu, who was thought of as a universal savior. The statue was perhaps a meter high, decorated in precious stones and chains and bearing a divine flute. An attractive piece of art, Oskar thought, but was it worth his exhausted, swollen feet?

Perhaps, he thought later, the destination had been not the statue, but the words he had heard along the way.

Several weeks later, three Brahmins, members of India's priest caste, visited the ashram. Dressed in loose-fitting, light-colored clothing, they wore their hair and beards long and had the thread, the long strip of white wool, slung over their right shoulders. This they had received as young initiates into one of the "twice born" castes in a ceremony called *upanayana.*

Oskar listened to their discussions and found them sincere and wise. When he was allowed to ask a question, he asked, "Why, if you are Hindu, does your teaching seem so similar to Christian tradition?"

"What does it matter?" one of the Brahmins answered.

"Well, you could pass for Christian missionaries. I say this as a Christian by birth. Don't you want to deliver a clear message?"

A second Brahmin answered. "We are not Christian missionaries, but tell us, did you ever read the Gospels?"

"As a matter of fact, I recently read two."

"Perhaps you came across a passage about fishing?"

"Yes, I did. And as a boy I fished in a river near my house."

"Excellent. And you announced to the fish that you were coming to catch them?"

"Well, no."

"So we don't need to announce who we are or attempt to catch followers like fish in a net. Even our religion doesn't matter. It's our way that's important. And if one needs to explain things, one must do so in a manner that does not try to convert or cause discomfort or a feeling of pressure on the part of the listener. Much better to cause comfort and bring strength to the listener."

"Much better," echoed another of the Brahmins.

The third raised a finger. "Have you ever heard of the Wheel of Buddha?"

"I, I think so."

"Do you understand its meaning?"

"Does it have something to do with karma?"

"It is a circle with a dot in its center and spokes directed outward. The outer areas represent our differences. All over the world, you witness this outer edge; people have different beliefs, behaviors, different ways—Christian, Muslim, Hindu, Jew. With those differences come conflict and strife, struggle and pain. But as we move more towards the center, these people and ways become more alike, and by the time we are in the center there is true unity with others and with yourself. The differences disappear and there is only commonality and an end to strife. No more theological arguments, no more differences. Everyone and all philosophies meet in the center."

Oskar had a vision of himself as a little boy cradled in his mother's arms along with his sister, Hilde.

"Which of you is Mother's most beloved?" Sophie had asked, teasing.

"Me! Me!" each had cried.

"No, sillies! I love you equally!"

"Anyone, from any religion, can find his way to the center?" Oskar asked the Brahmin.

"The starting point is unimportant."

"Everything at the starting point is illusion anyway," a second Brahmin chimed in. "We call this illusion *maya*."

Oskar knocked on a nearby desk. "But this is a hard desk. Very real, no?"

"Your perception of that desk depends on many things—time, for instance. When you were a boy it was one thing, a tree perhaps. Now you are a young man, and it is another. In fifty years it will be yet another thing, dust perhaps. Yet somehow it was always the same. *Maya* is man's illusion or perception based on his subjective place in time."

The first Brahmin spoke gently. "In the East, we look at things differently than you do in the West."

"But how do I overcome these illusions?"

The third Brahmin spoke more definitively than the others. "You cannot completely escape them. You are a product of your time. If you grew up in Nazi Germany, that shapes you. Think of the German word *Welt*, from the ancient Germanic words for man and old, perhaps, mmm?"

"So do I stay at the ashram? What's the best way for me?"

"We can only tell you what Brahmins do," said the first and most kindly of the Brahmins. "We are not hermits or monks, retreating from the world. We travel, we talk to people, we learn from them and share."

"And by doing so," said the second, "we move closer to the center of the circle."

15

"*N*amaste.*"* The ashram devotees bowed to Oskar, palms together at their chests.

"*Namaste,*" he responded, from a similar posture.

He asked Swami Shivananda what the greeting represented and whether that knowledge would be of help on his quest for fulfillment.

"One hand represents you, the other represents the one you are greeting." He brought his hands together to demonstrate. "You bow to the divine in that person, which is also the divine in yourself. And so, you are one."

Oskar asked Leela what the swami meant by "divine" and how such a concept might differ from "infinity."

"Before leaving Greece," she said, her cheekbones rounding as she remembered and smiled, "I joined a convent and became a nun, and one of the things I learned is that you have to come to your own understanding of such things."

"But is divine simply an infinity of time and space? You must have learned at the convent that God was absolute, omnipotent, omnipresent, as I learned in school."

"The more you search, the more you will come to your own understanding. What God is for you will become more clear as you search. It is very personal."

Unsatisfied, he went back to one of Swami Shivananda's assistant swamis, and asked about the meaning of the ashram.

"The ashram represents one of life's four *ashramas*, or stages: youthful study, marriage and family life, retreat and introspection, and finally the preparation for our passing. During this last stage we pass on wisdom to the next generation. That is what an ashram has come to symbolize."

"I don't think I'm at that stage yet," Oskar said. "My life is ongoing; I'm not ready for retreat and introspection, and certainly not preparing for my passing."

A few days later, Swami Shivananda fell ill with a lung ailment and sent for doctors from Delhi. Oskar was surprised that such a seemingly healthy man who practiced such rigorous breathing and hatha yoga exercises would request a doctor; in fact he was surprised that the swami would fall sick at all.

He asked Leela about the swami's health and care. "There is a kind of intoxication that comes with the breathing, especially if the exercises are overdone," she said. "The more you breathe this way, especially when you become very proficient, the more you want to do the exercises. Consequently, many of the swamis have developed throat and lung problems."

"Perhaps some of them are a bit addicted," Oskar suggested.

They sat for some time, as the birds in the green expanse of branches and leaves above them carried on animated conversations. Cloud formations floated above, their shapes briefly defined, then dissolved as they drifted away, the wind whispering at their edges.

"This isn't where I want to end my life," Oskar said. "I've got to go on."

Leela tilted her head to one side and gave a little nod, closing her eyes momentarily. Oskar could not tell if this were an expression of assent or of relief that he had finally come to a decision she had expected all along. "I'll give you the names of friends in Israel. If you are ever there, look them up."

"I'll take the names, but I don't think I'll be going to Israel anytime soon."

Once Swami Shivananda was well again, Oskar sought him out. "I've been honored by your invitation to stay here and am grateful for your help and teaching, but I've decided to go on with my search."

The swami nodded. "I'll be sorry to see you go, but I understand."

"I've sent a letter to my parents, asking for some money to pay you . . ."

"No, no. You have been working here all this time. That is the payment."

"But I have to pay you for the food, the accommodations. Please accept . . ."

"Well, perhaps something small. We can discuss this when your return letter arrives."

"I was wondering, Swami, if you can help me to better understand the different kinds of yoga, the jnana and bhakti, so I can take this knowledge with me."

The swami shook his head. "I don't think so. Imposing our views on you is not our way."

As he left the ashram, Oskar looked back and again saw the sign— Himalayan Forest University—but now the words held significance. The learning here had been less conventional and more universal than his previous education, and every bit as valuable.

The disciplines had been more attuned to the world of matter, the curriculum more concerned with the unity of body and soul than with details of the perceived world such as history, language, and science. How, he wondered, might the two curricula be combined? Might law and medicine be taught in concert with yoga? How might the ashram's motto "know thyself" be applied in western universities, and what might the role of the Bible be?

He remembered learning that Krishna had said: "All this yoga I have taught you will be of no avail without my grace."

Exactly what, Oskar wondered, is grace?

One of the assistants at the ashram had given him the name of a man in Delhi. Visit him, and ask about his guru, the assistant had said, giving Oskar a personal recommendation.

So he took a bus from the edge of the Ganges and then a train to Delhi. The man's name was Bhadra Sena. He was in his sixties, his hair and eyebrows were white; he lived in a modern home, dressed in simple though not poor clothing, and wore a turban. Upon hearing that Oskar had been recommended by members of the ashram and after listening to his intentions, Bhadra Sena welcomed Oskar and agreed to take him to visit his own teacher.

"We do not use the word 'guru,' however. This is an inflated, puffed-up word not meant for everyday teachers. Literally it means 'one who dispels your darkness and helps you to see the inner light of your soul' and truthfully, my teacher does exactly that."

On the way to the teacher's ashram, Bhadra Sena answered Oskar's questions. "My teacher has a normal job, working in a government office, he is married, and has a son. I think you will find our way different from anything you've seen so far."

They arrived at a neat, clean modern building in which the man's devotees had already begun to assemble. A tall turbaned man approached them and Bhadra Sena said, "This is my teacher, Master Kirpal Singh."

Master Singh greated Oskar graciously, with personal warmth and kindness, inviting him to stay, listen and, observe. Those listening to Master Singh appeared raptly attentive. "All Sikh men have the family name Singh," Bhadra Sena whispered. "It means 'lionhearted' and implies disciple, strength. The women are named Kaur, which means 'princess.'"

"God made man," Master Singh said, in his opening remarks to the group. "But man made religions. Every saint was born a sinner; but every sinner has the birthright to become a saint. We have only to work hard, perform service, and share the fruits of our labor." He seemed to look right at Oskar. "One ought not exchange one's own cultural background for that of another," he said. "Rather one ought return to one's own cultural background and fill it with inner light one receives from a living master."

He discussed the teachings of Guru Nanak, the founder of the Sikh religion, and the nine official gurus who followed him. He encouraged his listeners to earn their livelihoods through honest work, never by religious teachings, as profiting from spirituality corrupts one's soul and the teachings themselves.

"We do not require much," Master Singh explained. "We have no deities other than he who is the Creator, Sustainer, and Purifier— often referred to as Destroyer—of the universe. We worship no idols or statues and do not believe in human incarnations of the Creator. We do ask you to take a vow of absolute vegetarianism and abstinence from alcohol."

Oskar was introduced around and found the members of the Sikh community to be sociable and welcoming. He met an American his age named William, who was also new to Sikhism, and together they discussed what they had heard.

"I'm concerned about taking vows," Oskar said. "How can we project about the future and what a given situation will require?"

"You feel the vow might be restrictive," said William.

"What if there's an unnecessary hardship because of the vow? What if I am somewhere and I must eat something that does not precisely meet the vow's criteria?"

"Why not ask Master Singh?" William suggested, tipping his head in the direction of the teacher.

Oskar approached the teacher and explained his dilemma. "I am a vegetarian anyway, but I want to be a free man, able to follow my own convictions, rather than be a slave to a vow."

Master Singh gave Oskar an understanding smile. "Why don't you sleep on it."

At Bhadra Sena's home, before retiring for the night, Oskar's host asked to speak quietly to him, out of the family's earshot.

"My father is gravely ill, and if he summons me, I will have to leave and stay with him. I'm explaining this because if his time comes I may be caught up in the situation and may not have time to explain what all the activity is about."

The night passed uneventfully, and the following day Oskar accompanied Bhadra Sena to his teacher's ashram and explained that he had not changed his mind about the vow.

"Well," Master Singh said, after a moment's consideration, "if you are truly sincere about your vegetarianism, perhaps you will not need to take the vow."

"Well, I have to think about being initiated into your group," Oskar said.

Master Singh said he understood.

"He's a very generous, understanding teacher," Oskar said to Bhadra Sena, when they had returned to his home. "But I'm surprised he would so easily allow me to join without taking the vow."

"Whatever you decide is fine," Bhadra Sena said. "You're always welcome here, whatever happens with the master and your vow."

Oskar thanked his host. "Tell me about the Sikh religion's relationship to the Hindu religion and Islam."

"As Master Singh says: 'Keep your own cultural background and bring your inner light to bear.' I am Hindu, you know. This was my upbringing and I am comfortable with it. The Sikh religion is conciliatory towards that. It makes room for everything else; it was founded as a way of blending or reconciling Islam with Hinduism. As you heard last night: no statues, no pagan gods. This is monotheism—belief in the one Creator. We have our scripture and the gurus beginning with Guru Nanak but we do not elevate our teachers in the here and now. We believe in learning and discipline, in defending ourselves, in hard work. We are small in number but hold a high percentage of positions in the government and military because of our attitudes, our discipline."

"Are you an elite in your society?" Oskar asked, thinking of the Brahmin caste.

"We believe in complete equality. We are entirely against any caste system. We believe that women are the equals of men. Our scripture says of women: 'Why call her inferior, who gives birth to kings?' And while it is true we hold many jobs one might think of as elite, we are also taxi drivers and shopkeepers."

Bhadra Sena brought up the Wheel of Buddha, the differences between people on its outside and the perfect harmony at its center, and the symbolism of the cow and its "holy" virtues, both concepts with which Oskar was familiar, and host and guest marvelled at their common interests.

A knock came at the door and Bhadra Sena went to see who it was. When he came back, he was distracted and serious. "I have to go. It is my father's time."

Oskar said he would wait and read. He sat back with his Bible, enjoying the quiet, the voices occasionally intruding from the street, which was on the outskirts of Delhi. He especially enjoyed the children's shouts, which are joyful in any language. He reread the stories of Abraham and Jacob, and the voices of the children outside brought the stories to life so that they seemed immediate and real.

When Bhadra Sena returned, Oskar could see by his face that his father had died. He expressed his condolences and waited to see if his host desired privacy or company.

"He sat on the bed and called each of us to him," Bhadra Sena said, sitting down next to Oskar, but looking at the far wall. "He blessed us calmly, as though it were his choice at that moment, then he passed away."

"I'm so sorry," said Oskar.

"Perhaps it is strange," said Bhadra Sena, "but I am not sorry. Not for him, though perhaps a little for myself." He finally looked Oskar. "He had achieved fulfillment in this life."

"Did he know the Bible?" Oskar asked.

Bhadra Sena gave him a curious look. "Well, many years ago, he was given a New Testament."

"I meant the Books of Moses. The Old Testament."

"I don't know what that is. Why do you ask?"

"I was just reading about Abraham's grandson, Jacob. When Jacob felt his death approaching he called his family to him and they sat on his bed, and he gave his final blessing and passed away. It sounded so much like what you just described that I thought perhaps your father had read that story."

Bhadra Sena shook his head. "It is not an unusual passing here."

When he had gone, Oskar returned to his Bible, and the resonance of his experience with Bhadra Sena brought a vividness, a third dimension to his reading; in his mind the stories came alive.

Since his epiphany at the Berlin rail station, Oskar had searched and journeyed, analyzing and inspecting doctrines and dogmas, searching out inequalities and hypocrisies, filtering religions and political systems he saw through his own prism of disillusionment. Despite his own personal grief, Bhadra Sena invited Oskar to stay at least a few days more, and Oskar accepted but made a point of touring Old Delhi and New Delhi again on his own, seeing sights of interest and giving his host and his family privacy.

A museum had been made of the palace of a local raja who had had a personal interest in radios and owned some of the oldest, built by Edison, as well as the most modern German Grundig model. The palace was ornate, opulent, while outside beggars cried for alms; not far away lived a colony of lepers. He was surprised to see no sign of hatred or envy on the part of the poor. Perhaps they accepted their fate as the result of their own actions, their karma. He likened the attitude he saw in India's poor to Greek stoicism. Perhaps, he mused, the lack of poor on the street was simply a pragmatic matter: one cannot live under an umbrella in the cold.

When he told Bhadra Sena he would be leaving and thanked him for his hospitality under such difficult circumstances, his host suggested he visit a relative, Nehru, who was a pundit (sometimes referred to as a pandit, or one well versed in oral tradition), a professor at the University of Allahabad, a town between Delhi and Calcutta, and a relative of the prime minister of the same name.

Oskar had intended traveling in that direction, so after a short train ride, he found his way early one evening to a modest bungalow fronted by a small garden. Mrs. Nehru, a short woman with smiling eyes, invited Oskar in, explained that her husband was not yet home, and invited him to dinner. When Professor Nehru arrived, his wife met him at the door. Oskar watched as they bowed respectfully to one another and said, "*Namaste.*"

Clean shaven and in his early fifties, wearing loose-fitting Brahmin clothing, the professor seated himself alongside his wife on one side of the table; Oskar was invited to sit at the other side. A waiter placed plates before each of them and, after a moment's hesitation, Oskar said, "I'm very sorry. I hope it's not too much trouble. But I'm a vegetarian."

Mrs. Nehru summoned the servant in Urdu, and the dish was taken away. "Please wait a few minutes," she said politely. The servant returned five minutes later with a plate of eggs and vegetables. Oskar ate the vegetables and forced himself to eat a few bites of the eggs.

Dinner conversation was unfocused small talk. The professor's warm, shining eyes observed Oskar from a well of friendship and good humor. Nehru asked about his cousin, and Oskar asked about the local area and the garden, and described the fruit garden he had played in as a child. The professor asked Oskar to tell about himself and his life, and towards the end of the meal, the professor asked Oskar why, in his opinion, the Germans hated the Jews so much. Oskar tried to think of an answer but was able only to mumble something about the Jews being accused of usury and greed during the war.

"But you worked for a bank. Didn't you try to get the best salary for yourself? Didn't you try to make money? So what's wrong with a Jew doing the same? A man has to work."

"You're right," Oskar said, a little embarrassed. "That was a silly answer. I remember being told in elementary school that the Jews had to suffer for crucifying our Lord."

Nehru sat back. His wife was looking at him as though she knew he would have something to say. Oskar admired their obvious love and respect, the silent communications, the tacit understanding, the way each bowed to the divine in the other. How wonderful to be so connected spiritually and intellectually and with such love.

"The Jews suffering for the crucifixion? Well, if that's the case—and I'm not so sure it is—it's been two thousand years! A long time to hold a grudge, don't you think? What did the Nazis claim is currently wrong with Jews?"

"Perhaps they continue to justify the crucifixion," Oskar offered.

Now Nehru leaned forward, looking hard at Oskar with black eyes that seemed to grow darker still. "Tell me, why did you come to India?"

"Well, I was attracted by Gandhi. While we have had such terrible wars in Europe, your Gandhi, one small man with nothing backing him up, accomplished so much so peacefully."

"But it makes no sense!" Nehru exclaimed. "You came to India because you admire Gandhi, yet we did to him just what you claim the Jews did to Jesus! You ought to be anti-Indian. In fact, come to think of it, you ought to be anti-Greek, despite all of the cultural history of Greece. Look at what they did to Socrates!" He exchanged hidden smiles with his wife.

Oskar thought for some time before answering. "I remember, as a child, seeing a strange chicken put in with a group of chickens, where it was pecked to death. I also remember anyone different being disliked in Bavaria. Perhaps therein lies the answer."

"Well, I think there are differences," Nehru said. "Socrates and Gandhi were not killed for religious reasons, but the Jews, and Jesus for that matter, are a different story."

Oskar only half heard. He was looking at the vegetables and eggs on his plate, but his mind was far away.

The following day he boarded a train to Calcutta, his mind still on the previous evening's discussion and the beautiful relationship between the Nehrus. Was the crucifixion a religious matter while these other examples of bigotry and genocide were politics? He vowed to read both versions of the Bible to learn more.

An engineer who worked in a steel factory along the train route to Calcutta, in Shantiniketan, offered Oskar a place to stay. Long accustomed to Indian hospitality and having shed some of his European-bred suspicions, he accepted, and accompanied the tall, thirtyish engineer wearing the long white shirt to a small home in a modest neighborhood. The factory, the man explained, had been built by the Russians. Oskar looked around the living room, which was sparsely decorated, except for two enormous portraits hung next to one another on the one wall.

"I recognize Gandhi," said Oskar, "but who is the other one?"

"His name is Subhas Chandra Bhose, a Bengali, originally a disciple of Vivekananda. He also played a part in India's independence. After Gandhiji came from South Africa and began his campaign for freeing India nonviolently, Bhose agreed that we have to restore India's honor, but he advocated any means necessary, including violence. You are German?"

Oskar indicated that he was.

"Bhose bought weapons from Germany, including a submarine. Because he was so against England, in that sense he followed Hitler, perhaps even admired him."

"Don't you think it's contradictory to have a portrait of an admirer of Hitler's next to Gandhiji?"

The engineer stared at the portraits for a while, looking from one to the other; finally he gave a half nod. "I see what you mean, but both men have done a great deal for Indian independence."

"If I were to put up a portrait of Stalin and the Pope, no one in Europe would accept that."

"Well," said the engineer, "I'm not European, so that doesn't matter." Carefully, he lifted an instrument from a corner of the room. "If you don't mind, I'm going to play my sitar. Have you heard sitar music?" Oskar said he had and sat back to listen while the engineer played.

Within seconds Oskar was more comfortable; the two portraits and their contradictions vanished, and his consciousness moved with the music, grounded by its consistent rooted chords yet transported by the intricately woven melodies played high above, reaching and soaring while remaining true to the deeper constants of the foundation chords. The engineer played a theme, then strayed from it, with variations that were sometimes musical, sometimes emotional in their differences.

When he finally stopped, Oskar returned to the room and the present. "I can tell what you were feeling while you played," he said, once the silence had settled. "We took that trip together."

"That the music spoke so clearly to you, a European, is a compliment," said the engineer.

"To us both," Oskar laughed. "It's opened up my view, my whole trip in a way, and now we're kindred spirits."

When he went to bed, he was kept awake by a steady humming that filled the heavy humid air; he realized after an hour of insomnia that the noise was the drone of a multitude of mosquitoes. He pulled the white mosquito netting close around the bed, allowed his body to relax using a breathing technique he had learned at the ashram, and gradually fell asleep.

16

He watched the sky through the window of the train on the way to Calcutta the next day, remembering the first time he had read about Ramakrishna, remembering the nice lady at the American library at Erlangen who had referred the book to him. That book had watered that original seed of change that had brought him to this moment, traveling to the ashram of Ramakrishna in Dakineshevar. He watched high thin clouds float over arid acreage as the train approached the city, and he saw that his own experience was like that, that he was watching and experiencing physical and spiritual terrain, absorbing its essence as clouds absorb moisture.

The train pulled into the Calcutta station too late for a visit to the nearest ashram, so Oskar found the phone number of a hostel, and reserved a bed. He was standing at the edge of a bus stop when a tall, slim Indian man in his twenties caught his attention and began speaking to him in German.

The man, who wore European clothing, asked if he was visiting from Germany. Oskar merely looked at him, processing the fact that this Indian man was speaking German rather than the English normally spoken to foreigners by the locals.

"I said . . ."

"I heard you. Yes, how did you know?"

"Your jacket. Typical Bavarian alpine."

Oskar looked down at himself, then laughed. "I guess it is. How is it you speak German?"

"I studied there for a few years. Where are you going? Need directions?"

"I just made a reservation inside and will be going to the ashram in Dakineshevar tomorrow."

"You don't want to stay in that place. I live in Calcutta. I'm familiar with Germany. I'd be honored if you'd be my guest."

"Thanks, but I've already made a reservation."

"I'll take care of it." He put out his hand. "My name is Mukherjee."

They took a bus to a small house in a poor neighborhood in Calcutta and entered a tiny living area around the edges of which lay folded clothing and bedrolls. No one else was there. Mukherjee began preparing a sleeping area for him.

"I don't want to put anyone out," Oskar said.

"No, no, my family agrees. This is where you are to sleep."

Oskar looked around with raised eyebrows, wondering how they knew. Not wanting to offend his host or his family, he changed the subject. "How was your experience in Germany?"

Mukherjee hesitated, then answered slowly. "Oh, well, fine. The university was excellent. I studied engineering."

"But how did you find . . . Germany? Tell me truthfully."

Mukherjee's shoulders slumped, and he swallowed several times. "Since you asked, I felt very much a foreigner and an outsider. I went to restaurants and other public places, but when I sat down, people moved away. If I was alone, no one joined me. I would see people pointing and saying amongst themselves that blacks shouldn't be here."

"Why, then, would you invite a German into your home?"

"I decided to make a point of inviting foreigners in so no one would feel in India what I felt in Germany."

The following morning, Mukherjee took Oskar to Dakineshevar, a sprawling complex of temples, ashrams, and archeological excavations; Oskar found the place interesting but static. There was nothing new to be learned in this memorial, no living thought or active teaching. Ramakrishna and Vivekananda were long gone, and while monuments and mausoleums were nice tributes, they could not convey the insight Oskar sought.

After returning to Mukherjee's house for tea, Oskar explained that he would move on.

"My name is a common one," Mukherjee said, handing Oskar a stack of small white cards, "so give any foreigners coming this way my card. It has my address and phone number. Tell them they will always be welcome here."

Oskar headed for Risa with a planned stopover at Waltair, north of Madras. An acquaintance at the Shivananda ashram had given him the name of a man there and suggested he pay the man a visit. On the way, he stopped at Konarak near Orissa's capital to view the ruins of a sun worshippers' temple left over from the Middle Ages.

The walls of the temple were engraved with swastikas. There were few guests and no one guiding tours or answering visitors' questions, so Oskar asked a man standing nearby why the swastikas were part of this ancient temple.

"The symbol represents the wheel of the sun. This place was dedicated to sun worship."

"In Germany, I'm sure you know, this is the symbol of the Nazis."

"Except the Nazis got it backwards and upside down. This one is going counterclockwise, whereas you Germans had it going clockwise, and notice the way it sits on an edge rather than a solid base, giving the feeling of being a wheel rather than a square."

Oskar left the excavation remembering a book he had read in school, by Carl Jung, about the impact of symbols on the human consciousness.

The word "swastika," he later learned, was derived from Sanskrit, and its original meaning was "all is well."

"Where are you staying?" the man he had questioned about the swastika asked.

"I'm traveling," Oskar said.

"Why not stay for a day? I'm a farmer and could use a hand if you'd like to lend one."

Oskar went home with the farmer. The following morning Oskar said he was ready to help and wanted to know what he could do. "I'll be plowing that field over there with a small tractor." The farmer pointed past a line of trees toward neat rows of plants. They walked to where he kept his farm machines. "Do you know how to drive one of these?" He touched the seat of an old but workable tractor.

"Yes, I have a license," Oskar assured him.

"Well, then, let's go." The farmer led him to the field, showed Oskar where its boundaries were, and set the level of the plow. "When you're through, just drive back here. I'll find you."

Oskar set himself on the high, bouncy seat, looked over the controls, started the tractor, and set off, glancing behind him to make sure the plow was operating properly. He drove to the end of the row, managed to turn the plow around, and came back again. Fine sand sprayed out behind the thick tires' treads. Halfway down the next row the plow slowed and then stopped in a deep bed of sand. He tried a lower gear, but the tires spun and the tractor dug itself in deeper, until after a few minutes its gearbox was pressed into the ground.

Oskar turned off the engine, sat for a moment considering what to do, and then set off to find the farmer to explain what had happened.

At first the man shouted at him, demanding to know how such a thing could have occurred, since Oskar claimed to be an experienced, licensed tractor driver. Once he calmed down, he rounded up two oxen, followed Oskar to where the tractor sat in its sand pile, and, after shaking his head and walking circles around it for a few minutes, hitched up the oxen and pulled the tractor and plow free.

"It must be bad karma," the farmer was saying, more to himself than to Oskar.

"Look, I apologize for any damage to the tractor. I'll pay for it, of course."

"Hmm? No, that's not what I mean." He had begun to unhitch the ropes from the oxen and tractor. "This must be my own bad karma. It's my fault. Something I did in the past, but the question is . . . what." Again he fell to muttering to himself. Finally he turned to Oskar, rubbing his chin and glancing around in a disconcerted way. "I said my prayer and made my offerings this morning, so I thought everything would be fine. But then this."

"I don't see why I should be the instrument to punish you. Does that make sense?" Oskar said, trying to find some way to comfort him.

"Who knows? The gods have different ways of rebuking us, and I must accept it. I cannot take your offer to pay damages. I have to fix whatever is wrong with me." He turned to Oskar, and seemed to have found his way to an opinion. "You see, if I were entirely one with the spirit of the divine world, this kind of thing would not have happened. And as for you, well, maybe you also have something to work out. Maybe both our karmas are somehow wrong. Think about that." He began to shake a finger, a light of an idea in his eyes. "We became acquainted and you agreed to do a bit of work, and said you knew how to drive a tractor and yet apparently you did not. Or at least you did not know how to plow a field. Is this not true?"

"Quite true," Oskar had to admit. "I exaggerated my knowledge of plowing. Perhaps this is what was wrong with my karma."

"Well, don't be so fast," said the farmer. "I did not ask if you could plow fields, but if you could drive a tractor. Apparently you could drive a tractor, yet could not plow fields, at least not in this kind of deep sand, which was not even part of my question! So this is my own failure again!"

Oskar shook his head, astonished by the farmer's simple humility.

"I am quite sure," the farmer said, as they parted, "that there are many other things wrong with me, many failures for which I must account. I simply have to find them."

Mr. Naidoo was dark, long-limbed and spare, his face smooth and clean shaven. He lived in a little bungalow, whitewashed and built slightly off the ground, on the outskirts of Waltair. In front of the house was a neat, well-kept garden.

When he explained who he was and that he had been at the Shivananda ashram, Oskar was warmly welcomed and invited to stay. Mrs. Naidoo was small and round; she welcomed Oskar, then retreated to the kitchen, where she remained for much of his stay. Oskar caught a glimpse of a daughter in her twenties, dark hair knotted behind her head, colorful sari swirling as she walked circles around a tree in the backyard.

When asked at dinner about his experiences in India, Oskar related the story of his dinner with Mr. Nehru, his refusal to take Master Singh's vow of vegetarianism and how he had reluctantly eaten the eggs put before him in Nehru's home.

"I did not want to cause him personal inconvenience," Oskar explained.

Naidoo looked fleetingly puzzled, then disappointed. "It's a pity you had to deny your convictions. It would have been a good thing for them to see a European who was faithful to himself."

The following morning, Oskar happened to glance out a window as he passed, and what he saw made him stop and watch. Naidoo's daughter was again in the garden, walking circles around the same tree, first in one direction then the other, intoning what sounded like prayers. Oskar listened and tried to make sense of the words, but could not.

At breakfast he asked Naidoo what his daughter was doing.

"Offering thanks."

"To a tree?"

"She was very ill recently, the doctors could do nothing for her, but one of the local sadhus—spiritual, holy men—came and meditated and instructed her to pluck the leaves of this tree and prepare them in a particular way, and this would be her cure. And that is exactly what happened." He gave the scene outside a satisfied, paternal smile. "And so now she offers her thanks."

"I see why she is thankful, and please don't take the question as disrespectful, but praying to a tree—isn't this a kind of idol worshipping?"

"Perhaps it is," Naidoo admitted.

"But suppose I had given her a box of pills made by a pharmacy. Would she prostrate herself before it?"

"Why not?"

"Even though pills are made by people in a factory?"

"If God wants to heal her through pills or some other remedy, why not give thanks to him through them—pills, tree, whatever?"

"Well," Oskar said after a few minutes of watching Naidoo's daughter, "I suppose it's more a kind of giving thanks to the vehicle, the transport. Rather beautiful, different from the Catholic friends of my childhood who bowed before statues of Joseph and Mary. She's bowing to what's behind the statues." He thought a moment. "Perhaps they were, as well."

"I know my daughter is well, and so I am thankful. The rest. . . ?" He made a gesture of dismissal with his fingers.

"You know, you are so tolerant in this country. I think of the bloodshed between Christians throughout history, and I see all the different idols—which are apparently not what I thought of as idols—and deities and how tolerant you are towards others' beliefs and I am amazed and humbled. Much food for thought."

He and Naidoo sat up late, reflecting on the nature of religion and creation, which is ongoing. Naidoo described aspects of Hindu and pre-Hindu history Oskar had never known. He explained the concept of nothingness, or no-thingness, the reality based on nonexistence which, through the act of creation, becomes reality, or Brahman, with qualities or existence as we know them. Oskar's mind whirled around the new concepts, examining the theories and ideas the way a child turns over a new toy in his small hands, looking at them from every angle and holding them up to the light of his mind for examination. He relished such stimulating discussions, yet they were impersonal and theoretical. Still only discussions.

Naidoo drew parallels between western biblical teachings and Indian historical and religious perspectives Oskar found interesting and affecting since they drew from ideas which were part of his childhood and which had shape and form and even color and feel in his personal memory. Yet they were still part of the past mixed in with theory.

Naidoo explained the coming of Buddha, telling of the epiphany and revelation Gotama (the man who came to be known as Buddha) had while sitting under a tree in Bodh Gaya, and Oskar remembered visiting that place, that fig tree, which the Buddhist monks there had pointed out.

They argued into the night about whether Buddha was an atheist, which was what Oskar had thought. Not exactly right, Naidoo corrected. Buddha did not deny the existence of God; he refused to discuss the subject. How can we, with our limited abilities to understand the universe, possibly understand or intelligently discuss the infinite? We would find out about that if and when the time came, Buddha taught. And even if we could understand God, how could we reduce knowledge of the infinite to an abstraction so as to communicate it to others? Impossible.

Better to teach about what we can observe—best to be present in this moment, our only reality. Buddha thus trained himself and his disciples to learn to focus on the moment, ridding themselves of all distractions. There is only now. Reality is direct experience, and the eightfold path of truth will lead you there.

Oskar listened with animated eyes, then sat back and stared into the distance for some time, absorbing all he had heard. "You know, I spend much of my free time reading the Five Books of Moses, and what I read that's so very different is the personal relationship between Abraham and Jacob and Moses and their God. They walk and talk together, they disagree and have . . ." He brought the fingers of both hands together, interlocking them so his hands were one unit. "They have an interaction, a relationship like a father with a son."

Naidoo shrugged. "I don't know about this."

"Well, I'm not a parent as you are, but I get the feeling there is a love there, such as a parent feels for a child, and it goes both ways. The parent understands the child's frailties and faults, so there is a deep bond that is more than one can put into words." Now he felt he was onto something, an idea, perhaps a revelation that was just beyond his grasp.

"You have beautiful, attractive teachings and a tolerance that has moved me deeply in my travels. The prayers your daughter offers and what we've talked about and the things I've seen have taught me so very much. Only . . . it is not connected to my daily life. When I was a little boy I had questions about religion and I used to bother the monks, trying to understand. They were the personal questions of a little boy. Then when I was perhaps fourteen or so, I was angry with my parents because I felt I could not trust them. I couldn't understand the larger picture, their dilemmas, but I was hurt and angry. This was a personal pain, and it's never been addressed by religion, anywhere or at any time in my life. And it isn't for lack of looking! I have yet to find a religion or belief that speaks to that little boy's questions or to that teenager whose feelings were hurt."

"Perhaps none exists," Naidoo suggested. "After all, life is filled with pain, and it is asking a great deal to expect a child to grasp the meaning of a religion."

Oskar remembered from Genesis the story of Jacob, who seemed so human and alive. His story was filled with betrayal, temptation, anger, and fear, and for that reason, his great love and even greater faith were that much more touching and impressive. A verse from a psalm appeared in his memory and he recited it: "This is a generation that seeks after Him, that seeks the face of the God of Jacob" (Psalm 24:6). The words stayed with him as though they were not in his mind but in the night sky, as though they were meant for him personally.

"Are you all right?" Naidoo asked.

Oskar had been sitting back, his eyes wide and unfocussed, his gaze upwards toward the spot on the ceiling where he seemed to see the letters. Now he leaned suddenly forward, his eyes cast down, his breath heavy and in the top of his chest.

He appreciated Naidoo's attitude toward the tree, which he might once have considered idolatry but was plainly not. His appreciation was like that for a work of art, admired from outside. Now he knew where the difference lay and why it was so important to him. In the Bible, God spoke directly to Abraham, Moses, and David. The directness was a comfort and the instruction was specific. He remembered a passage in the Book of Deuteronomy regarding lending money and receiving collateral, a coat, for instance. If the borrower does not pay the lender back, he is to return the coat for the night so that the lender might keep warm, despite the debt. And this, the Bible said, "shall be a righteousness unto thee before the Lord thy God" (Deuteronomy 24:13). What a difference, he concluded, between the mundane law he had learned at the university and the law of Moses!

As he rolled and pitched and tossed, trying to sleep but too filled with ideas and revelations to do so, he remembered something Leela had said. If ever he were interested in visiting Israel, he could write her and she would give him all he needed.

The following morning he wrote her, explaining his thoughts and feelings, confident she would understand. He would indeed be interested in visiting Israel, the land and people of this so-called Old Testament. He would be in Madras soon, and could receive her reply there.

As he was writing, something else came to him, a memory of a man he had met in Delhi but had forgotten about because the meeting, while impressive, had not seemed significant enough to remember. The man's name was Cameroon, and he was of mixed descent, half-Sikh, half-Jewish, born in Trinidad. He was a beautiful young man, with long dark hair and penetrating eyes, a traveler who spoke softly yet profoundly. He had suggested that Oskar read a particular portion of the Bible since his family name, Eder, appeared there. It was in the Book of Chronicles, he had claimed, a section of the Bible Oskar had not read, since ancient geneology held no interest for him. But now he went back and read the sections with interest, and what he read added to his awakening.

He hoped Leela was still at the ashram, that she would receive his letter, and that she would remember and write back.

Asher said good-bye to Mr. Naidoo and went on a whirlwind tour of southern India, visiting places he had long thought about seeing. Mr. Naidoo refused any offer of money, so Oskar arranged to have his father send a coffee machine, an offer Naidoo, who loved coffee, joyfully accepted.

He visited Tanjore and Mysore, where the British influence was noticeable, and in a museum in Tanjore he saw a sculpture of Nataraj, the dancing Shiva, and two figures inside and outside a ring of fire. The inside figure smiled while the outside figure suffered, and he remembered the Wheel of Buddha and wondered if those inside the circle might be purified by the same fire that burns those without.

He braved the heat in Trichinopoly, where he was impressed by stone deities and sculptures which appeared to have erotic meaning. He had two cameras with him and wanted pictures of the statues, but knew that pictures in a spiritual, religiously important site would be unpopular if not forbidden. He devised a plan; he would leave and come back around again to the entrance, his smaller camera hidden in his hand. When no one was looking, he would quickly snap his photos.

But once in position, the camera ready, he pressed the shutter, and it would not work. He pushed harder, until he was certain the camera would break, but it refused to take the picture. Thinking perhaps a grain of sand had gotten into the mechanism, he looked around, saw a sadhu staring at him, and rushed from the building and into the town, looking for a camera shop. Before going inside, he raised the camera and tried one last time to take a picture. The camera worked perfectly.

Madras was one of the larger cities in southern India. It was considered the burial place of the apostle St. Thomas, and Oskar found the city and its surrounding landscape breathtaking. He made sure to get out in the early morning to take advantage of what little cool air there was, and it was then that he saw the trucks and ox carts hauling to incinerators those who had died of disease and starvation the previous night, an incongruous, disturbing sight which drove Oskar back indoors.

He went to the post office the first day and found a letter from Leela waiting. Whether it was Oskar's heart or mind that had finally been attracted to Israel did not matter to her, only that he was going. He was to find enclosed in her letter the names of two sisters who lived in Jerusalem, along with a land route that would take him to a Jordanian border point called the Mandelbaum Gate; in Hebrew it is Sha'ar Mandelbaum, the word *sha'ar* meaning gate. Mandelbaum is "almond tree" in English, but the place was apparently named after the man on whose former property the military outpost was now located.

Oskar wrote to the Israeli consulate in Bombay, applying for a visa to Israel; he explained the route he wished to take and said who had recommended him and that he would likely arrive in six months or so. He also described his interest in the biblical story of Jacob, its connection to modern Israel and his own curiosity about the place. Perhaps he might retrieve an answer in Cochin, for he was planning to stop next in its capital, Ernakulam.

He traveled southwest by train and bus, toward a Jewish community Leela had recommended he visit before going to Israel. He saw the Nilgiris, known as the Blue Hills, along the southwest coast of India. After arriving in Ernakulam, he waited at the bus terminal, needing to change a few traveler's checks, but all the banks and shops were closed as it was a local holiday. Having only a few coins in his pocket, he waited for a bus, hoping it would take him to the Jewish community.

No bus came, but a rickshaw driver approached and motioned him aboard. Oskar showed him his empty wallet and the driver left him alone. After he had stood there for an hour or so, a woman carrying a baby came over. Both were emaciated, and the baby seemed faint from hunger. Remembering women in India who begged with babies and kept what they received for themselves, leaving the babies to starve, Oskar hesitated. He gave the few pennies in his pocket to a passing peddler for a cup of warm milk, which he gave to the mother, who shared it with her baby. As they drank, the rickshaw driver appeared again and motioned Oskar into the rickshaw. Oskar again showed him his empty wallet but this time the driver insisted and he was on his way to the Jewish community.

The rickshaw left him at the entrance to a synagogue compound and Oskar approached an attendant and explained that he would like to have a tour. When asked if he was Jewish, he said that he was not and told the attendant the story of Leela and his application for a visa to Israel. Oskar explained that he would not be able to pay for his tour until the holiday was over. The attendant showed him to a guest room and together they went out to an inexpensive local restaurant.

The following morning the same attendant gave him a tour of the synagogue, showing him the ark, its Torah scrolls, skullcaps, prayer shawls, and an impressive quantity of decorative silver. Oskar did not entirely understand what he was seeing. He knew only the Five Books of Moses and he did his best to explain this to the attendant.

The attendant nodded and said in broken English: "Five Books of Moses . . . *Torah*."

When the tour was over, the attendant asked if he would like to see the "other Jewish community."

"What other Jewish community?" Oskar asked.

"The black one."

Oskar agreed, and they went together on a second tour, visiting Jews who traced their ancestry to the time of King Solomon. Their color did not surprise Oskar, who had himself darkened several shades since his arrival in India. Why would it not be possible for Jews from Solomon's time, who traded with southern India, to emigrate to this place and grow darker over the millennium? The connection between these people and his newly discovered biblical stories was exciting, though the separation of the two Jewish groups bothered him; he tried to imagine a dark Catholic group suddenly appearing in Germany and how they might be treated.

He was told about the most "severe" day of the Jewish year, Yom Kippur, a day of atonement and fasting. No entertainment or work was permitted. Oskar wondered if in this raucous country such an observance might be difficult, but the attendant explained that several hundred years ago a local maharaja had decreed that the Jews would have religious freedom and their holidays would be respected.

When Oskar brought up the subject of anti-Semitism, he was told that the Jews here knew of such things only from books.

At the post office a letter was waiting from the Israeli consulate in

Bombay—there was not, as yet, an embassy—explaining that his request for a visa had been forwarded to the Ministry of Foreign Affairs in Tel Aviv. If approved, the letter said, the visa would await him at the Mandelbaum Gate. Sending a visa directly would be problematic, since his having an Israeli visa would itself prohibit him from traveling there. No Arab country would allow entrance to anyone with an Israeli visa, and the route to the Mandelbaum Gate was through several Arab nations.

Buoyed by the news, Oskar went back to his Bible in earnest, rereading the stories of Isaac and Jacob, who had been renamed Israel. Were these ancient writings merely stories, he wondered, or actual history? Searching for connections between modern Israel and its biblical namesake, he began fervently reading the books of the prophets.

17

Vinoba Bhave was a small, chocolate-colored man whose eyes communicated the intensity of his commitment while his fine hands and delicate fingers seemed at odds with the dreary work asked of them. In his loose, white shirt and pants he led a multicultural, colorfully dressed group of regulars and part-timers in a *bhoodan yatra*, which means, literally, a land donation pilgrimage. He would become known as India's "walking saint."

He was an unlicensed teacher (and jailed several times for it) who had worked closely with Gandhi. After the assassination, he traveled around India asking the wealthy to donate their idle lands to the poor and then teaching the poor how to maintain and cultivate their new property.

Offered the opportunity to join the *yatra*, Oskar immediately agreed. He watched the diminutive leader, who was always surrounded by a wide and varied spectrum of humanity and was always trailing reporters and writers who questioned his thoughts, decisions, and actions. Sanitation, Bhave explained, was one of the greatest challenges for the poor. He pointed to the outskirts of the fields.

"Our people just walk off a hundred meters and leave their excrements, which then lie out in the hot sun." He shook his head, his long white hair swirling. "Then the pigs eat the excrement and someone eats the pigs, and he gets sick. So teaching our people to keep even a rudimentary toilet facility is a high priority." He motioned to a youthful Japanese man standing a short distance away. "Come, *gopal bhai*. Help me lift the container." The two walked to either side of a large vat. Reporters scurried after him.

Oskar turned to a man nearby. "Is that his name or does it mean something?"

"*Gopal bhai* means brother shepherd," the man said, and followed the crowd.

They found Vinoba Bhave cleaning human excrement from the vat with his hands.

"Why are you doing that yourself?" One of the reporters looked around as though someone might stop the little leader. The reporter leaned forward as though about to pull him away from the container, but could not bring himself to reach out. "Can't you delegate that work to someone else?"

Bhave smiled with good humor, his voice gentle yet imbued with purpose. "I can fill it up, so I can clean it out." He went back to work.

As soon as Bhave was free, Oskar explained who he was and why he had come and asked if he might spend a day or two with the group.

"Of course," said Bhave.

Whenever Bhave and his followers approached a new village, the elders of that village would walk out to meet them, prostrate themselves on the ground, and present Bhave with a chain of flowers. Bhave would ask if there was land to donate that he might redistribute and whether the poor who would be receiving the land needed training in its maintenance and cultivation.

Vinoba awoke at two A.M. each morning and meditated until three, at which time the rest of Bhave's people would awaken and meditate for a half hour. Soon after, Bhave would conduct the morning meeting, which consisted of a short lecture or sermon. On some mornings, as the sun came up, another of the group's twenty-five or thirty members might discuss his or her background or religion. The nomadic aspect of the group, its charismatic spiritual leader, and the outdoor work in the bright tropical sun all gave Oskar a feeling that he was living centuries earlier, and was following Abraham, Moses, or Jesus. After the meeting the focus would be on the village's sanitation, followed by a breakfast, usually arranged by the villagers in gratitude for the help they had just received.

When there had been a donation of land, Bhave would leave behind a member of the *yatra* to oversee its administration and the education of the poor in keeping it.

On the fourth day after Oskar's arrival, a delegation arrived from a nearby village seeking Bhave's help in a different kind of matter. Theirs and a neighboring village had been carrying on a blood feud for generations. Each year someone in one or the other town was murdered. Could Bhave help to settle their differences?

After conferring with his supporters and followers, Bhave agreed. He would return in a few days.

Oskar enjoyed the company of Bhave's followers and admired their mission. He was quickly at ease, talking about his background, asking about theirs, and helping out with the day's tasks. He began taking notice of a regal Indian woman, a few years his junior. His regard had been fleeting at first, but he became more attentive as his admiration grew. She was graceful without the slightest air of superiority, and her unawareness of her allure made her that much more charming. Unfortunately, she spoke primarily Tamil, very little English.

One of his new friends had seen him looking at her out of the corner of his eye. "Do you want me to arrange a meeting?"

Oskar continued to watch the woman. "She has a royal soul."

"She is from a well-known family. Very well respected and admired. Who knows? Maybe something can be worked out."

Oskar blushed. "Oh, I wouldn't know how to go about that."

"Leave it to me and my friends. We'll arrange the whole thing."

In the meantime, Bhave had returned from the feuding villages and explained that the problem had been solved. The villages were at peace. All it had taken was a little listening on both sides, and putting aside hurt feelings. Oskar looked with new respect at the wiry man with the delicate fingers and invisible ego.

The next day he was approached by his friend and told that a meeting with the young woman had been arranged. His heart racing, and having no idea of what he might say to her, he allowed himself to be led to where she was waiting with a few of her friends. When Oskar was introduced, everyone else moved tactfully away.

Their meeting was short. Both Oskar and the young woman were shy; neither had much to say. But Oskar was so taken with her beauty and sweetness that despite his sudden diffidence he became preoccupied with the idea of a future with her.

The following day, his friend came to him and explained that he had spoken with Bhave, who would be willing to perform a marriage if the couple wished.

Oskar thanked his new friend and sat alone, thoughts swirling, emotions in turmoil. He still had no idea of where and under what circumstances he wished to settle for the long term. With this regal young woman, he would have to stay in India, possibly without completing his own search, certainly without visiting Israel. The few westerners he could think of who had converted to Hinduism had seemed unhappy, never true Hindus. His recent visit with the gentleman who had felt so unwelcome in Germany surfaced in his memory. How happy would she be in Germany? he wondered. What was the fair choice?

He sent a message to Bhave that he appreciated the offer, but he preferred to wait.

Oskar was asked to speak to the group about Christianity, since that was the religion of his upbringing. He protested that he was searching for a spiritual base and was not focused on Christianity. So much the better, he was told, and was encouraged to speak instead about his search.

So he described his childhood impressions of Christianity and his confusion about the Lord's Prayer, how he had asked about the phrase "Hallowed be thy name" and the priest's unconvincing answer. He explained his uncertainty about the phrase "Thy kingdom come" and ended his lecture with the question of what that kingdom might be like. Would it be of earth or of another world, and would it involve the coming of a prophet or messiah?

Vinoba Bhave thanked him for speaking from his heart. "If the Indian people follow my way and Gandhi's teaching," Bhave said, "then my kingdom will be of both this world and the other world."

The words "my kingdom" resonated in Oskar's mind, causing him to consider all of Vinoba Bhave's good works. He was a peacemaker; he brought equality, yet he would do even the most menial work, such as cleaning human waste with his bare hands. One rarely saw such high principles and goals alongside such humility. Might he be . . . the messiah? If so, perhaps there was no need to go to Israel or back to Germany. And in that case, perhaps he might yet stay here and marry the young Indian woman.

He looked at her sitting opposite him; their eyes met for a moment, and he forced himself to look away, as his heart did somersaults.

His thoughts were everywhere, and, as he sought an answer, a direction, and could find none, Oskar decided to make no decision at all. If he could not determine that Bhave was a prophet or the messiah, he would continue to contemplate the matter from afar. The following day he informed Bhave that he would be on his way again. Bhave thanked him and said he would be always welcome to return.

It was late spring, and the arid air lay heavily on the flat, dusty land; when Oskar put on his shirt, he was startled by its heat against his shoulders.

His next stop was the Sevagram Ashram of Gandhiji, which was in a primitive village in south-central India on the Deccan plateau. To keep the ashram's inhabitants in line with those they served, no electricity or modernity of any kind was allowed. The poorest of the poor (the *harijan*), Gandhi had believed, were the people of God. The ashram's name, Sevagram, came from *seva* (place) and *gram* (to serve).

A place to serve.

Everyone at the ashram shared expenses and work. Oskar was given a job mending sandals in a leather workshop, a job he took to quickly. After a few days of practice he was told to fashion a pair of sandals for a woman named Ashadevi, who was scheduled to begin a lecture tour. He searched the shop for the proper leather, found what he needed on an enormous roll and sliced off what he thought he would need for the woman's sandals. Using a drawing of her feet, he set to work stitching and forming the footwear, which he presented to the shoemaker after several hours of work. The shoemaker eyed the shoes, then slapped Oskar in the face with them.

"Are you crazy? You made two left feet, and you used the wrong leather. This thick hide is for mountain walking, not for a lady in a town. What a waste of time, not to mention materials."

"I'll replace the material, of course," offered Oskar.

"But the customer has no sandals!" The shoemaker was shaking his hands in the air. "Come on, we'll work together. I'll cut the material and you stitch them up."

By the light of a single kerosene lamp, they put together the woman's sandals and handed them to her—on time.

Soon after, an English couple who had long been Gandhi supporters and residents of the ashram invited Oskar to stay with them. While they were an integral part of the ashram, the couple retained a somewhat European lifestyle. While England's former colonialism was never discussed, the English remained culturally and politically apart from the Indians at the ashram. It was unspoken yet understood that their participation was appreciated, but would always be that of outsiders. Just as Oskar had noticed with converts to Hinduism, the non-Indians were welcome, appreciated, yet always apart, never to be full-fledged members.

One evening the couple took out a gramophone along with records they had brought from England, and asked if Oskar would like to hear Bach's *Brandenburg Concertos*.

Oskar enthusiastically replied that he particularly loved the first, second, and fifth concertos, but when he sat back and listened, his connection to the music was not what it had once been, and he pondered this while his hosts wondered about his insensitivity to such brilliant music. Perhaps his newfound appreciation of Indian music and its subtle variations in mood and color at different times of day had somehow detracted from his love for western classical music, which can be played to similar effect at any hour.

The following day he was invited to meet with Shri E. W. Aryanayakam, who had been a general secretary to Gandhiji. Oskar thanked Aryanayakam for seeing him and was asked why he had come to India.

"Most of all," Oskar said, when he was near the end of his story, "I have such admiration for Gandhiji and his principle of nonviolence, especially coming as I do from Germany."

Aryanayakam folded his hands together. "The English translation of this principle is quite inaccurate, you know. The Indian word *ahimsa*, commonly translated simply as nonviolence, is a double negative, meaning nondisharmony. The concept is to avoid confronting disharmonic actions, such as totalitarian or colonial rule, with further disharmony. You cannot fight disharmony with more disharmony. You must find a nondisharmonic way."

"Well then, how do you confront disharmony? If for instance"— Oskar thought for a moment—"the English put people in jail for teaching illegally, which is a kind of disharmony—"

"Most certainly."

"How do you confront that with a positive?"

Aryanayakam nodded, his eyes nearly closed. "First, we teach everyone to stand on their own legs, to be free of dependence on supermarkets and other extensions of the colonial power. Spinning and weaving are examples of crafts and skills that Gandhiji supported, to make one independent. Bringing back an apparently outdated tool like the spinning wheel and founding the All-India Spinners' Association brought previously powerless people some self-reliance and reduced British economic dominance."

"And you broke the English salt monopoly by taking salt directly from the ocean?"

"We do not want to fight violently, as Hitler did, but to try to become independent. If the English were to stop making profits from us, they would cease dominating us. Without profits, you see, they will lose interest. We don't hate the English, only their rule of us."

Oskar was impressed. "Suppose," he went on, "Gandhiji had become prime minister of India and had even gained, say, 95 percent of the world's support, but suppose that one or two minorities who disagreed with Gandhi used violence to try to take over and rebel. How would Gandhi deal with such a violent threat? Could he have remained faithful to his nonviolent principles while governing?"

Aryanayakam lowered his head and sat quietly while Oskar waited. Finally he looked up. "Gandhi enjoyed divine grace, and expected to die for his ideals when the time came."

It was not the answer Oskar had expected. He was reminded of Vinoba Bhave's remarks that "my kingdom will be of this world and the next" if his teachings were properly followed. He had expected a direct answer, and, as he had been with Bhave's comments, he was motivated to be on his way, promising to meditate and study these ideas as he traveled further. Where would such a kingdom be and what would it be like, and what would the result be if his teachings were not properly followed? Perhaps the solitude and serenity of the Himalayas would be conducive to finding the answers to these cryptic words.

He left some money with the Gandhiji ashram, and as he rode the bus towards the Himalayas, Oskar watched the Indian faces on the roadsides and tried to understand their motives. Indian history ran through his mind's eye, and he considered Gandhi's insistence on nonviolence and the magnitude of his following. He likened the diversity of the Indian people to the landscape he saw through the window: here were lofty Himalayan peaks, there were low, hot, workaday plains of the Ganges, and still further on were malaria-infested, snake-filled swamps, which called to mind violent Hindu groups who had been behind the great pacifist's murder.

He saw what Aryanayakam meant: that Gandhi's death for his principles at the right moment in history was itself divine grace. But such grace had been interwoven with the partitioning of India, the deaths of multitudes. He still wondered about the roles of religion and politics: was there ever a synchronicity between the two, or were religion and spirituality an opiate, a means of sending thinking people into caves and lives of prayer, abstinence, and yoga?

He remembered his visa application and, like a roadblock, his thoughts ran up against the story of Jacob and the name Israel, given to both the man and the nation.

As he traveled northward, Oskar visited the famous Taj Mahal in Agra, but its magnificence and splendor were lost on him. His mind was overwhelmed with Vinoba Bhave's claim of kingdoms in this and another world, and with Aryanayakam's remark about the divine grace of Gandhi's death. He remembered the mystic teaching known as an Upanishad: "Know the One, and you will know all."

He traveled towards Delhi, with teachings and ideas flashing through his mind as quickly as the scenery outside his window. He thought of the Bible: "Hear o Israel, the Lord is our God, the Lord is One" (Deuteronomy 6:4). He was bewildered when he read, "Thus spoke the Lord . . ." (various citations apply, e.g., Exodus 20:1,

Numbers 11:23, Deuteronomy 31:14), whether to Moses, Isaiah, or to other prophets. What had been abstractions, mere words on a page, took on greater possibilities. The Bible seemed to speak not only abstractly about the One, but depicted Him speaking directly to humans. Was such communication two-way? And if so, how could anyone—especially Moses—predict the exile and regathering of the people of Israel thousands of years in advance? Were the prophets simply superintelligent, precognitive humans, or were they indeed the recipients of the genuine Word of the Creator?

An anticipation and excitement welled in him as he saw that a trip back into the Indian mountains was unnecessary. He would go to Israel, to find the answers for himself.

Once in Delhi, instead of boarding a train north toward the Himalayas, he bought a ticket for Amritsar, and began making his way inexorably toward what was colloquially known as Israel's Mandelbaum Gate.

Amritsar was the center of the Sikh community on the border of India and Pakistan, and after wandering for a day there, Oskar crossed into Pakistan, where he immediately noticed a difference in the people's temperament and style. The difference reminded him of one he had noticed when he was young and had traveled to Holland from Germany. The sensibility, the very air was different. Like their holy symbol, the cow, the people he had met in India were relaxed, easygoing, less forward or aggressive than their Pakistani neighbors. And the aggressiveness he noticed on the part of Pakistanis was not necessarily unfriendly; it might be an anxiousness to be friendly. Individuals in both countries might be friendly or not; it was the style, the energy with which they displayed their friendship or indifference that was where the cultural personality lay. Such was his initial impression of Lahore, the first town he came to in Pakistan after leaving India.

He sat down for lunch at a street restaurant and became fascinated by the people passing by and stopping to eat. After being served a simple meal, he offered a short prayer of thanks, and then was soon distracted by a man who was sitting next to him. The man was looking at him, but did not say anything, so Oskar continued eating, glancing at the man now and then. When he finished his meal, the man finally spoke up. "You speak English?" he asked.

Oskar indicated that he did, and for a while they spoke about Oskar's travels and the city of Lahore.

"As someone interested in culture and religion, you might be interested in the Ahmadiyya."

"What are they?" Oskar had not heard of the Ahmadiyya before.

"They're a Muslim group. I'm a member. Would you like to learn?"

"Are you trying to convince me to join?"

"Actually, I was observing you and was amazed to see you, obviously a European, praying. I'd never seen a European pray, and I thought you might find our group interesting, and now that I know you've never heard of us, I know you will."

They drove together northwest to Rabwah, the spiritual center of the Ahmadiyya.

Devotees of Ahmadiyya, in contrast to most Muslims, who believe Muhammad is the only prophet after Moses and Jesus, believe that the Quran predicted the coming of a prophet named Ahmad. In the late 1800s, a Pakistani named Ghulam Ahmad laid claim to that prophecy, and became the leader of the Ahmadiyya movement.

Oskar accepted their insistence that if he were to study the Quran, he must do so in its original Arabic. Lacking the facility to do so, he set out to begin with the help of his new teachers by reading and studying an English translation produced by the Ahmadiyya.

He hoped to learn more about Islam and the Quran and compare that knowledge to what he knew of Christianity, Hinduism, Buddhism, and what little he had gleaned from the Five Books of Moses, the original Bible. He was impressed by the beauty of the Quran's opening *Sura*, which had become the daily prayer, the *El Fatch*. As he studied and read and learned, he came away impressed, but from a distance. He felt that, as with Christianity, the pronouncements of the Quran about Allah seemed to come from so far on high that he, and the rest of mankind, were insignificant. While the passages were beautiful, they contained, besides illumination and inspiration, terrifying descriptions of hell's torments. He began to realize that for him, personally, the Bible was like a personal letter of love from the Heavenly Father.

The Quran's approach was both charming and foreign to him, and he struggled to accept its teachings. Perhaps because of Oskar's own background—his childhood questions about the church, his teenage disaffection with his parents—he remained attracted to the direct and personal relationship between Jacob, Abraham, and Moses, and their God, who spoke directly to them, whether he was promising or punishing.

He wondered about the fear his own study of the Quran might engender, whether it might lead to revelation and understanding as it had with his Sufi teacher, Pir Vilayat Khan, or frustration and extremism if taught by a less open-minded teacher. He remembered what the hermit in the cave high in the Himalayas had told him. He need not join another religion to find the object of his search. Then, one day, he felt the hermit's advice validated by a passage in the Quran praising and giving value to the Bible as a source of guidance. He reminded himself not to judge all of Islam after only a few weeks of study.

One morning when Oskar was half asleep, he had a vivid dream that two enormous glowing feet stood before him and from high above a voice ordered him to leave Rabwah that day. He awoke confused and out of sorts, and wondered how he might leave so quickly without offending his hosts. He thought of the visa, which he hoped was waiting in Israel; more than ever he wanted to travel there. As he said good morning to his hosts, several said he looked strange, distracted. Oskar answered that he had much to think about and was going to spend some time traveling alone. They offered to put together a tour for him within a few days, but he insisted on leaving immediately. He cut his breakfast short and quickly left the Ahmadiyyans, assuring his hosts he would return; his books and clothing remained in his room.

Someone had suggested that he visit the city of Peshawar, near the Afghan border, where the Indians had met Alexander the Great. He was hungry, and rather than wait for the kind of food his body was accustomed to, he bought some vegetables fried in oil from a street kiosk, then wandered for the remainder of the day, with little thought as to what he might do next. He stayed overnight at a hostel and by morning was desperately sick to his stomach. He returned to the Ahmadiyya Center in Rabwah, where he was given herbal tea and told to rest, but neither helped. Severe stomach pain was compounded by ongoing constipation until he was given English salt to swallow with water, which finally brought some measure of relief.

It was early October of 1956, and after accepting a pair of loose-fitting pants and insisting that his hosts take a few dollars with which to do good works for the needy, Oskar was on his way again, this time north to Kabul, via Quetta and Kandahar.

To avoid the sweltering Balochistan desert he maneuvered over the mountainous border into Afghanistan. Little of his strength had returned by the time he reached Kabul, and he marveled that he had not been sick for a year and a half, yet here he was, miserable. Perhaps, he thought, his failure to immediately obey the voice in his dream had caused the illness. He began to pray for forgiveness, while carefully monitoring his food intake. He remembered the kiosk and the ugly-looking oil his food had been cooked in, likely used many times over, perhaps to cook meat. Avoiding meat in Afghanistan might not be so easy, he thought, as it was a staple, often eaten two or three times each day.

He realized that he could take advantage of the recent harvest; the street vendors' carts were full of produce, so he bought an enormous bunch of grapes from a friendly vendor who asked if he would prefer to eat them right away. When Oskar said he would, the vendor dipped the grapes into a channel that flowed through Kabul and held them out, smiling.

Oskar glanced upstream and saw a woman washing her laundry in the channel; beyond her he saw a restaurant which dumped its garbage there, and still further upstream someone was urinating into the water. The vendor watched his expression. "Don't worry. Flowing water purifies." Not wanting to offend him, Oskar bought the grapes, but once he was out of the vendor's sight, he threw them away.

The pain in his abdomen was increasing and he had to find a bathroom, so he made his way to a public rest room, collapsed on the floor and blacked out. He awoke in a puddle of his own blood. He began searching for a doctor, and managed to find one who spoke German. The doctor gave him a prescription and within a few days his abdominal bleeding had stopped.

Still weak, Oskar stayed in Kabul and visited a few sites, including

the king's palace. He met an official at the Russian embassy, a confirmed Communist who had nothing positive to say about any religion. People's needs could be met, unemployment and war con-
quered, all via Communism. Of course, that was the theory, the
Russian said. It might never actually occur.

"Why not?" Oskar asked.

"We have a planned system," the Russian answered. "Five-year
plans, everything ordered and determined for the future. But agriculture is variable, as it is dependent on nature. We cannot plan for the
weather, droughts or floods. Agriculture is out of our control and
humans are not machines." The man sighed. "What a wonderful
dream, though."

The Russian impressed him as a man of good will who truly hoped
the world might be bettered through Communism. He thought of the
saying "The road to hell is paved with good intentions." He also
remembered the phrase "peace on earth to men of good will" from
his childhood studies, the Gospel of Luke, he thought. Years later he
would learn that he had read one of many mistranslations. The
phrase had been "Glory to God in the highest, and on earth peace to
men on whom His favor rests" (Luke 2:14). Perhaps "on whom His
favor rests" was shortened to "God's will," which had then become
the commonly used "good will."

Trucks piled high with loosely tied goods slammed into potholes
on the north road. Men sat astride the goods, and when the trucks
stopped they would jump down, adding to the clouds of dust explod-
ing around the trucks. Afghanistan seemed to Oskar to be little more
than hills and dust. The people in the trucks were polite and usually
invited Oskar to sit in the cab with the driver once he had negotiated a
ride at one of the bus and truck terminals. The new shirt he had

bought in Kabul was quickly sweated through and shredded in back from the friction of the truck's bumping and jostling.

He found a ride the second day with four people in a Jeep. They started off in the afternoon, Oskar seated next to the driver. In the evening they looked for someplace to stay but found nothing and continued driving into the night. Oskar dozed.

When he awoke, he was lying at the side of the road, surrounded by a crowd. He asked if he had been robbed and was told that the Jeep in which he had been riding had been in an accident. As they had maneuvered down a steep grade, the driver had lost control and bounced over a rock. Oskar had been thrown clear, hit his head, and been knocked unconscious.

A truck came for the wounded passengers, but Oskar was pronounced well enough to remain. He was given a drink, allowed to sleep a while, and told to climb aboard another truck bound for Herat, where he hoped, but failed, to find honey for his tea to bring him some energy. While he was interested in Herat, one of the holiest cities of Islam, he decided to head for Mashhad, in Iran.

Northern Iran, or Persia, differed from the south in that the countryside was more hilly and not nearly as arid; hints of greenery showed against bare hills. An Englishwoman approached him and perhaps sensed that he was not in the best of conditions; she asked if he would like to stay a day or two with her and her husband, as they frequently took in guests.

He was offered tea or coffee, and when he accepted the tea, was surprised and delighted to find it had been mixed with honey.

"It will give you a bit of a boost," the woman said, and it did.

After a few days' rest, the Englishwoman arranged for him to board a truck for Teheran, where he met a Persian named Atarhov, who invited him into his home.

He and his wife had fallen sick, Atarhov explained, soon after the second of their children was born. The doctors could not help them, but changing their diets to only raw vegetarian foods had done them wonders. His wife had conceived again, at age forty-five, and they had a third child, an extraordinarily beautiful girl who was now fourteen. This daughter had never eaten anything but raw vegetarian foods, and she drank only fruit juices. In school she could tell by smell what was appropriate to eat. Atarhov had written a book on raw foods and he gave Oskar a copy.

Oskar spent a few days in Baghdad, visiting museums and viewing artifacts. Excavations, particularly one of ancient Babylon where Abraham was said to have dwelled, made a powerful spiritual impression on him, and brought life to the biblical stories in his memories.

He met young Iraqis, followers of John the Baptist, who insisted they were neither Christians nor Jews, but Essenes. Oskar did not know what to make of them.

He traveled through the Syrian desert towards Jordan and Jerusalem, less intimidated by the five-hundred-mile stretch of sand than he had been when he traveled through the area on his way to India. On that first trip, the unknown, rather than the desert, had been the cause of his fear. The desert sky blanketed him, and he saw himself as a grain of sand before the immensity of the universe. Perhaps the illusion was caused by the lack of boundaries; the sky seemed to go on even further than the desert because of the desert's flatness and his being on the ground, whereas the sky arched over him, emphasizing its enormity and his own insignificance.

And the daytime heat was as endless as the sky.

He had time to muse and ponder and consider; his ideas had time to coalesce beneath inspiring stars and to simmer under daylight's swelter until his thoughts wilted and his mind burned. He remembered a passage in the Quran, something akin to "we have appointed for every nation a holy rite that they should perform," and marveled at the variety of landscapes, climates, races, religions, and nations, all made by the one Creator. He dozed, dreaming of a Christmas tree in swirling, sweltering sand. He awoke smiling, just as the bus driver announced their arrival in Amman, the enormous desert village of palaces and street bazaars.

He strolled in the street, his eyes everywhere, but recoiled suddenly at a loud noise. Before he could react further, a hand had pulled him into a shop. He began to protest that he was only looking, not buying, but the man who had grabbed him said, "Just stay here and be quiet." Outside in the street a motorcade roared past. "The king," the man said, nodding after the fading tumult. "His motorcade is preceded by men on horseback who club anyone in their way."

Oskar left Amman as quickly as he could, boarding a bus to Jericho, bound for Jerusalem.

18

Oskar looked down from the six-thousand-year-old tell, one of the oldest excavations on earth and his first stop in Jericho. From the hillside he saw tall, vibrant palms and lush fields surrounding the historic site, aware that below his feet centuries of settlements, sites of construction, war and reconstruction had all come and gone. Surrounding the oasis of Jericho lay the barren Jordan valley, flanked to the east by the mountains of Moab and to the west by the rocky hills of the Judean desert. He had a dizzying awareness, as he had had at the Babylon excavations in Iraq, of rich history beneath his feet, but modernity intruded and soured the moment.

Oskar met a young Arab at the hostel in which he was staying, and, when he expressed an interest in seeing Jericho, the young man agreed to become his guide. To Jericho's immediate north and south were crowded refugee camps overflowing with young men much like himself, the guide explained. Their population dwarfed that of Jericho, and Oskar wanted to see them for himself, not from the top of the excavation's hill, but in detail, as a visitor. His young guide agreed.

"The Jordanian government blames us for their losses in the 1948 war; it's their justification for keeping us here."

"If you can't work, what do you eat?" Oskar asked.

"Whatever the United Nations brings, which isn't much. People think of creative ways to get food, things to tell the authorities to get us fed, like claiming births of twins, not recording deaths and so forth."

"Why don't the refugees just leave?"

The young man looked at Oskar with heavy-lidded eyes. "There was a settlement before 1948 called Kalia, which lay between Jericho and the tip of the Dead Sea. The Jews had somehow managed to grow food there, so some refugees tried it. They grew cucumbers and tomatoes, but the authorities chased them off, saying it wasn't their land and they had to either buy it or go back to the camps. Well, they couldn't buy it."

"What do the Jews have to do with all this? Why fight them if it was the local authorities who were keeping you from your land?"

"Make no mistake, the Jews took our land," Oskar's guide insisted.

Oskar was confused. "But you just said the authorities here, the king, I suppose you mean, pushed you off the land."

"A necessity for the Jordanian army in attempting to recoup their lands. They pushed us off that previous Jewish settlement, Kalia, but all these refugees had to flee the 1948 war."

Oskar crossed his arms and considered what the young man was saying. "The Quran stresses the Bible's importance and praises the Jews."

"What you call the Bible," the young man answered, "is a Zionist forgery."

"I know only one Bible," Oskar answered. "I have seen many translations and there are slight differences in wording, but they agree with one another."

His tour guide gave him a harsh look; his voice was rising. "It's a forgery. You know it as well as I. We have been persecuted for centuries, victimized by your Bible. Look at the Crusades, at the way the British treated us. Go back to the time of the Romans if you have to."

Oskar held out an open palm, signalling his understanding and desire for peace.

Each refugee family had built a cramped, one-room mud hut. Cooking, washing, laundry were done out-of-doors. Water was available from one of the three natural sources of Jericho: the famous Jericho well, located between the original village and the camps, and the two waterways which originate at the edge of the Judean desert.

Oskar learned from other young Arabs at the hostel and at restaurants that the refugees had been told by Radio Damascus and Arab military broadcasts that advancing Arab armies would disburse any settlements in their path, and if the refugees would clear a path for the armies they would later be allowed to reoccupy their lands, as well as those of the previous Jewish owners.

He took a bus toward Jerusalem, a steep ride of several hours from the lows of Jericho and the Dead Sea, which are several hundred yards below sea level, to the Mount of Olives and Jerusalem, which are hundreds of yards above.

At a stop for tea in Bethany, Oskar struck up a conversation with a group of nuns who lived on the eastern slope of the Mount of Olives. He mentioned Leela, the only nun he knew, and was suprised to find that the nuns knew her well. He was invited to stay at their convent, and when he asked the cost, the nuns replied that no payment was necessary.

It was fall, and the nuns harvested olives at nearby orchards, where they were often pelted with stones thrown by Arab youths. The nuns hoped that a man in their midst might protect them. Oskar accompanied them to the olive groves, enjoying the sun and the spreading trees with their characteristic trunks and egg-shaped, dark green leaves, all the while making certain he was easily visible.

The nuns explained that the Israeli border was closed because of the recent war with Egypt, so, from the convent, Oskar traveled by bus to East Jerusalem, which was in Jordanian hands. After finding a hostel, he spent several days orienting himself to the narrow, winding streets of the ancient city.

Cameroon, the half-Sikh, half-Jew who had taught Oskar how to find his family name in the Bible, had suggested he visit an Ethiopian monastery at Mount Calvary. In A.D. 326, Queen Helena, the mother of the Roman emperor Constantine, who had converted to Christianity, had the Church of the Holy Sepulcher built on a rocky hill she called Golgotha, where Jesus was said to have been crucified. Since then it had been damaged and reconstructed several times and was thought to be one of the world's most important Christian sites.

Oskar learned that the enormous grey stone church housed six Christian denominations: Greek, Armenian, Catholic, Copt, Assyrian, and Ethiopian. He found the long-standing quarrels and deep rifts among the denominations disconcerting and confusing, particularly on the heels of his experiences in India, where he had witnessed widespread tolerance.

The Ethiopians Cameroon had suggested he visit had no full share of the church building proper but had built a monastery called Deir-es-Sultan (meaning the residence of or given by the sultan) on one of the building's low terraces. Several hundred years earlier they had been driven out of the inner church, and the sultan at that time had decreed that this monastery and its poverty-stricken monks would occupy its current place.

The Ethiopian monks, who radiated a peaceful dignity, knew and respected Cameroon, and his recommendation of Oskar to them carried weight enough to bring an invitation for him to stay in one of their cells. His room was about the size of his quarters in the Rishikesh Himalayan ashram, enough space for a bed and a chair. Outside the room was a common kitchen and bathroom. Oskar gratefully accepted the monks' offer.

He spent his free time reading his Bible and discussing local geography, politics, and religion with the monks, whom he found forthcoming but shy. Their attitude was favorable towards Jews and the State of Israel; they were frightened of the Arabs and kept to themselves. Certain practices of theirs were similar to Jewish customs; their priests were circumcised, and a differentiation was made between clean and unclean animals with respect to diet, particularly regarding the pig.

Oskar noticed that many of the cars on the streets of East Jerusalem were German-made Mercedes. He approached some of their owners and asked why they bought German cars, and was told that they wished to support Germany, which had been a good friend. Oskar visited the German ambassador in Amman. The official purpose of the visit, he said, was to record his presence here as a German, and to discuss his travels with the ambassador.

Once in the ambassador's office, Oskar asked what the official thought about the widespread Arab preference for German cars. When the ambassador asked that he explain himself, Oskar conveyed his concern, even shock, that locals wanted to do business with Germany in support of what Germany had done to the Jews.

The ambassador was annoyed. "Well, I don't know about that," he said.

"I imagine you don't," Oskar said. "That's why I'm here. To explain it to you so you will know it."

The ambassador examined Oskar, looking him up and down. "And just who are you?"

"Doctor Oskar Eder."

"Well, I don't know you. Besides, the time I have for you is up. I'm a busy man." The ambassador rang for a servant to show Oskar out.

Upon his return to the monastery, Oskar wrote and sent a letter to the German Ministry of Foreign Affairs complaining of the situation; he never received a reply.

The Ethiopian monks changed his view of Christianity, which he had thought unfeeling and impersonal because of his experiences as a child. The monks were understanding, empathetic, and open-minded. His repeated reading about Jacob in the Bible had aroused in Oskar a great curiosity and interest in Israel. He had come this far, but animosity between the Arabs and Jews had kept him from what he had come for. The monks helped him find his way through the final obstacles.

They told Oskar that there would be a festival in a few days, and if he were careful he could go to a gate in the military zone and see over its top.

Oskar went to the heavily guarded gate on a cool evening, and explained that he wanted to have a look at the other side. He stood on his toes, peered over the wall, and could just make out the uppermost stones of the Western Wall and the Dome of the Rock towards the east, but what caught his attention on that chilly December evening was to the west: a glowing light from a great candelabra, the meaning of which he did not yet know, and the melodious sounds of a joyful, festive crowd. He had read in the Bible about a seven-branched candelabra and was confused by the one he saw now, which appeared to have nine branches. He turned around and watched the Arabs behind him, noticing a nervousness, even fear, among them, as though the Jewish excitement on the other side of the wall might bring with it an immediate danger.

Silently he watched the lighting of the eight branches from the torch of its ninth, elevated branch, and beheld the singing and dancing in the flickering yellow light.

Oskar visited as many places as he could, led by young Arabs happy to show a German the sights. He visited Nablus and Jacob's Well, cut from solid rock, below which flowed an underground river which could be seen with a flashlight, glittering through a crevice. He wondered, as he looked down at the ancient water source, about the veracity of biblical stories. Isaac, he remembered, had been known as a well digger.

His guide took him to a Samaritan community, a picturesque bus ride which left him fascinated. He remembered reading in the Gospel of John that Jesus passed by Shechern, later called Nablus, and spoke with Samaritan women. He was also confused. The priest at the Samaritan community knew nothing of any Bible except the Five Books of Moses. Their priests, he said, were descended from Aaron, and had nothing to do with Christianity.

He learned of the Byzantine persecution of the Samaritans and their near extinction, and came away bewildered that after centuries of Arab-Christian animosity those groups managed to coexist in the Holy Land, while the Samaritans had been reduced to a fringe minority.

He was impressed by the serenity of the Patriarch's Mosque in Hebron, the Haram-el-Halil mosque in Arabic, whose name refers to Abraham as the "friend of God" or "beloved of God." He was appalled by several Arabs who greeted him as "German, good friend," and claimed to want to finish what Germany had started. They were visibly taken aback when Oskar told them he could not befriend murderers.

Christmas was approaching and Oskar visited the Church of the

Nativity and participated in its holiday service. When the congregation prostrated itself before a representation of the baby Jesus, Oskar flashed back to a childhood incident during a Pentecostal procession in Forchheim during which citizens prostrated themselves before icons that were held aloft. Those who did not had their hats knocked off, which encouraged them to bend to the ground, thereby paying their respects. He realized just how estranged he was from western Christianity.

He had planned to stay a few more days, but learned that the border between Israel and Jordan would soon open. It was a few days after the western New Year and Oskar was excitedly preparing his belongings for crossing into Israeli Jerusalem. He wanted to be one of the first.

It was a few minutes after eight o'clock on a morning in early January of 1957, at the Mandelbaum Gate, a military checkpoint a short distance north of the more renowned, ancient, castle-like Damascus Gate, one of the entrances to Jerusalem's walled Old City.

The Mandelbaum (meaning almond tree) Gate was named for the original owner of the land upon which it stood. A pair of simple army barracks and a bit of barbed wire were all that now stood between the two countries; a narrow fenced entranceway led into one of the buildings. Inside were several small offices. Except for a thin moustache, the Jordanian officer in charge looked like any other in his red-and-white-dotted *keffiyeh*. Oskar explained to the guard that he wished to cross into Israel.

"Where is your passport? Your visa?"

He handed over his passport. "My visa is waiting for me on the other side."

The Jordanian shook his head with half a smile. "I can't take a chance on letting you through. The other side won't let you in, and I won't be able to let you back. You'll be caught between. Besides, you're a German. Think twice about what you're doing. Those Jews will beat you up, and worse."

"My visa is arranged. The rest is my problem." He looked the guard in the eye and spoke as forcefully as he could, but in truth he was frightened and intimidated. The consulate in Bombay had said the visa, if granted, would be waiting, but at that moment he was far from certain.

After twenty minutes of wrangling and intimidation, Oskar's papers were stamped and he was allowed to pass the barbed-wire fence and the twenty yards of no-man's-land into the white Israeli border post. He found a simple room with a shelf, a table, and several chairs, in one of which sat a middle-aged Israeli in street clothes. He looked at Oskar's passport and asked for his visa.

"I was told it . . . might be waiting for me here."

"Just a minute." The man went to a shelf and looked through some papers. "It's been waiting a long time. What took you?"

"The border was closed."

The guard looked over Oskar's papers, then returned his attention to Oskar. "Why would you come to Israel? What are you looking for?" The questions held no hostility, only avid curiosity and interest.

Oskar told the man of his interest in Gandhi, his travels in India, and his recent reading of the Bible. What impressed him about the Israeli border guard was his understanding and nonjudgmental interest. This was no philosopher or swami; he was a simple guard, yet he listened without prejudice, drew no quick conclusions, and was able to discuss Oskar's experiences and interests with open intelligence born not of books but of life experience. Despite his own background, and despite recent warnings to the contrary he had heard from Jordanians, Oskar felt no threat.

The border guard related to Oskar on a personal level, two people sharing one place and moment, communicating. And through that effort: understanding.

Oskar felt he had met a true human being.

By the time he left the outpost, it was nearly noon. He was at the edge of Mea She'arim, the orthodox quarter, dominated by black hats and furs, long robes, curls and side locks. Such persistent adherence to tradition over the course of centuries spoke of a depth of belief, a substance, to Oskar. The stability and permanence attracted him, a man who had experienced little of either. He wandered the quarter for several hours.

He was looking for an address in Talbieh, a quarter in western Jerusalem that had once been mixed, where Arab and Jewish homes had stood side by side, until the Arab owners fled during and after the 1948 war. Since then, the attractive, tree-shaded neighborhood had become a tidy Jewish suburb. He found what he sought on Disraeli Street; it was a small, first-floor apartment in a long building opposite a quiet park.

As it had in so many places, Oskar's friendship with Leela opened doors in Israel. Elsa Ehricke and Martha Cohn-Ehricke were German refugees and sisters. Elsa was a writer of prose and poetry; Martha was a widow, hence her hyphenated name. They belonged to a circle of acquaintances that included Professor Magnes, Professor Ernst Simon, Professor Hugo Bergman, the first rector of Hebrew University, and the author, philosopher, and noted political scientist Martin Buber, who was working for peace with Israel's Arab neighbors, and who had sought advice on the subject from Gandhi through a series of letters.

As he had been in Jordan, Oskar was recognized on the streets as European by his clothing, particularly his Tyrolean coat. People asked what he was looking for, why he had come, who he was. Once he spoke they realized he was German, and most turned away. There was no hostility, only an immediate distancing, as though a door had shut against him.

In India and Pakistan he had been quick to develop enough rapport with those he met on the streets and in restaurants to find a place to stay or a tour guide. In his first days in Jerusalem, Oskar did the same, approaching waiters, bus drivers and the average person on the street with the open honesty, bordering on naïveté, that came so easily to him. The difference in Jerusalem was that many of these average, workaday people were knowledgeable about biblical history, culture, and philosophy, and Oskar quickly ascertained that their knowledge was not separate from their daily lives but was an integral part of it. There was a direct personal connection between who these people were—in America they would be called "blue collar"—and their spirituality and religion. Their connection to the source, however, varied, as each individual seemed to grapple in his or her way with finding meaning and spiritual connection. Despite such differences and struggles, it was all one, and was tremendously attractive to Oskar, who had never had that experience; in fact his life had been characterized by exactly the opposite: the ripping away of such connections.

In his new acquaintances Oskar found interested listeners and friends who enjoyed discussion and the examination of ideas. Comparisons between modern Israel's struggles with its neighbors and Oskar's experiences in Germany were frequent topics, and Oskar's memories were invited and his opinion valued, though he sensed a reluctance on the part of his listeners to relate their feelings about their European experiences.

Once he became accustomed to Jerusalem's narrow tangled lanes and purposefully striding pedestrians, Oskar was taken to the home of Professor Bergman, a Czech refugee and philosophy professor at Hebrew University (later its first rector); he had developed a large circle of learned friends who met at *onegs*, Sabbath get-togethers, for lively discussion and discourse. At that time, Oskar was not interested in, nor was he invited to, synagogue services.

They met in the professor's apartment, a single-floor building with two side-by-side flats, on Rambam Street in Rehavia, a section of Jerusalem populated primarily by Jews from Central Europe. The quarter was quiet at that time, its shaded gardens offering solace and rest. On his first visit, Oskar came in from the bright sunlight that lit the red tiled roof of the house next door, made his way down a darkened hallway, and was greeted by the large, slow-moving, and even slower-talking professor.

They discussed Jewish religion and thought, and the professor gave him a Jewish prayer book containing both Hebrew and German translations. Oskar took the book back to the sisters' house, and, with Martha and Elsa's help, struggled to understand it. He found the prayers dense, foreign, and difficult. Martha and Elsa's explanations helped him to see a glimmer of meaning in the prayers, which he connected with the biblical stories he had been reading and the excavations he had visited. Branches and limbs—historical, religious, and spiritual—were coming together in the spreading tree of Oskar's consciousness.

Professor Bergman was patient with Oskar, considering his guest's questions and carefully weighing his answers, showing respect and always encouraging Oskar's interest.

Oskar was introduced to Rav Braun, a small middle-aged man who wore a *kippah* and black clothing, and who lived in a modest, book-filled ground-floor apartment on crowded Zephania Street, not far from Mea She'arim.

Rav Braun invited Oskar and the two German sisters to visit, moving books from tabletops and chairs to make room for his guests. They spoke at length about Oskar's experiences in Pakistan and Jordan, focusing on Islamic culture and society. Rav Braun had asked that Oskar bring the three-volume Quran commentary he had received in Rabwah from the Ahmadiyya. Since Oskar had little interest in becoming an Islamic scholar, he gave the books to his host.

Rav Braun explained that, after the restoration to the divine order, three languages would be spoken by people on earth: one's mother tongue, English as an international language, and Hebrew, which would be the holy language. Oskar asked whether the speech one hears in restaurants and buses is that same holy tongue.

"Well, yes. It is the same language, but with some differences. The style of biblical language is . . ." The rav made a gesture upwards, to the heavens, then leaned toward his guest. "Just as you do not speak like Goethe in your daily conversations."

Oskar wanted to make sure he understood correctly. "So, as to the words, the Bible's Hebrew is the same Hebrew as that which is spoken here."

"I only hope," Rav Braun said, "it will not be profaned."

Jerusalem slowed on Friday afternoons, its noise dissipated and its atmosphere transformed. While neither Martha nor Elsa was orthodox, they did observe the Sabbath, lighting candles and preparing a festive dinner. Oskar enjoyed the peace and relaxation of Shabbat, the preparations for and anticipation of a special day. He was a welcome part of it all, in spite of his German background. That this same observance, relaxation, and warmth was occurring in nearly every house for miles around in the middle of the twentieth century aroused in him a sense of wonder and appreciation.

At the Oneg Shabbat, the informal gathering that was a regular part of the Bergman household's Saturday afternoon observance, Professor Bergman invited Oskar to discuss his experiences.

After sundown, the professor's wife lit Havdalah candles, signifying the end of Shabbat and the beginning of the work week. Oskar found a beauty in the ritual, despite his lack of any deep understanding of Shabbat. Electricity, which had been turned off prior to the Sabbath, was turned on again. Oskar mused about the professor's Shabbat observance and that of Jerusalem's citizens in general. The peace of the observance and the joy so many people seemed to take in faith, family, and friends made an impression. As he turned his thoughts towards the Sundays of his upbringing, the professor interrupted and asked Oskar to return the following week.

"I have a book you might find interesting," Professor Bergman said. "You have heard of Martin Buber? Well, I have some of his work here. Borrow it, read it; tell me what you think. His work derives from his experiences in Europe, particularly Germany, and discusses many of the issues we've covered in our talks."

During the next few days, between his walks around Jerusalem, his discussions with Martha and Elsa, and his reading of his new German/Hebrew prayer book, Oskar somehow found time to read the prize-winning author and philosopher's work. When he told Professor Bergman his reaction, the professor contacted Buber and arranged for an invitation to the author's home, which was located between Martha and Elsa's apartment and Professor Bergman's.

"I'm afraid I did not agree with much of what you wrote in your book about two faiths or creeds," Oskar explained to Buber, "particularly with regard to Christianity."

"Tell me more about your thoughts and experiences," the middle-aged philosopher asked. What little hair he had was graying, as was his long beard. His eyes were dark and insistent.

Oskar described his introduction to Christianity—dogmatic, institutional, and impersonal, though softened somewhat by his experience with the Ethiopian monks at the Church of the Holy Sepulcher. In his childhood, Oskar's connection was not so much with the Holy Trinity as with demanding monks and priests who seemed to show little interest in his soul, except for trying to save it from damnation. He explained his childhood confusion about loving one's neighbor and the position of the Sabbath in the week and his questions about the nature of the soul. He described his searches and travels in India, Asia, and the Middle East.

Buber was impressed and interested. "And what of Judaism? What is your understanding and knowledge of the Jewish way of life?"

"Very little," Oskar answered. "I'm interested in modern Israel as a continuation of the biblical stories. So far, I feel good about it, particularly Shabbat. But that is a practical attraction."

"You seem to be leaning more towards the Jewish way than the Christian, if you don't mind my saying so," Buber observed.

In Buber's view, it was the dialogue between God and man that was central to Judaism, the same quality that struck Oskar in the biblical story of Jacob. Oskar suggested that perhaps he was not estranged so much from Christianity as he was from the "Churchianity" that had been forced on him as a boy.

The Jewish thinker's comment about Oskar's leaning toward Judaism was a watershed moment, a chord that would grow into a Jewish symphony.

19

Oskar stood near the window looking out into the street, which was tinged yellow by the afternoon light. "Israeli Jerusalem is so much more humane than I was told it would be." He turned to his host. "I wonder if it's just Jerusalem or if everyone in Israel is so straightforward and thoughtful."

The professor, who was nearly as tall sitting down as Oskar was standing up, measured his words. "Perhaps Kibbutz Hazorea, a kibbutz of German Jews . . ." He focused on Oskar and stretched his lips into a smile. "Yes, a good idea. Have you heard this word 'kibbutz'?"

"I don't think so."

"Kibbutzim have evolved into rural communities in the truest sense of the word. Hazorea was organized in the 1930s, and like most kibbutzim, it is separated into zones: residential, industrial, educational, and so forth."

"So a kibbutz differs from a farm in that this is not an individual whose home is attached to his fields and livestock, but a cooperative. I met a Russian fellow who . . ."

"It isn't communist, but you may find socialist elements, yes. If you take the train towards Tel Aviv, I think you'll find the ride picturesque, and your stay at Kibbutz Hazorea instructive, though whether you'll conclude that Jerusalem's people are representative of Israel is another matter. You'll have to decide that for yourself."

Tel Aviv was a modern city which at that time held little interest for Oskar, so he boarded a train due north for Haifa Bay. He pressed his face against the window and watched the desert give way to orange and grapefruit orchards surrounded by cyprus trees which served as windbreaks. Wild shrubs dotted the red-brown soil of the coastal plain.

Another passenger, an American sitting opposite Oskar, also watched the scenery. Oskar heard him say, "It was barren, nothing there; and now . . . the Garden of Eden."

That someone would speak such words aloud was deeply moving to Oskar, and gave him greater inner understanding of place, time, and psyche than a long, direct conversation might have otherwise. In his reading the previous evening, he had come upon a prediction in the Book of Ezekiel that at the time of the regathering of the dispersed children of Israel, words such as these would be spoken (Ezekiel 36:35).

He thought back to his childhood confusion over the Lord's Prayer, particularly over the word "hallowed." He now thought that perhaps the word meant "sanctify." His reading the previous night mentioned that the prophet said that the Lord would, at the time of Israel's regathering, sanctify the people, and sanctify his name (Ezekiel 36:21–23, 38:23).

While he was excited and motivated by the sudden appearance of answers to what had been very old and personal questions, Oskar was startled as well.

A Canadian woman sitting nearby engaged Oskar in conversation about himself and his interest in Israel. She hoped to show him around

Haifa, she said, as their conversation deepened. He tried to share his new thoughts with her, especially about Shabbat and the meaning of "Hallowed be thy name," but the woman did not seem to share his enthusiasm. She claimed that the Jews needed to find Jesus to be saved. Oskar did not answer her; he wanted to find out for himself.

He sat up reading his Bible on his only night in Haifa, with the blue bay behind, the city on all sides, and the green slopes of Mount Carmel before him. He fell asleep content, and had a dream unlike any he had ever had: it contained no images, nothing visual at all, only a sound more beautiful than any he had ever heard. He thought of it as "the music of the spheres."

The dream played a faint overture in his memory the following day as he arrived in the fertile Jezreel Valley at the foot of the Menashe Hills, named after the tribe who had settled there in biblical times. The kibbutz office was a bare room in a plain wooden building. Two men and a woman were talking when Oskar knocked tentatively on the office door. He showed them the note he had brought from Professor Bergman and summoned up his courage. "I'd like to learn about kibbutz life, about new Israel and collective settlements." Before he finished, one of the young men had pushed past him and was motioning for him to follow.

He was led to a row of small wooden barracks. "You'll stay here," he was told, and the young man began walking back towards the office.

"I don't want to just hang around," Oskar called after him. "Can you put me to work?"

The young man turned and smiled for the first time. "Don't worry. There will be plenty to do tomorrow."

In the crowded dining hall with its rows of tables, he ate little and observed the people around him chattering in English and Hebrew and a smattering of German. Though he could not hear the details of their conversations, he could tell by their intent expressions and forceful phrasing that they were people with purpose . . . though he had to admit that they did not look like any farmers he had ever seen.

The kibbutz consisted of several hundred people, families doubled up in barracks somewhat larger than Oskar's. They were on the main road from Haifa to Megiddo Junction and the fields and orchards were all on the other side of that road. Oskar was told that after the time of the Crusaders, the entire Jezreel Valley had become a malaria-infested swamp, and was sanitized and cultivated by "Zionists" who had purchased the land from its Arab owners.

The following morning he was led across the street to an orchard and asked to try out a hand scythe. If left uncut, the long grass surrounding the trees would use up the water from the soil, leaving too little for the trees to bear fruit.

After watching for a few minutes, Oskar tried his own hand with the scythe, clumsily at first, and then with more facility, until he began to relax and enjoy himself. He worked his way to the end of the row, turned, and began on the next, focusing on the blade's arc and finding just the right position for his legs and body. A desert wind was gathering from the east, hot air that whipped the sand into a hazy curtain; it blew in gradually and, intent on his work, Oskar never noticed. By the time he neared the end of the third row he could see only one or two trees in front of him.

He called into the wind but no one answered. He had experienced worse heat in India, so he continued on to the fourth row, but within a few minutes he could no longer see and had to give up. He found the kibbutz by feeling for the fence at the orchard's outskirts and edging his way along it to the opening that faced the road opposite the living area.

The dining hall was empty. As he was leaving, a young woman walked in. "What are you doing here?" she asked.

"I came in from the fields and was hoping for something to drink."

The woman was taken aback. "You were working . . . in that?"

"Well, why not?" He was suddenly on the defensive.

"No one works during the *chamsin!*"

"What's a 'hamseen'?"

She pronounced the word again. "It's Arabic, meaning fifty, because this hot wind springs up about fifty days each year, blowing fine dust in from the desert, making it too hot to work. Everyone's resting, waiting for it to pass." She found him a bowl of soup and a hunk of bread. "When you're done, Oskar—Oskar, right?—get some rest."

At dinner that night he could sense a change in the way he was perceived by the kibbutz members. He saw their approving glances and a few direct smiles. A young man and woman sat down to eat with him. After a few minutes the young man looked at him. "If you're willing to work in the *chamsin*, you must really love us."

He took the statement as friendly, if a little confusing. Later he learned that in the formative years of the kibbutzim, work and love had often been equated. Within a decade, once war became pervasive, the association would be less commonplace.

Mordechai Tel-Tsur taught a morning Hebrew language class. In the afternoons his students worked the fields and orchards. Tall and lean, with arms and shoulders sinewy from years of hard work, Mordechai divided his time between his specialty and whatever the kibbutz required. Electricians might clean cow stables, a secretary might pick oranges and keep his administrative job only a year or two so as to avoid an imbalance of political power. Everyone did what was needed, sharing work equally.

Mordechai's family name had been changed, in accordance with the custom of the kibbutz founders, from the German Schelzer to Tel-Tsur, which had a similar sound. He described life, or torture as he called it, as a Jew in Germany, and Oskar remembered a comment another friend, also a German Jew, had made. That man had endured being spit at in the street, with little recourse beyond the typical Jewish response: a glance at the sky and a comment about the "untimely rain." Unlike the situation for non-Jewish Germans of that time, there had been no hiding in German society for these men.

At first Oskar imagined that his own response had he been Jewish might have been different. He envisioned himself standing up to the Nazis, but quickly realized that doing so would only have brought more abuse, and worse. The thought sickened him. He had been part of that culture; he had been a leader of future Nazis in the *Jungvolk*.

Mordechai described the pain and shame of fleeing his own country, for his life, to Israel. He watched Oskar's face. Oskar looked into his new friend's eyes; for a moment he searched for words. "Thank you for telling me all this . . . so frankly."

For Oskar, anti-Semitism was no longer only a word, a statistical phenomenon; it was this man Mordechai's personal shame and horror. It was the spit he wiped from his sunburned cheek. Not once, but many times.

That night Oskar stared at the ceiling, unable to sleep. *Where was I,* he wondered, and then remembered where he had been. He asked himself how he of all people had arrived at this kibbutz to find himself with German Holocaust survivors. He wondered what would become of him, and when he finally slept, he dreamt of millions of lifeless eyes, and heard the beating of millions of hearts, and each beat asked him, as God had asked Adam, "Where are you?"

The following morning he ran to find Mordechai, not sure what he wanted to say but knowing he had to beg forgiveness. Jumbled words,

German and English, poured from him, expressing how sorry he was for having been a part of such a society. Mordechai listened, waited a moment, then said, "If you ever want to learn Hebrew, the root of our culture, you will be welcome in my *Ulpan*." His weathered face broke into a smile. "Learning Hebrew helps one's understanding. It's a standing invitation," Mordechai said.

"I may take you up on it," Oskar said.

As he met and came to know more survivors and relatives of Jews killed in the camps, he saw the unspeakable loss and confusion in their eyes, which seemed to belong to drowning victims grasping at some reality, some fragment of civilization to hold on to. They searched Oskar's eyes, desperate to know how such horror could possibly have been allowed to occur.

His visa was for a few short months, so to use his time wisely, Oskar left Kibbutz Hazorea and headed for Tiberias, on the treelined shores of the Lake of Galilee. Best known as the "town of Mishna," Tiberias is the resting place of some of history's great rabbinical scholars, including the Rabbi Akiba and Rambam, known to the rest of the world as Maimonides.

He quickly found work on a nearby kibbutz, meeting and making friends and working in banana fields, enjoying the overripe, unmarketable fruits of his labor.

He loved working the land and was developing a bond with the work, the landscape and the ground itself. The people he met were straightforward and honest and Oskar discovered he could be open with them despite their cultural differences. Gone were the suspicions of his childhood and teen years; gone was the cultural confusion that had kept much of India at a distance. The seed of his original journey had blossomed and flourished, watered by years of search, travel, and introspection, until it too germinated, planting a seed of its own. The seed was an idea: to settle in Israel.

He had read through his prayer book, his siddur, and had begun reading it a second time. It remained dense and confusing, but the prayers appealed to him in some new way he could not yet verbalize or quantify, as the land and people of Israel did.

He traveled to Safed, in the Upper Galilee, and saw bare hills covered with sprouting trees, the beginning of a reforestation project. He met dozens of new people, and admired their grasp of everyday circumstance, their attention to real life—their heads were just above their feet, not off in the clouds. But he never failed to notice how restrained they were towards him. Polite, direct, even friendly, but restrained.

In the spring of 1957, when the weather warmed and coats gave way to short sleeves, he began noticing tattooed numbers on many left forearms. Each time he saw one he felt a small earthquake, as though a heavy slab of sadness and shame had shifted, announcing itself, beneath his feet.

It was early May, Independence Day in Israel. His visa extended, Oskar was able to travel to Haifa to see the parade. Legions of uniformed youth filed past, and when an army division of women marched by, rifles over their shoulders, the reality of modern Israel's need for self-defense was driven home. He remembered hearing the mufti Amin el-Husseini, who had styled himself the Grand-Mufti of Palestine on Radio Berlin during the war, broadcast that killing Jews was pleasing to Allah. As that image and his experiences in Jordan obscured the pageantry before him, he wept quietly, the crowd and marchers a blurry curtain of tears.

The war had never ended.

So much went through his mind as he watched that Independence Day parade in 1957, as he wept for generations of lost Jews. He remembered being told as a boy that the Jews had killed Christ and would have to suffer for it. He thought of chickens, which attacked any not of their own group. He remembered his unwillingness to marry an Indian woman for fear of the abuse her dark skin would bring her in Germany. He remembered his experiences with so many Indians, friendly and warm, but living amidst horrific poverty.

He had read that Paul once said to the Corinthians that if your brother is hurt by what you eat, you are no longer walking in love. The Jews, he realized, had kept their dietary laws, their way of life, their faith, despite centuries of vilification and hostility. Their commitment impressed Oskar, for whom permanence had never existed.

He wanted to learn more.

Oskar had been in contact with his parents and with acquaintances in Germany by mail, and had received an invitation to lecture about Germany's past from an educational institution that worked with youth groups. Never one to make quick decisions, he thought a respite from his experience in Israel might give him the perspective to decide if this were the place where he would ultimately settle. He might be able to help someone, a young person perhaps, struggling to cope with his or her German identity.

He had no interest in traveling by ship, and passenger planes were far less appealing to him than the smaller variety he had flown years before, so he went to the Lebanese border, hoping to cross, but found it open only to diplomats. From there he went back to Jerusalem and the Mandelbaum Gate, where he was told by the British consulate that had taken over certain Jordanian affairs that another visa would be impossible. A combination of persistent pleading and arguing finally yielded the visa, and Oskar said good-bye to the friends he had made in Jerusalem.

One of them was Professor David Flusser, a short man with round cheeks, greenish-brown eyes, and quick gestures. The professor lived on the ground floor of an attractive four-story home with a lovely garden owned by an Armenian who, because of the separation between east and west Jerusalem, had moved to the Jordanian side. The flat had been rented by the Hebrew University, and rent was paid to a government office for abandoned property, the collected rents along with those from many "abandoned" houses forming a fund to be used for compensating previous owners in a hoped-for peace treaty. The professor's specialty was history, specifically that of the period of the Second Temple, but he had a wide breadth of knowledge, encompassing much of European history and civilization.

As they said their good-byes, Professor Flusser sternly admonished Oskar to shave his beard. Anyone from Israel wearing a beard would be assumed to be Jewish and would be treated accordingly, which would be dangerous in Arab countries.

Oskar went to a mirror, looked at himself, and was ashamed, thinking of the brave stalwarts of Mea She'arim who never shaved, even when attacked. And here he was so worried about the possibility of being identified as a Jew that he was considering changing his appearance.

If he looked like a Jew, he determined, let that be their problem.

He went back to the Church of the Sepulcher and renewed his acquaintance with the Ethiopian monks who had shown him such kindness on his way to Israel. He saw a young Arab he had met before who had converted to Christianity. When Oskar did not answer questions about his return and intentions, the young Arab lowered his head. A shopkeeper he had befriended before also turned away.

Realizing he had little business in eastern Jerusalem, he went to Amman and found a room in a small hotel. That evening a group of young people struck up a conversation with him and, noticing his accent, expressed their support for Germany and dislike of Jews. Oskar pointed out that the Quran speaks of the Jews as the originators of the Bible, and predicts the return of the exiled Jews. Nowhere, as far as he could see, does the Quran contradict the promise of the Jews' return. The young people began to argue amongst themselves. Some called Oskar a traitor and wanted him to leave, accusing the hotel proprietor of hosting an Israeli spy. Others claimed Oskar was a guest and defended his right to stay. A fistfight ensued, with four or five on each side. Chairs were broken, and their legs taken up as clubs.

Oskar shouted over the melee that this was not a Muslim way to behave, especially towards a guest. He was left alone after that, the fight spilling out into the street.

Oskar asked the proprietor to bring tea at six. He would pay and be on his way in the morning. When his tea arrived, he was afraid to venture outside, worried that the anti-Semitic among the fighters might be waiting for him. At eleven o'clock, he carefully peeked out, found the way clear, and boarded a bus for Damascus.

The elderly man seated next to him wore traditional Muslim attire. Oskar hesitated. "English?" he asked.

The elderly man nodded.

"I was wondering if you could tell me about the role the messiah plays in your religion. I read in the Quran that Jesus was considered a messiah."

The Arab looked surprised, though whether his reaction was to the question or to the fact that a German had been reading the Quran Oskar could not tell.

"This concept, the messiah, does not play a big role in my religion."

"But," said Oskar, "but isn't Ahmad something of a messiah in your religion, at least to the Ahmadiyya branch?"

"Not in the sense you might think."

The driver had started the bus's engines and the elderly Arab turned toward the window as they started moving. After a few minutes he turned back to Oskar. "Perhaps a messiah is simply one who roams or travels a great deal."

Oskar was about to tell him what a primitive answer he thought this was, but considered the question more carefully. A messiah might be someone who is not provincial, who had been around and was more than a simple villager. Jesus and Muhammad were not only inspired but were well traveled. If more young people were encouraged to travel as part of their courses of study, they might come of age with a sense of perspective about their culture's place in the world, which might reduce conflict. If such logic were followed further, the Jewish people being nomadic and traveling involuntarily throughout history might be part of their being "chosen"; or, vice versa, perhaps their travels had been divinely chosen.

He looked at the man beside him with new respect. The man caught Oskar's eye and smiled back.

Oskar did not stay in Damascus long. The Syrian border posed no difficulties, but in the main square he came across a six-foot-high poster depicting a Jew with an enormous curved nose, ugly eyes, thick lips, and a heavy beard. The Jew was lying on the street with his head on the sidewalk. Stepping on the Jew's head was the boot of a Syrian soldier. The poster said, "Beware of Jews. They are enemies," in Arabic and English.

Oskar took out a camera, determined to take a picture of the poster to show his family and friends in Germany, but as he was about to click the shutter, something slammed into his hand and the camera was dashed to the ground. A voice shouted, "You are not allowed to take a picture here!"

"I see no sign forbidding it," Oskar protested.

The man who had slapped his camera away was still yelling, threatening to drag him to the police station. Oskar calmed the man by placing the camera in his bag and walking quietly away. He decided to leave Syria as quickly as he could, and went directly to a train station, where he saw similar anti-Jewish posters.

In Turkey he went north by bus through Adana and Tarsus, birthplace of Paul (formerly Saul), Mersin, and Anamur, where he met a hospitable local gentleman. He went on to picturesque Side and Antalya on the coast. The following day he crossed the mountains between Korkuteli and Denizli by foot and arrived at a village near Laodicea, hoping to see the place mentioned in the Revelation of John. He wanted to see the places he had read about in the New Testament, especially in the Book of Revelation. When he explained to the locals that he had crossed the mountains by foot, he was called crazy, since those mountains were full of wolves.

A local teacher invited him to stay the night, and when Oskar explained that he hoped to visit Laodicea, he was told that no bus ran to the ancient ruins, but he was offered the use of the man's bicycle, which Oskar recognized as a generous offer, given that a bicycle was then a valuable commodity. He offered to leave his watch as collateral but the teacher refused, insisting that he trusted Oskar.

At Laodicea Oskar reflected quietly on the transience of all things; here was one of the founding places of Christianity, in ruins. He rode back to the teacher's home, thanked him, and traveled on towards Izmir, a larger, more modern town.

On his way he visited all the ruins and historical sites he could find, admiring urban and church architecture, examining artifacts, and, under a store's porch, finding a bag of ancient Roman coins mixed with Turkish lira. He looked around, worried that the money had been left by thieves who might still be in the vicinity. Perhaps he would even be mistaken for a thief. But after a while he calmed down, grew more confident, and decided to keep the money. The coins made excellent keepsakes and he could always use the lira.

Seeing the ancient Christian ruins left him with a feeling that even the mighty Christian Church, which had exerted such control over his life when he was a child, was not above being judged or punished. Time will wear on even the most influential church in history, he thought, as he visited the ruins of Smyrna, Pergamos, and Sardes, all mentioned in the Book of Revelation.

He returned to Izmir, and took a night boat to Athens, expecting to be uplifted by the sunrise at Piraeus and by the sight of the ancient Greek ruins. He stood at the ferry's bow as the night's deep blue gave way to the morning's orange and the silhouette of the Acropolis rose over the ancient Greek city. He waited for the surge of emotion, the rush of excitement and awe. It never came. In its place was a creeping horror, a fear that the ground would open and swallow him whole as he arrived in a pagan land.

20

He boarded a bus for Thessaloníki, where he toured the city's ancient churches and applied for a permit to travel to Mount Athos, an autonomous territory on a mountainous peninsula which had been referred to as the Monks' Republic since its inception during the fourth century. It housed monasteries of various ethnicities: Russian, Rumanian, Serb, Bulgarian, and an assortment of Greek origin. Many had been built at the feet of mountains or at the water's edge, providing scenic fodder for meditation or inspiration. As in the Himalayas, hermits dwelled at higher elevations.

Most of the men disembarked at the pier. Women who had accompanied male relatives returned to the boat with the crew, since no women were permitted at Mount Athos. Even female animals were turned away.

Detached, secluded, and tranquil, it was the perfect retreat. Western philosophers and scientists sought out the refuge to enhance their concentration. As at the Church of the Sepulcher, divisiveness was apparent in that Catholic monks and priests were prohibited entirely from the community of monasteries.

During his first full day, Oskar attended a three-hour prayer service beginning at 2:30 A.M. at a Russian monastery named for the saint Panteleimon, followed by work in the fields and gardens, a short breakfast, biblical study, and more prayer and contemplation. Afternoon gardening was followed by a light evening meal and a few hours of sleep. The monks taught prayers in English and German, including a beautiful "prayer of the heart."

He found books in the monastery's library containing records from the early fathers of the church, many of which exhibited anti-Jewish sentiments. The monks discussed the schism between the eastern and western churches, endorsed politically by Charlemagne, who had neglected the eastern church. His own capital, Aachen, was geographically nearer to Rome, Charles reasoned, so he would follow its teachings rather than Constantinople's. Later, the monks explained, the Crusaders took the schism literally and decimated the followers of the eastern church.

The imagery of the eastern churches was less realistic, more two dimensional than that of western churches. Abstract icons appeared throughout. These were not representative works meant as portraits or even tributes. When one observes western religious art, one appreciates its aesthetic value; one may even be spiritually inspired. But the appreciation, the relationship, is in one direction, that of viewer towards the art. With eastern religious icons, a dimensional relationship is considered. Where is the viewer, for instance, in relation to paradise or the saint? The viewer becomes part of a bigger picture, part of the art, and one's perception of that relationship transcends the viewer/art relationship. The stylizations of western art would be a distraction from this eastern perspective.

Jesus was never depicted as a baby in eastern religious art, but as the stern ruler of the universe. Muhammad was welcomed by Christians, the monks explained. His coming had been foretold, and it was when he denied the crucifixion of Christ that Rome denounced him.

Oskar hiked up into the higher elevations, hoping to learn more from the hermits who resided there. He visited a few, one of whom spoke at length about his ideas and experiences. At the entrance to his cave, near where the hermit took his meals, were the skulls of hermits who had lived there previously.

He stayed in his cave, sleeping on a straw mat, meditating, and descending the mountain only once each week to attend church services at one of the Greek monasteries, where he was given two loaves of bread which were to last the week; he took his water from a mountain stream.

"How do you keep warm?" Oskar wanted to know.

"Inner heat," the hermit answered.

The hermit created two-dimensional icons and Oskar asked if the hermit might make him one. The hermit agreed, provided he stay another week, which he did.

After visiting nearly two dozen monasteries, Oskar concluded that the monastic life, prayerful, contemplative, and pious, was admirable, and the locale inspirational, but it did not suit him as a permanent solution to the human condition. He had read that Adam, and humankind, for that matter, existed to subdue the earth in the image and name of the Creator, to till the soil, to live in harmony with one another and with the earth's bounty. Fleeing or withdrawing, even for the most admirable, spiritual goals, might be a temporary solution, a respite perhaps, but was not a goal in and of itself.

Such was the conclusion Oskar reached for himself and his own future, so he took his belongings, including the icon of Paul that the hermit had made for him, which was going to be a gift to his mother, and made his way from Greece to Yugoslavia, toward home.

After vivid Mount Athos, Yugoslavia seemed drab and washed out; the streets of Sarajevo, where the spark of World War I had been struck, were dreary and chilly, but the reception he would receive in this, the first Communist country he had visited for any length of time, would be even colder than the local climate.

He was famished and scoured the marketplace stands for decent fruit. Most of what he found was half rotten or unripe, and he remembered the conversation with the Russian he had met in Afghanistan, who had predicted the downfall of Communism through the failure of its agricultural system. He was beginning a second trip through the marketplace when he felt a hand on his shoulder and heard sharp words barked at him in the local tongue. He turned to find an irate policeman accosting him in an accusatory tone.

Oskar laughed. "I'm just trying to find some decent vegetables."

The policeman repeated himself and Oskar realized he was being accused of spying. He tried to explain himself again, but was taken roughly by the arm to the local police station, where his backpack was emptied. The officer triumphantly snatched up Oskar's cameras.

"They don't have any film," Oskar protested. "Go ahead. Open them." He demonstrated his point, then protested and cajoled until the police were convinced and allowed him to leave, whereupon Oskar left Sarajevo and Yugoslavia, sans fruit, as quickly as he could.

He arrived home, to his parents' delight, tried and failed to explain his spiritual journey, and gave in to the simple pleasure of being among his family again.

"I have a surprise," his father said, the following morning. "I applied to the tax authorities on your behalf, Oggie, and we've arranged to write off your entire journey as a study trip. Most of the taxes you paid when you were with the bank in Frankfurt have been refunded and are in a sizeable account in your name."

"It would be easy, I'm sure," said Sophie, "for you to set up again as a lawyer or banker."

Oskar had been holding an envelope, which he now opened, drawing out a piece of stationery. "I've been invited to teach at an educational institute, to talk about my experiences and ideas, and about the war . . ."

"But the bank . . ." Sophie looked from the letter to her son's eyes. She looked to Wilhelm for support, but Oskar's father was content, as usual, to observe without comment. "Teaching is an estimable profession," she managed to say.

Forchheim was more than a town in Germany—it was Oskar's memories, it was the angst all teenagers struggle with against a backdrop none should ever have to. Something he had read, a biblical passage, had been working on him, and came floating to the surface of his consciousness, like a fisherman's bobbin.

Be reconciled to thy brother.

It was part of a passage from the Sermon on the Mount in the Gospel of Matthew; the words had floated up from his distant memory and remained with him, asserting themselves in his consciousness.

Experiencing the old streets of Forchheim again had an alchemic effect which, along with those haunting words, engendered a desire in him to make amends. How could he have a complete, spiritual life in Israel, or anywhere else, without making amends to those he had harmed?

He walked the streets, remembering his old life and the feelings that had gone with it. He remembered a boy he had hit whose tooth he had broken. The boy had worked in a butcher shop. Not sure what he would say, Oskar found the shop and asked for the boy.

"What do you want with him?"

Oskar stammered out his plan, his hope for forgiveness.

"You cannot talk to him," said the owner, whom Oskar remembered as a stout Catholic.

"But I only want to . . ."

"He was killed in the Battle of Stalingrad."

Oskar stared at the shop's owner, unsure of what to do or say. The owner's face softened. "It's okay. He held no grudge. I'm sure he would forgive you."

He walked home, somewhat relieved, and realized he had to find Theo, the boy he had taunted and beaten up at school for being a teacher's pet. Theo's father had been a tailor, he remembered, and the next day, Oskar managed to locate him and asked where he could find his son.

"What do you want with Theo?"

"To have a personal talk. Please, it's important."

"He's in Bamberg, studying to become a priest."

Oskar took a train to the theological school in Bamberg, found Theo, and reminded the young man of the way he had treated him. "I'm trying to change my ways," Oskar explained. "I'm not there yet, but I'm trying to clear up anything I've done. I hope you'll forgive me."

Theo looked right through him. "I forgive you," he said, mechanically.

Oskar left, chiding himself for having unrealistic expectations, telling himself he had done his best.

Over the next week he found more of his old friends, but felt little connection to them. One had been duped into signing up for the SS while drunk, had been in prison, and was now an outcast due to his prior affiliation. That boy had been drunk on the wrong day, Oskar told himself.

After he had spent a week in Forchheim, listening to conversations on the streets and in shops and visiting old acquaintances, it became apparent that his personal redemption lay elsewhere, and that de-Nazification had changed little in Germany.

Germany was still back on its heels; many had not yet found their footing and moved about the country in search of jobs, roots, and identities. Oskar had decided to travel in ways that allowed him to meet people and derive some sense of time and place. He hitchhiked towards the educational institute to which he had been invited in the town of Vlotho. On the way, he met an elderly man, and the conversation quickly turned to religious matters.

"Do you often pray from the heart?" the man asked.

Oskar was startled. "What do you mean by 'from the heart'?"

"I mean doing something more than reciting prewritten texts. I mean really praying, from your heart. It's vital to get used to it. Come with me, I'll show you what I mean."

They arrived in a village not far from Vlotho that evening, and the man took Oskar to a stone cottage and led him to a room which Oskar could sense was somehow apart from the rest of the living quarters. The man knelt and prayed, urging Oskar to do the same. They stayed that way together until the prayers came easily, like one side of a familiar conversation. Afterwards the elderly man suggested Oskar help himself to coffee, tea, or water. There was no further talk. The man said goodnight, explained that he might be gone when Oskar woke in the morning, and retired.

When Oskar woke up he did find himself alone, so he made a cup of tea and found the institute he was seeking in a castle that dated from the Middle Ages; it had become a youth hostel and more recently an education center. Weeklong classes, weekend retreats, and adult seminars were offered and were well attended.

The atmosphere was one of curiosity and discovery. The administrators asked Oskar to lecture on India, Gandhi, eastern religion, Israel, and the Jews. These seemed to be the first Germans interested in facing the collapse of their way of life beyond the superficialities surrounding the war itself. Oskar was engaged and enthusiastic.

The administrators requested that he shave his beard, and when he asked why, he was told that it was disturbing to some of the staff, and to most of the students, especially those of the elder generation who came for weekend classes.

Beards were uncommon in Germany; he had not seen one while hitchhiking to the institute. Why not send anyone who disapproved to him personally? he asked. He would explain his appearance to them directly. The institute's leader, a broad, tall, former SS man who had been "de-Nazified" and found innocent of war crimes, said that would be impossible. The school would lose students and customers, and would be unable to survive.

Classes were scheduled to begin. Putting the disagreement aside, Oskar began to teach.

As Christmas approached, students and teachers, most of whom were Protestants, put up a tree, lit candles, baked cookies, and gathered one evening to sing and celebrate. An elderly woman had written a poem for the occasion; it told of the baby Jesus, born in Bethlehem, a beautiful blond boy with blue eyes who played near a rushing stream in the forest. If he were here today, the poem claimed, little Jesus would have cookies and gifts bestowed upon him.

Oskar asked permission to speak; he looked over the students and teachers surrounded by glittering holiday trimmings. "I'm confused by your poem and by how well we claim we would treat the baby Jesus today. Just a few years ago all the Jewish baby boys born here were herded off to the gas chamber, not fed cookies and chocolates. You even have trouble with my beard! Can you imagine if a person showed up here who really looked Jewish, not just with a beard but with a black hat and side locks? How would you treat him?"

His comments brought a quick end to the evening and to his stay at the institute.

A person may be driven by a complex mixture of needs, some hereditary or learned as behaviors from parents or other early environmental influences. To these are added one's experiences during the years of maturation, especially those that occur in difficult, stress-filled times. Oskar had been searching for a way of life, a philosophy and day-to-day existence worth devoting himself to. Israel—its people, land, political origins, and primary religion—all filled the voids in his heart and mind. As a student, a lawyer, a banker, he had always been thorough, so to be certain before making such a momentous decision, he had gone back to Europe to give his former life a chance.

But he went back for another reason. He was driven by a need to understand the underbelly of his origins, the way a scientist or a boy will turn over rocks in search of whatever creatures live beneath it and hide from the light. The notion that the Five Books of Moses, the bedrock of the Jewish religion, had given birth to two of the world's most popular religions, which had then, so far as he could see, discarded the parent religion, was confusing to him. So he returned to Europe to verify his hypothesis, for he had not yet decided for himself whether it was true.

As important as Oskar's need to be absolutely certain of his new direction was, and as curious as he had become about the independent natures of Christianity and Islam, there may have been an even more significant reason for his return to Europe, one which perhaps he was not aware of: the human need for fulfillment, validation, permanence . . . and love.

The Bruderhof Community was founded in Sannerz, Germany, in the 1920s, and based the life of its members on Jesus' Sermon on the Mount, especially its espousal of nonviolence, love of one's neighbors and enemies alike, and sexual purity. The community's members were from all walks of life and nationalities and shared labor and property in the manner and style of Gandhi.

Nazi persecution had driven the Bruderhof to Holland and Great Britain. A branch had been established in the United States, and after the war, a small number had gone back to Germany to reestablish the community and attempt to recoup confiscated property.

Oskar spent a few days with them, finding them pleasant and their atmosphere reflective of everything they claimed, but he felt that they were cut off from the rest of the world and therefore unable to address the challenges of greater society such as Germany's social and economic problems. Israel, which was growing in importance to Oskar, was not on their agenda.

He learned of a small Catholic community near Bebra in central Germany, presided over by a woman descended from German nobility. They were an independent-thinking collection of Catholics with an in-house priest who agreed to discuss the issues of concern to Oskar, though he did not answer his new guest's questions about the history behind and reasons for the changes that allowed Christians to eat pork, replace biblical holidays with new ones, and work on Saturdays. He let Oskar air his views and opinions and did not offer much at all in response.

At the community's Sunday mass, Oskar took a seat in the back row, more interested in watching people than in participating in the service. When it was time to offer Communion, the priest did not invite the congregation to come forward but left his pulpit and offered wafers to each individual. When he came to the back and held the wafer out, Oskar refused.

"You don't want it?"

Oskar shook his head.

Afterwards, the priest sought him out. "Are your disagreements with the church so serious that you cannot be a part of our community?"

"It's more serious than that. Before I left Germany, I would have readily taken part, but now that I've learned that the church changed the original commandments, well, it's changed my whole outlook. No one's given me the reason. How can I possibly participate when the observance is clearly arbitrary and has deserted the original intent? This is not a game for me, and I hope you'll respect that."

"I have to respect your belief," he said, looking hard at Oskar, "but please respect mine."

Oskar took the priest's hint and left the next day.

An invitation to speak in East Germany arrived a few weeks later.

Oskar brought with him a weekly newspaper he had been given in the Jewish community of Cologne. At the East German checkpoint, the police officer went through Oskar's overnight bag, removing and replacing his pajamas, washing implements, and Bible. Upon examining the Jewish weekly, the policeman held it up and demanded to know why Oskar would bring such forbidden propaganda into the country.

"I don't think of this as propaganda, and I did not know it was forbidden."

"You'll have to go back."

Oskar had dealt with such people before. "I have a valid visa and there's no reason not to allow me entry. If you have a problem with me, bring me before your commander." His newspaper confiscated, Oskar was brought before the commander, and after displaying his usual stubbornness, the commander was worn down and Oskar allowed entry.

He arrived at his destination, a town in Mecklenburg, which is in northeast Germany between Berlin and the Baltic Sea, where he was welcomed by his hosts and immediately reported himself to the police, as was required of all western visitors. On the official questionnaire, he was asked to write down his profession, and, no longer considering himself a lawyer or banker, he wrote "teacher."

The following day, an official came to question him as to what he was planning to teach. Oskar described his travels to India and the Middle East, his thoughts about Gandhi, and his feelings about pacifism. The policeman was not only interested but thought Oskar's story worth hearing by the rest of the force. If the officer's superior consented, would Oskar be willing to talk to the police? The approval, however, might take a week, since the superior was in Leipzig.

Oskar agreed. While he stayed with his East German hosts, a few visitors were invited in each day to meet and listen to him, so that large gatherings, which were forbidden, were avoided.

Oskar found East Germany monotonous and dreary, like Yugoslavia, a painting with its hues and colors drained away. The hosts were honestly interested and sincere, like the Afghani Russian; they were seeking a way to cleanse the wreckage of their collective past.

The exchanges were two-way in that his hosts taught Oskar the historical justifications for Marxism. Oskar wondered about whether the word "freedom" referred to an external circumstance or one's attitude. He had certainly seen little of anything that could be called freedom in Sarajevo or in the confiscation of his Jewish weekly. His hosts argued that society must protect itself before freedom can be allowed. Religion, they claimed, was an opiate which dulled the senses of the poor, allowing the rich to rule and therefore subverting real freedom.

There followed discussions about Stalin and Darwin and evolution; Oskar remembered the words "God spoke . . ." from his Bible, and suggested that therefore language was of divine origin and not developed from matter, as suggested by atheistic materialism. The exchanges were the only vibrant experience to be found in East Germany.

The approval for his lecture to the police had not yet arrived by the time his visa expired, and, having provided his agreed-upon lectures in one-on-one form, Oskar returned to West Germany.

21

The little town of Hamm, not to be confused with the larger city of the same name to its north, is a village in the district of Sieg, which is also the name of one of the Rhine's tributaries. Towards the town's center Oskar found a large house in which lived a couple in their sixties. Heinrich was reticent and thin, his bony face encircling large brown eyes that said more than his words. His wife, Hedwig, was taller, slightly corpulent, and with wise, warm, welcoming eyes. They had no children of their own, and the six they had adopted after the war were already grown, married, and on their own.

The couple received Oskar graciously and invited him to spend the night in their home, where he enjoyed simple, healthy food. He left the next morning, having found the devout Protestant couple agreeable but no more attractive to him in the long term than anyone else, except that their diet was healthier than most.

The morning was sunny and temperate and Oskar prepared to hitchhike to parts unknown, surrounded by chattering birds, schoolchildren, and townspeople readying for their workdays. He felt a sudden reluctance as he started out on the main road, and the more he tried to flag down passing cars or trucks, the less interested he became in leaving. His attention, on some level he could not control, kept drifting back to the little town and the home of the couple he had met the night before. Eventually he gave up and went back to their house to find Heinrich and Hedwig waiting, not the least bit surprised to see him. When he explained that he had been unable to continue on his way, they looked at one another. "We thought you might be back," said Heinrich.

Oskar stayed with the couple for a year and a half.

That first morning Hedwig sat down with Oskar and explained their backgrounds and how they were attempting to help people in Hamm. She was the daughter of a businessman and had inherited a grocery shop from her parents. In the late 1920s and early 1930s, after the First World War, Hedwig had tried to help the jobless and alcoholics by teaching them the benefit of a healthier diet. Once they ate better, she reasoned, they would think more clearly, spend their money more responsibly, and be more likely to help themselves. She was a vegetarian who had developed delicious, nourishing recipes from easily acquired natural ingredients. The authorities at that time appreciated her work, and arranged for her to teach seminars on healthy eating.

Early on, the Nazis emphasized fitness and physical health, and Hedwig had been invited to join the party. Like Oskar she had been seduced at first, particularly by the Nazis' apparent concern for the poor and unemployed; she was idealistic and optimistic, and continued teaching. But in 1934, with the boycotting of Jewish shops and growing persecution and violence, she realized something was wrong. Her mother had taught her that the Bible singled out the Jews as special. Since the Third Reich was against the Jews, Hedwig concluded, the Nazis must be against the Bible.

She and her husband, who was a coal miner, had been studying the Scriptures, and came upon the Decalogue and the commandment "Thou shalt keep the Sabbath." So she applied to the local authorities to be allowed to close the shop on Saturday, which she and her husband believed to be the true holy day. Her Bible edition appeared to confirm her conclusion.

The Nazis did close her shop on Saturday, and on every other day; her store was forcibly shut down.

The couple was left with no income, and only pittance for savings. Heinrich had contracted lung disease in the mines and had retired with a pension. They began selling the remnants of their store, anything not confiscated, and soon found that their clientele included the town's Jewish population. While Jewish customers could not visit their shop, they could buy surreptitiously, if the couple delivered to them. The arrangement became a mainstay of their meager income.

With the advent in 1935 of the Nuremberg Laws, Heinrich and Hedwig saw the handwriting on the wall and warned their Jewish neighbors to leave Germany. At least one family took their advice, and the couple remained on close terms with those who stayed.

When the war broke out, underground groups of all kinds were formed, and through a Bible study and prayer group, the couple became the locus of a pocket of resistance. Other, larger, such groups existed, such as the White Rose in Munich, but they had no means of communicating, no structure for coalescing into a more sizable and effective force.

They wrote and distributed leaflets based on biblical teachings, demonstrating the anti-Christian, anti-Bible nature of the Nazi Party and its propaganda.

One afternoon soon after the war with Russia had begun, the couple was sitting in an upstairs room, concentrating on their writing, when two policemen entered unannounced. They had forgotten to lock the door. The police accused them of writing anti-Nazi propaganda and organizing illegal underground operations. They waved a court-ordered search warrant.

"Our hearts were beating up to our tongues," Hedwig explained, with a shake of her head at the memory.

The couple was ordered into separate corners while the police tore apart the room, searching everywhere but on the table where they had been writing. Beds were overturned and ripped apart, carpets were torn up, but not a glance was turned towards what was under the Nazis' very noses. When the police left without a shred of evidence, the couple felt they had been protected by God, who had blinded the Nazis. They went right back to work, albeit a bit more cautiously.

After the war's end, grateful for their divine protection, they decided to adopt German children, refugees who had no place else to turn.

But the end of the war did not put a stop to misery. Young people drank and smoked, trying to forget the losses that permeated their lives, and the couple wanted to help. The local church considered them obscure outsiders, so they began conducting independent afternoon religious services, open to local youth, which were based on biblical teachings and had an emphasis on healthy living.

"What's in there?" Oskar asked, pointing to a box on the wall of the reception room.

"A charity box for children of people who have no jobs, for orphans, for the poor."

"Have you thought of putting up a box for Jewish Holocaust survivors?" Oskar asked.

The couple looked at one another. "We'll put up another box next to that one," Hedwig said. "An Israel charity box."

Oskar stayed on, and was enthusiastic about the couple's charity. They formed a support group for Jews who had been injured by Nazi medical experiments, and a separate support group for those who had been at a small camp in Rumania called Wapniarka where the Jewish prisoners had had their nervous systems damaged by an experimental treatment with a kind of pea not meant for human consumption.

The couple demonstrated a remarkable quality of faith. On a sweltering summer afternoon, during a thunderstorm so violent that Heinrich feared the houses and fields would be damaged, he went upstairs to his room to pray for their safety. The storm continued, unabated, so the frail old man threw open a window, leaned out and shouted his prayers into the downpour, being all but drowned out by the wind and thunder. Within moments the rain stopped, the clouds fled, and the village was lit with sunshine. Oskar was stunned, but Heinrich and Hedwig did not seem to give the matter a second thought; it was as if Heinrich had fixed a leaky faucet.

Hedwig left one afternoon for the funeral of a woman she knew, and when she returned, her face glowed. "No one wore black," she explained to Oskar, "only white, and everyone was in such a wonderful mood." She went on, like a little girl with a secret, "Let me tell you why. When the old woman was on her death bed, half unconscious, she opened her eyes, and said, 'Oh how beautiful it is,' and then passed away. Everyone was so moved. We knew, you see, that death in this world is not really the end, so we rejoiced for the rest of the funeral."

When Oskar's parents learned he was no longer teaching at the educational institute in Vlotho, their relationship grew strained. He had not resumed his legal practice, he lived with a bizarre elderly couple, and he was growing a beard. Worst of all, talk had begun circulating around Forchheim that he might have done something wrong, perhaps at the bank, and was hiding. What other reasonable explanation could there be for such behavior?

Such rumors were hard on the parents of a "lost son," as Sophie had begun calling him. She and Wilhelm had started a correspondence with a lawyer with whom Oskar had worked before beginning his employment at the bank in Frankfurt, a man descended from nobility, who had a fine reputation and an unmarried daughter Oskar's age. Sophie hoped Oskar would take an interest in her.

Perhaps if Hilde had not been so far away, his sister might have been a bridge or buffer between parents and son, who viewed the German status quo so differently. Hilde understood both sides and the good intentions behind them, and her gentle manner might have brought them together. But she was unreachable except by mail.

When he was alone and his time unoccupied, Oskar wondered about his future. His parents were right in that his vocational training, his means of earning a respectable income in Germany, were in the legal and banking systems, while his travels and new understanding flew in the face of such a choice.

He wondered if he might stay with Heinrich and Hedwig—good, generous, pious people he had come to respect—but working in Heinrich's gardens and fields, where he learned organic agriculture, was not a long-term alternative. He thought about starting his own reform movement but had no idea of how to begin without some preexisting base of support and the requisite organizational knowledge. Reform movements grow from historical, social necessity. They arise naturally. Rarely do they come from a single individual's need for direction, except when this need is shared by others with a mutual awareness.

Besides, first the church had broken with Judaism, then the schism had divided the church into east and west. He had seen just a few splinters of these differences at Mount Athos. After Martin Luther, the Protestants had divided as well. Did Germany need yet another sect?

He had been struggling to read Martin Buber's translation of the Bible, which contained new words and phrases designed to bring clarity from the original Hebrew to the German. It was a valiant attempt at an impossible task. For instance, the Hebrew word *ruach* might translate as wind, air, or spirit—hence Buber's German translation of Genesis 1:2, in which God's "wind-noise-spirit" hovered above the abyss. Translation diluted the Bible's meaning, despite all good and scholarly intentions to the contrary. The answer, which had come to Oskar as a response to other questions at other times, was to read only in the original Hebrew. He remembered his friend Rav Braun's prediction that someday Hebrew would be utilized universally in the reading of Scripture.

He was nearly certain his future lay in Israel. Life with Heinrich and Hedwig had been interesting and fulfilling but was not a long-term solution. Before making arrangements to leave, he had heard of a religious organization that sounded interesting, followers of the Bible rather than of organizational church teachings. Wanting to leave no stone unturned, he hitchhiked to Freiburg to visit the Dawn, whose leaders welcomed him.

Quickly, Oskar voiced his questions. If the Dawn's precepts were based solely on the Bible, why did they observe the Sabbath on Sunday? Why did they ignore commandments, eat unclean foods, and consider themselves as the exclusive true believers?

The Dawn's members stood up for their beliefs, claiming he was "Judaising" the Bible, and Oskar's answer was to cite the Sermon on the Mount: "Whosoever neglects even the least of the Commandments shall be the least in the Kingdom of God." He asked how it was that they claimed to love their neighbors.

The discussion, and his visit, ended there.

He had been in Germany for two years and had exhausted his

search for a spiritual future outside of Israel. He and a young acquaintance, Wolfgang Glauche, decided to travel together. Oskar arranged with the Israeli embassy in Bonn for a visa to be forwarded to the Mandelbaum Gate by the end of 1959. He said good-bye to Heinrich and Hedwig, who were at once encouraging and sorry to see him go. His parents were confused by his plans but not surprised, and promised him a warm bed anytime he wanted to return.

They began hitchhiking in Stuttgart, where Glauche lived, and quickly traveled through southern Germany and Austria into Yugoslavia, arriving in a small village whose citizens had been terrorized by the German army during the war. Oskar expressed sorrow over the incident and explained that he and his friend were not tourists but spiritual seekers, he on his way to Israel, his friend traveling further east. The villagers said this was the first instance they had experienced of a German taking responsibility for his country's part in the war. Oskar and Wolfgang were told about other sad, shocking incidents that had occurred in neighboring villages, perpetrated by Nazis and a Nazi-affiliated Croat group called Ustacha.

A middle-aged man came forward and invited the two travelers to stay at his home, and they accepted. The man had a wife and two children who were glad to have visitors, though surprised that neither would eat meat. A meal of cheese, vegetables, and potatoes was provided and gratefully accepted.

The following morning they thanked their hosts and hitchhiked through the bluffs and ramparts of Montenegro's mountains, pausing at overlooks and headlands to watch the flow of rivers and estuaries. The two traversed Greece towards Turkey, craning their necks from gats and spits of land, shading their eyes to view the high peaks against the yellow Mediterranean sun.

Oskar's future possibilities had narrowed somewhat; he was glad to be on his way again with his new friend, who had asked that he no longer be called Wolfgang but Johannes. They ate plain vegetarian fare as they walked, and Oskar pointed out where he had been and what he had seen on his earlier trips. In the evenings they read their Bibles together.

"We're making good time," Oskar said one night. "We'll probably get to Syria sometime tomorrow."

Johannes looked up from his Bible. "Do you think they'll give us trouble at the border?"

Oskar shook his head, started to answer, then pointed at his friend's face. "You're reading without glasses."

Glauche thought a moment, glanced around, then gave a surprised laugh. "Well, that's right. I guess I am. My eyes feel good and I can see whatever I try to—" He began peering at Oskar and at his own hands, trying to see them at different distances. "I don't think I need them anymore!"

Oskar nodded knowingly. "Shows what a good, spiritual life will do for you. And, as Hedwig would say, a healthy vegetarian diet!"

They stopped in a town just across the Syrian border, attracting an immediate crowd. Someone suggested that the two strangers might like to meet a local sheik.

The sheik, whose name was Kailani, was a Sufi, a dervish—hospitable and friendly. He invited the travelers in for a discussion, which was quickly extended to dinner and an overnight stay. Before accepting, Oskar carefully explained that the two were strict vegetarians, and would not touch meat, despite its being a local staple.

"Not a problem at all," the sheik assured him. "It is all arranged."

The following day Johannes traveled to the excavations of Palmyra in eastern Syria while Oskar, having had his fill of digs, stayed behind with the sheik. Oskar engaged his host in historical and religious conversation, covering the world's major religions and the Quran's views on the Bible, the Gospels, and especially Jesus and the prophets.

Inevitably, the talk turned to politics and the relatively new State of Israel and its volatile relationship with its neighbors. Oskar and the sheik readily agreed that a people's religious origins, even in secular states, could not help but influence their politics. Comparisons were made between Israel's difficulties and the animosity between eastern and western Christianity. The sheik was fascinated by the discussion and asked if Oskar would agree to his inviting in a larger group the following day for a broader discussion. Again citing his disinclination to eat meat, Oskar agreed.

That evening, the sheik took Oskar upstairs into a specially prepared room for his Sufi prayers and Oskar explained that he had also been a Sufi, a *mureed*, which means disciple or student.

The following evening they were joined by approximately ten dinner guests. Once Oskar was introduced as a German, one of the guests, a relative of the sheik and a ranking official in the Syrian Ministry for Immigration and Emigration, began praising Hitler and the accomplishments of the Nazis with specific regard to German infrastructure.

Oskar listened politely. "He may have built highways and factories, but so did Egypt, which the Quran refers to rather unfavorably. And it is interesting that Hitler and the pharaoh both turned out to be murderers. The difference was that the Egyptians only murdered male babies, whereas Hitler murdered them all, from baby to grandparents."

"Oh, come now," the sheik's relative said. "Hitler wasn't so bad. What he did to the Jews was really necessary, if you think about it."

Oskar stood up, looking at the sheik, hoping he might intervene. "You've invited us for discussion, not for praising murderers. I don't care who this guy is, friend, relative, official, whatever. One of us has to leave."

The sheik didn't answer right away.

"Or," Oskar offered, "he can stop praising Hitler. I won't listen to that."

"Calm down," the sheik implored. "Don't take what he's saying so personally."

"I do take it personally. It's impossible for me to listen to such things."

The sheik motioned his relative into another room, and, when they came back, talk slowly resumed about more polite matters. But the atmosphere had been poisoned and remained emotionally charged.

The sheik invited everyone to sit at a long table that had been ornately set. Oskar was given a seat next to the sheik. Servants brought platters of rice and vegetables followed by a lamb which the sheik had ordered slaughtered. When Oskar took only a cucumber, faces turned his way, disapproving eyes glanced towards his plate, then at their host.

"Why don't you eat?" the sheik wanted to know.

"I told you several times, very clearly, that I'm a vegetarian. Everything here, even the vegetables and rice, has been cooked with lamb."

"But you are my guest, this is a festive meal. You should try to enjoy it."

"You know I can't do that under these circumstances."

"You offend us by making such a fuss."

Oskar's voice was rising. "Let's think about who's offended. You knew . . . and agreed. My plate stays clean of meat, and vegetables cooked in meat."

"But can't you see my guests are uncomfortable?"

"They can stare all they want. I made this clear. You didn't have to agree."

The sheik stood up, his eyes on Oskar. "I'll be back. I have to think it over."

The other guests began eating quietly, avoiding Oskar's eyes. He took a tentative bite of his cucumber.

After a few minutes the sheik returned and stood at the head of the table. "My dear friends, I was very insulted at first, but I must confess that I have learned a tremendous lesson: we Muslims have forgotten that our prophet Muhammad was a vegetarian. It is written that he lived on dates and other vegetables and allowed us to eat meat only because we are weak. If we want to be strong, and if we want to enjoy peace on earth, we should follow his example. We ought to either live by our scriptures or consider discarding them altogether. Please finish your meal, as it has been prepared, but I ask you to think about what I've said and take a lesson from this situation."

He ordered a meal of fresh fruit and nuts to be served to Oskar, and the tension dissipated. After the guests had left, the sheik sat down with Oskar. "Perhaps we ought to consider gathering a group of followers and starting a reform movement. The way our country is run now isn't right. Your way would catch on."

"If you start with fighting and revolutions, that's what you end with," Oskar countered. "As the Gospels say, he who takes up the sword will perish by it. From my own experience, violence just brings more of the same. My thought is to start slowly, teaching what you read in your scriptures, but slowly, nonviolently, like leavening bread."

"How long do you think you might stay?"

A tension in the sheik's tone gave him pause, and Oskar remembered the status of the man he had argued with and wondered if his border crossing would be safe.

"Until tomorrow."

"By what route will you leave?"

"Jordan, to Jerusalem."

"There's a bus at 5 A.M. to Damascus. You can easily get from there to Amman."

22

Oskar arrived in Amman and then East Jerusalem, looked for Johannes in the agreed-upon cafe and, not finding him, strolled the old city, including the abandoned Jewish quarter. After Johannes arrived, the two compared notes, shared a cup of tea and a meal together, and went their separate ways. On November 30, 1959, Oskar passed without incident through the Mandelbaum Gate into West Jerusalem and went directly to Martha and Elsa's home to tell the sisters he had returned and was hoping to study Hebrew. The sisters suggested he quickly return to Kibbutz Hazorea and register with Mordechai's *Ulpan*, where classes would begin in January.

After a visit with friends he had met through Professor Bergman, Oskar traveled back to the kibbutz and sought out Mordechai, who greeted him warmly. "Why didn't you write and let me know? I would have saved you a place in the class."

"I didn't know when I was coming back. I was figuring it all out for myself as I went along. You might have wasted my place, had you saved it. I understand if I have to wait."

Mordechai clapped him on the shoulder. "Didn't I tell you there's always a place for you?"

Oskar's excitement at returning to the kibbutz and finally beginning Hebrew studies was tempered by Mordechai's departure for America, where he was to encourage and help organize *aliyah*, the return of Jews to Israel.

His replacement, Arnon Fishman, reminded the students that they aspired not only to speak Hebrew but also to become active participants in Israeli society. Choosing a Hebrew name would be an important step in that direction, though the decision was, of course, left to each individual. Oskar was uncertain what name he would choose if he were to make the change, and asked his new teacher's advice.

"The name 'Asher' sounds a bit like Oskar and means 'blessed' or 'happy one,'" Arnon explained. "And it's the name of one of Jacob's twelve sons, the leader of a tribe."

Perhaps it was the association with Jacob, whose story had always resonated for him, or perhaps it was the name's meaning, but Oskar took to his new name as much as he had to his new life. The two came together, coalescing into a new identity: he became Asher Eder, resident of Kibbutz Hazorea, Hebrew language student.

He was the only non-Jew in a class of thirty to forty young, hopeful immigrants, primarily Americans along with a few Europeans who had lost family in the Holocaust. The days were divided in half: school in the morning, kibbutz work in the afternoon. A week later the schedule would be reversed.

The Hebrew was difficult in that it had no similarity to any language he knew. The class utilized the Book of Genesis as a language and grammar reference, which was helpful since he had German and English editions and had more than a passing familiarity with the text. The language class supported his Bible study and vice versa. The going was slow and difficult, but he was an enthusiastic, determined student.

Originally, the kibbutz had been founded by German Jews, disciples of Buber who had arrived in the mid-1930s determined to build their society through collaborative work; doctors would double as farmers, lawyers as street cleaners. The idea was in part a response to the rampant anti-Semitism in Europe and Russian pogroms. Collaboration and fraternity would supercede class division and bigotry.

Despite his growing attraction to Judaism and the official disavowal of religion at the kibbutz, Asher felt at home at Kibbutz Hazorea. While his new identity had been forged by the war and its aftermath and his journey through Asia, he had in a sense been born at the kibbutz. The kibbutzim and all of Israel were attempting to start a new society, as he was beginning a new life.

He learned that many of the challenges Israel would face had been anticipated by Theodore Herzl, who stressed that, though Jewish in origin, Israel ought not be a religious society but a secular and entirely independent, free state. Industry, agriculture, economics, and even a military must be included as critical components if such a grand experiment were to succeed.

A painting by Marc Chagall symbolized to Asher the challenges facing the new country; it included a head bearing two faces—one a religious countenance, the other that of a laborer. Yet each was part of one whole: Israel.

As Passover approached, excitement pervaded the kibbutz, with everyone pitching in, preparing food and decorating the dining hall for the holiday. Asher read the corresponding biblical stories and considered the nature of freedom, whether from Egyptian or the more modern European or Russian tyranny. In India he had seen rural workers who had no day of rest, save the occasional festival, and realized that the Sabbath, a weekly day of rest, might be one of the great social innovations of all time. The Sabbath brought a freedom from work for one day, freedom to worship and celebrate one's family. Pesach, or Passover, was a celebration of that freedom, and he looked forward to participating, along with Jews the world over.

The dining hall had been decorated in tree-green and at one end a huge banner read, "We Celebrate Our Exodus from Europe."

"I'm surprised you'd put up a banner saying that," Asher said to a sunburned young man sitting nearby.

The man looked up at the banner and shrugged. "Why? It looks pretty good to me."

"Well, you claim to be atheists but it's a quote from the prophets."

The young man's angular face broke into a smile. "If you call the decoration committee prophets."

"Even though it refers to recent history," Asher continued, "the same words were written by Jeremiah over twenty-five hundred years ago. I'm paraphrasing: there will come a time when the Jewish people won't only celebrate their exodus from Egypt but from the countries to the north" (Jeremiah 3:18, 16:14, 15; Isaiah 49:12).

Still smiling, the young man rolled his eyes heavenward.

While those he met at the kibbutz claimed to be atheists, Asher sensed in them the same spirituality he derived from reading his Bible. That they were connected to the land, to history, and to one another was evident in the simplest of routines. Upon entering the dining hall, no one congregated in cliques; everyone sat and ate and discoursed with everyone else. While individuals had their differences, even frictions, there was an overarching sense of purpose and togetherness.

He worked in the steaming kitchen at first, amidst a sea of chrome cauldrons, pots, and cutlery, a job few wanted but which he did not mind. Washing dishes and cutlery can focus the mind, which becomes absorbed by the task, relaxed and at peace.

He was rotated outdoors to the gardens and found himself weeding and tending plants under the open sky. The Englishman, John, also a non-Jew, was put in charge of the nursery, and he soon brought Asher in to work with him. Asher took to the tree nursery and was quickly grafting and budding almonds, peaches, anything in demand and of commercial value. And in return, the work nurtured him; his study of grafting brought a fresh understanding to his reading—the obscure parable of the olive tree, in the Epistle to the Romans, took on new meaning after he had spent a few days in the nursery.

Work was punctuated by stimulating conversations that included differing opinions. While those with urban backgrounds struggled more with the rigors of the outdoor labor, the atmosphere was a positive one of fellowship and shared work and purpose.

Asher worked in the long rows of crops and trees, preparing the soil alongside an enormous piece of machinery, which he found distasteful until he considered it more carefully. Israel, he reasoned, would not flourish without modern machinery. The land could not be cultivated with preindustrial techniques, by donkeys and animal-pulled plows. Perhaps, he reasoned, machines had been created with divine help so that this formerly barren land might become fruitful. Widespread deforestation during the Roman-dominated era had left the land vulnerable, and rains eventually washed off much of the topsoil. Rocks had to be hoisted up steep slopes to allow replanting of forests, a task beyond the capability of men's and women's bare hands.

The only land allotted the Jews since World War I had been these barren rocks, yet Israel's soil had been ingeniously cultivated with the use of whatever means were at hand . . . including modern technology.

His Hebrew studies brought greater understanding of everyday life and made the Bible's stories come alive. Now when he read the

Psalms of David, the verses were no longer the words of one man, but resonated as the soul of Israel.

As Hebrew class ended late one morning and students stretched their legs and began filing out, Arnon motioned for Asher to wait. "Asher, this is difficult . . . you know that many of our people lost family in the Holocaust." He looked directly at Asher. "The presence here of a German who had been in the . . . in the German army and who continues to speak German hurts them. I'm sorry to have to be the one to talk to you about it. You're a good student and personally I like you."

For a moment Asher heard only his own heart, beating in his ears. "I don't want to hurt anyone or be a burden of any kind." He took a step toward the door. "I should leave, and the sooner the better."

Arnon stood up and put a hand on Asher's shoulder. "That's not what I meant. You're our guest. In fact, you're more than that. You're a member of the kibbutz. Anyway, the problem's not that simple. Our feelings about this remind us that we are German Jews and have to come to grips with post-Holocaust Germany." He squeezed Asher's shoulder. "Stay, Asher, for all our sakes."

Asher flushed, feeling the Gospels' teaching of loving one's enemy manifested in these supposedly atheist yet so very spiritual kibbutz people. He did not know what to say. Finally, he directed the conversation away from what he was feeling. "Why do you have to deal with the German government?"

"Some degree of financial restitution has been arranged for survivors. Adenauer and Ben-Gurion worked something out, but many don't want anything to do with German money, while others might accept something but can't decide if it ought to be private money or if it should go to the kibbutz. Either way, we beg you to stay. We know it's difficult for some of us and of course for you, but facing it will help us grow and learn more about ourselves."

Unable to put words to his feelings, Asher stumbled outside and sat down, his forearms on his knees, and wept.

The following day he sought out Arnon and agreed to stay through the end of the language course, which would provide him with enough communications skills for him to get by on his own without using English or the more offensive German.

As the Hebrew course wore on, he wondered what he would do at its end. Arnon led him to believe that he could stay at the kibbutz, a life which he was learning to like very much. He had developed close friendships with a few classmates. On the other hand, he would not miss the seemingly endless committee and subcommittee meetings that droned on every afternoon and evening.

In his free time he visited a neighboring village he had read about in the Book of Joshua. Called Yoqneam, it was a place of trees near pure green hills, and valleys sprinkled with flowers. As he had every-where else, he spoke to whomever he met, asking unabashed ques-tions with the curiosity of a schoolboy. One of those he met was a pro-fessor from Haifa named Rubinstein who suggested that upon completion of his *Ulpan*, his Hebrew study, he might find work at a children's orphanage called Ahava, after the Hebrew word for love. The orphanage was in nearby Kiryat Bialik, named for Israel's poet laureate, who was one of those credited with bringing back Hebrew. At that time Kiryat Bialik was a small, rural town, and Asher enjoyed taking long walks through the valleys and hills, examining shrubs and plants, often spending entire afternoons reveling in the Israeli countryside, forgetting the past and trying not to think too hard about the future.

He met with Hanni Ulmann, the director, and was pleased to learn that the orphanage had been founded in Berlin but had emigrated intact in the early 1930s, with many of its members, to Palestine. Hanni herself had been attracted to the singing, dancing, and camaraderie, learning at home from her father who had studied Jewish culture at the University of Berlin. After a long, in-depth conversation, Hanni invited him to become a volunteer at the home once he finished his studies.

But it would be a temporary home for him, just as it was for all the children there. What would he do when he outgrew it? The thought nagged at him on his walks, until one day he remembered Cameroon, who in India so long ago had told him that his family name had been in the Bible. He had been right. Why not settle where his biblical namesakes, the Eders, had lived? He sat and read and reread until he found what he was looking for: the very place he was seeking was Yoqneam, where he had met Professor Rubinstein, who had suggested he apply to work at Ahava.

He had no idea of what to do next, so he followed his heart, and began taking long inspired walks over the land on which he imagined his biblical namesakes had lived, through the breathtaking Yoqneam landscape on the southwestern side of the kibbutz. The land was all the more beautiful because he sensed he was supposed to be there. The walks left him at peace and with a sense of purpose, but as yet no way to achieve it.

In the meantime, his class ended; he said sad good-byes to his friends at Kibbutz Hazorea, and took what little he owned to Kiryat Bialik to join the Ahava children's home.

Hanni Ulmann sat in her office, the echoes of children's voices filtering in from filled rooms just down the hall. She looked up now and then from the forms on her desk and glanced out the window as though expecting someone.

Josef, who worked in the kitchen, peeked in. "They tell me you're letting him work here?"

"I trust Professor Rubinstein's opinion."

He turned away, as though at a noise down the hall; when he turned back his expression was grave. "Jewish refugees who have no place else to go are one thing, but a Luftwaffe pilot?"

"He is a student at Kibbutz Hazorea, no longer a Luftwaffe pilot. He wants to make up for those days. Professor Rubinstein must have had some way to determine his worth or he would not have recommended this young man." The look she gave him sent him back to the kitchen.

Forty minutes later there was a knock on her door and Hanni put her paperwork aside.

She smiled to herself. She had forgotten since their one meeting how very German he looked. His erect bearing and china blue eyes would stand out in this home filled with brown-eyed European Jews. His red cheeks and suntan spoke of time in the fields at Hazorea and perhaps elsewhere. He wore plain khaki pants and a loose shirt and sandals. Most surprising was his scraggly beard.

They looked at one another for a few minutes. Finally Hanni held out a hand. "Welcome, Asher. Come, we'll get a bite to eat."

The dining room had been a raucous playground, but when Hanni and Asher entered, the room grew silent. All eyes were on the newcomer as they sat down with plates of fruit. "They'll get used to you," Hanni assured him, as she began sprinkling sugar on a plate of strawberries.

Asher was looking at what she was doing. "Why are you doing that?" he asked.

"Haven't you tried them this way? Strawberries are delicious with sugar."

He gave her a severe look. "God knows what tastes good."

A few days later a local newspaper story appeared with the headline "Former Luftwaffe Pilot to Work at Ahava."

Few workers, particularly the German Jews at the home, would speak to him. Josef was slow to prepare the vegetarian dishes he requested. The children called him "the pilot," though rarely to his face. He was thought of as distant, strange, a hermit—a point of view seemingly confirmed by his clothing and beard.

It was the children who came around first. Asher was so gentle, so soft-spoken, that one by one they approached him, first with a touch or a word, a greeting to make sure he wouldn't bite or speak sharply. They no more knew a non-Jewish German than little Oskar had known a Jew so many decades earlier.

When not with the children, Asher worked hard: cleaning streets and helping out any way he could, as much to gain trust as to straighten up the orphanage. As at Kibbutz Hazorea, he won over a doubting public through diligent hard work and a respect for his fellows.

The children's ages ranged from five—some were barely more than toddlers—to fifteen years or older. None had anyplace to go or anyone to look after them. Asher understood that for them to trust him would take time and effort on his part. For them to trust anyone after the difficult lives they had had would be asking a great deal.

Once they had established a rapport, he became a kind of dorm father, living amongst the children, looking after them and giving them work to do in the garden, which had become his specialty. In his idealism and enthusiasm he was a big child himself.

And in return they taught him Hebrew. Children are, he quickly learned, the best teachers; their understanding is innate, their lessons in touch with the way one absorbs information, never abstract. He had heard an Israeli saying: in foreign countries the mother tongue is that learned from the mother; in Israel it is that which the mother learns from the child.

For Sukkoth everyone would have a short vacation; children would visit relatives and only those old enough to require no supervision would be staying. Hanni recommended that Asher take time for himself, a holiday. He decided to return to Jerusalem and visit Martha and Elsa and Rav Braun and all the friends he had made through Professor Bergman and his Shabbat Onegs. He left a few days early and walked and hitched through the hills, visiting the Jucker family, whom he had come to know during his initial visit to Yoqneam, when he had met Professor Rubinstein.

The Juckers asked him to stay overnight, then pointed him toward Kibbutz Ramat haShophet. He made his way through a hollow with a meandering rivulet surrounded by rich vegetation of all sizes and kinds, from stout trees to moderate shrubs to fine glade grasses. After an hour or so, the valley opened into a wide basin-shaped area where Tilda Jucker had told him to turn left towards the next kibbutz. On a whim he instead turned right, towards a treeless meadow of low grass, found himself a dry, beaten-down spot, turned to face the way he had come, and sat down. He breathed in the landscape, heard it, felt it sink through his skin to the marrow of his bones.

An idea danced just below his consciousness, making him smile, teasing his thoughts and not quite becoming a question. Finally it surfaced. Might he stay at the children's home permanently, helping these innocents build a new way of life?

Before he could properly consider what was not really even a question, the idea danced away again and he refocused on the landscape, of which he was now a part. The rest of the walk, through the hills of Menashe and then of Judea, passed quickly; each parcel of land, each segment was its own experience with its own natural beauty and symmetry.

He arrived in Jerusalem and was drawn to the main public Sukkoth structure in which happy crowds were eating, singing, and dancing. He loved the dancing best. That the same joy that inspired such song and dance permeated the experience in synagogue, the hoisting of Torah scrolls, which were after all the original Bible rather than leaves in a book, was at once moving, exhilarating, and inspiring.

An astonishing quality he found in his new friends in Jerusalem was that they somehow knew his heart before he himself did. Martin Buber had known he would be predisposed towards Judaism. And now, Professor Bergman, who greeted him so warmly and made him feel as though he were arriving again in his own home, observed within a few minutes of conversation that he must settle in a natural, vegetarian life, one connected with the land. If he had thought about it—and he had in a roundabout, unfocused way—he might have come to the same conclusion, but Professor Bergman had put the jumble of thoughts and experiences together into a simple plan for his future after only a few moments of conversation.

"On your way back, visit my old friend Nathan Chofshi, who lives in a settlement in the Jezreel Valley." The professor's eyes were alive with avid intent and good humor. "He's an organic farmer, a vegetarian. He'll help you find the right spot. And tell him I sent you, with love."

After Sukkoth, Asher sought out Nathan Chofshi, who told him to visit a young Rumanian named Adrian, who was also seeking a vegetarian, natural lifestyle. Asher agreed, but he did not hurry back the way he had come, anxious as he was. He wanted to walk through the open valley and again drink in all that beauty.

23

"If you like the valley as much as you say," Tilde Jucker said emphatically, "stay here. The people of Yoqneam would welcome you."

"Do you really think so?"

"Esther Krenski owns several plots of land in the valley," said her husband, Isidore. "I wouldn't be surprised if she would be happy to sell one to you and Adrian."

"We could talk to her," Tilde went on. "We raise cattle in the same valley, so we're neighbors of sorts." Isidore nodded, his eyebrows raised as though Esther Krenski were in the room and had already agreed.

"I'll see if Adrian will have a look with me." Asher was already breathless with excitement. He stood up and began pacing back and forth. Tilde and Isidore followed him with their eyes.

"I'll speak with Esther, meanwhile," Tilde offered.

Asher was back the following day. "We walked all around and agreed the valley would be ideal."

"Adrian went as well?"

Asher nodded. "And he'll pay half. Of course, now I have to find my half, but anyway, Adrian makes a good point. We don't know what kind of land this particular plot will be—on a slope, at the base of the valley, what its vegetation is like, and so forth."

"Listen to what Tilde just learned." Isidor pointed towards his wife.

Tilde's face was alight with news. "Esther agrees! She'll sell you the land!"

"I've got to go." Asher stood up and started for the door.

"But you've just gotten here. You don't even know which plot it is."

"I just remembered, I have bank accounts in Germany with money refunded from my trip to India." He saw the blank looks on his hosts' faces. "Never mind. I'll tell you later. I have to write my father, right away."

In the last months of 1960, Wilhelm wrote Asher agreeing to send him one thousand marks towards building a life of his choosing in Israel. He would also make the necessary arrangements with the land registry for the appropriate title to his land.

Asher returned to the children's home at Ahava, and shared with Hanni, her husband, Ernst, and everyone in sight the news of his planned purchase and settlement.

He had been discussing ideas for farming with Adrian. One of these involved growing fruit trees that would yield healthy, marketable fruit without the use of pesticides. A new Hebrew word, *Pardes*, from an ancient reference to paradise, was associated with these orchards. They were known literally as "watered orchards," and their fruit was known as the "paradise apple." He had been horrified to see signs on fences surrounding orchards sporting skulls and crossbones, indicating poisonous pesticides. He and Adrian would grow their crops differently.

Ernst listened to Asher describe his hopes and plans for farming and marketing the fruits of his and Adrian's labor. "I never dreamed I would be a farmer in Israel." Asher chuckled softly.

"Do you know why our country is called Israel?" Ernst asked.

"Something to do with the story of Jacob and the angel of Esau," Asher said.

"In part, yes, but the more recent reason is that the Nazis stamped the cards and passports of Jews with the letter 'J.' On women's cards they also stamped 'Sarah' and on men's they stamped 'Israel.' Ben-Gurion turned this former symbol of shame into a symbol of pride."

"So Israel was a name given by two antagonists—first the angel of Esau gave it to Jacob, and later the Nazis gave it to the nation of Israel."

"It means God will rule or contend, and the people will witness," Tilde said. "Think of the price that was paid: centuries of hatred and of pogroms, then the Holocaust and now survivors from broken families."

"A nation built on broken families," Asher mused. "A phoenix rising from the ashes of World War II, Auschwitz, and Hiroshima."

When he went back to work he paid more attention to the children, searching their eyes for evidence of loss. So much had been sacrificed for them to come here. He was chilled by a sudden fear. Towards what future had they come, with enemies on every side?

He frequently walked among the valley's trees, remembering his own childhood, the European woods, and the pain of believing the foundation beneath the stories his mother had told him about ancient castles of Bavaria and King Ludwig. The trust of a little boy had grown into a naive and, in retrospect, humiliating belief in speeches, newspaper reports, radio programs, and columns of strong marching men who had done the unspeakable.

In hindsight, his life was invisible. A life begins, blossoms, grows deep roots and stretching boughs. But his own roots lay flat against cold, impenetrable stone. His boughs had finally found the air and water they had sought after decades of poison, and now they searched for a place to sink more permanent roots. He had found good earth and a people who had persevered through the worst that history could throw at them, a people and a life that could be relied on not to abandon the trust of little boys.

Here there were other challenges, not all so immediate or understood. The challenge began with a primary constituency that had been oppressed in Europe and Russia for centuries, that had to contend with enormous open-door immigration issues. The challenges continued with hostile neighbors, with dealing fairly with a population that grew more varied every day, and with religious and historical claims on land and custom, claims not so easily reconciled. Challenges to come would include handling hostile enclaves and segments of the population and claims defended with violence, even suicide. How does a modern democracy cope with what one side calls terrorism and the other a desperate struggle for freedom?

For the present, the challenge of modern technology was enough—television was broadcast in Arab countries but, until now, not in Israel. Why should Israelis see only hostile television?

Asher pressed his lips together when he saw the programs children watched after Havdalah, when the electricity came on and the children were permitted to watch. He would not have been able to explain exactly why he did not like the programs, and he did not suggest that the children stop watching. To them he was an enigma, friendly but different, eating only vegetables even on Shabbat, when everyone else ate meat. He was given double portions of salad and vegetables; more than a few children were jealous.

"Ernst, come in here." Hanni waited until her husband had sat down next to her at one of the tables in Ahava's dining room. She fixed Asher with steady strong brown eyes. "Now, tell Ernst what you told me."

"I've bought a plot of land in the valley with that Rumanian boy you saw me with before Shabbat and I'm going to live there."

"Is that all?" Ernst asked, and he was up again and on his way back to his spot under the light, already picking up the history book he'd been reading.

Hanni followed him. "Did you know about this?"

"I knew he was doing it, but not when."

"And you don't want to know why he's unhappy with us?"

Ernst was nonplussed. "That's his problem. Anyway, who says he's unhappy with us? Asher, you said that?"

Asher was taken aback; he looked stricken. "I never said such a thing. At least I never meant to."

"Well, why else would you leave? Don't you like working with the children anymore?" Hanni turned helplessly to her husband. "Who doesn't like working with children?"

"I love the children," Asher assured her. "But Ernst is right in his way. It is my problem. I have to work things out for myself by being on my own, with nature."

"You see how he is with the plants," Ernst pointed out.

"And you see how he is with the children," said Hanni. She was about to ask if Asher had thought about the effect his leaving would have on the children, but his words had begun to sink in, and instead she looked from Asher to her husband and said, "I'm going to have a cup of tea."

The two young men now had two acres of land in a fertile valley, but no home to live in and no money or materials with which to build one. They considered pitching tents, but Tilde Jucker mentioned that on the next hill, overlooking the basin containing their land, was a watchtower dating from the late 1930s, and if permission were granted by the local authorities, they might stay there. The tower had no latrine or heat but it was, at least, solid shelter.

Once permission was granted, Asher and Adrian set about cleaning the two-story structure, which was littered with debris and animal leavings. After the first few days of living together, their differences became apparent. Adrian was a naturalist; he went to sleep when the sun went down and awoke when it rose. Asher studied and read by kerosene lamp at night, which disturbed Adrian, so the two decided that Adrian would stay in the lower part of the tower and Asher in the upper.

Their new home was hard and cold, with neither electricity nor water, and they had no money for food or accoutrements of any kind. The two took turns walking to Yoqneam and hiring themselves out for whatever work they could find. Each worked the land on his day off, weeding and rooting and preparing the ground for the planting of fruit trees in the coming months.

With winter came periods of rain and a long planting season that would stretch through February.

Adrian wanted to plant an orchard of apricots; Asher thought of his childhood garden and declared he would plant an assortment of fruit trees, which would provide a store of dried fruit for the following winter. So another disagreement developed.

Their solution mimicked Solomon; each worked one acre, bringing water and food on his day off from Yoqneam.

Life was difficult but well grounded in nature.

"I've got something to show you," Adrian had poked his head above the top steps.

"What is it?"

"Come and see it for yourself."

Asher followed his housemate to a spot between two low bushes. Adrian knelt, cleared away fistfuls of dirt from a stone ring, then stood up proudly, waiting for Asher's response.

"A well? Is it. . . ?"

Adrian handed him a wide, flat stone. "Drop it in."

He did and they listened; the sound held the beauty of a Renaissance painting.

"It isn't very deep," Adrian ventured.

"Did you try to reach in?"

"I was waiting for you."

Adrian, who was the taller of the two, reached down, then sat up and lowered a long leg over the side. "It's cold, and I think it's moving."

Some members of Kibbutz Ramat haShophet were unhappy about Asher and Adrian using the well, but a crisis was averted when everyone agreed that the National Water Authority would hold the well's title, and Asher and Adrian could have use of it as long as they did nothing to alter its natural condition, such as installing an electric pump or pipes or any construction requiring a permit.

The fruit tree saplings were in the ground by Tu B'Shevat, the annual tree-planting festival, which Asher learned was a "tree New Year." That spring, Hanni and Ernst invited Asher to Passover at Ahava; he arrived the day before the seder. That evening, erev seder, the dining hall was in full regalia, tables set and decorated with seder plates, the children wearing their holiday clothes. A visiting American rabbi, Ahron Singer, told the story of Passover, the Jews' escape from Egypt, in the simplest terms so that even the littlest child understood the symbolism of each item on the table.

While Asher had read Exodus in the Bible, the rabbi's telling was vivid and accessible and when he broke the piece of matzoh referred to as the *afikomen*, Asher remembered reading about Jesus being recognized only after breaking bread, which he did while surrounded by disciples.

He had changed where and how he was living, and now was breaking bread with a rabbi and a grandmother and a multitude of children. He sensed a profound shift in his life, a kind of "becoming," as he participated in the seder. This was no abstract ceremony but a centuries-old Jewish meal, vibrant and alive, commemorating the ancient Exodus while resonating with the more modern escape from Europe. His participation was recognized and approved by the rabbi and everyone else.

Yet he was separate, not a Jew, neither circumcised nor converted. The thought came and went in the emotion of the moment, quickly forgotten as he thanked the rabbi, not knowing of the long friendship that would develop between them.

He went back to his newly planted field and his bare room in the watchtower a spiritually changed man, his course altered. He had been set in a general direction that had been corrected, adjusted and honed by events. Like a ship that has finally sighted land, Asher's life shifted happily towards a new goal.

When he returned home he found his and Adrian's saplings destroyed, apparently eaten by a herd of goats or sheep. Though it was against their nature to mar the pristine landscape, he and Adrian put up a fence made of wooden posts connected with wire, along with a sign designating this their private planting field. The season was nearly over, so they hurried to replant, but once the new trees sprouted they were again eaten. The shepherd must have lifted the wires to allow his herd in, they reasoned. The season and their investment had been lost.

They built another, stronger fence, its wire set tight and close together so that not even a lamb might pass through.

The problem and its solution left Asher pondering the problems of antiquity; similar clashes between shepherds and farmers might have escalated into wars if the Jewish kings, Saul, David, and Solomon, had not interceded wisely. Asher wondered how such naturally occurring conflicts were navigated, how enemies who might not have considered seeing beyond their own interests were educated about the wisdom of acquiescing to the interests of the greater good.

Professor Rubinstein was visiting Ahava with members of an international organization called Service Civic Internationale, which performed volunteer services and worked towards mutual understanding and peace. He invited Asher to join them.

After a week of hard work and frank discussions, the organization's leaders wondered how best to entertain their people on Shabbat. Hanni suggested that the non-Jews visit the Galilee to learn about the country, with Asher as their guide. When the Jewish volunteers and the orphanage children learned of the outing, all wanted to go. Hanni explained that the Sabbath had to be observed by the Jewish among them, hence the division. The children were disappointed.

A festive meal was laid out in the dining hall on Friday night. Afterwards, Asher sat with Hanni and the organization's leaders. "Leaving the children behind tomorrow," Asher said, "may teach them to associate Shabbat with disappointment, instead of fun and rest."

"If you lead tomorrow's tour," said Hanni, "you can talk about your experiences in Israel."

Asher slept poorly that night, in his mind taking first one position, then the other. It was well after midnight before he finally fell asleep. He awoke before dawn and sat alone, meditating and praying. Eventually, an answer came to him; he prayed that if the sun was shining at the time the bus was to leave, it would be a sign that he should take the foreigners to the Galilee.

That morning, the sun was out and the sky completely clear as Asher showered and walked to breakfast. When he arrived at the dining hall, a wind blew dark clouds overhead and within minutes a cloudburst drenched the orphanage. Asher stood at the dining hall's doorway, awestruck at nature's display.

He sat down next to one of the organization's leaders, an associate of Rubinstein's from Haifa named Elimelech. "I've decided not to go because of the rain," Asher said.

Elimelech wrinkled his forehead. "You're afraid of a little rain?" he mocked. "But we'll be in the bus most of the time and the rest, well, we'll figure something out. It's just rain."

"It's not the rain, it's what's behind it." Asher explained how he had made his decision.

The volunteer sat stock still for a long moment. Without changing expression he looked at Asher. "I won't go either," he said.

The entrance door swung open and in swept Hanni, beaming, stopping short when she saw their faces. "Why aren't you excited about your wonderful day trip?"

Elimelech told her what Asher had just told him. "Wait just a minute." She quickly returned, the smile back on her face. "I called some friends nearby, in Haifa and Naharia, and it's beautiful in both places. No chance of rain."

Asher turned to Elimelech. "If that's the case then we certainly shouldn't go."

"What do you mean?"

"Think about it." Asher gave him a hard look. "It's only raining here."

Hanni threw her hands in the air. "What are we going to do with all those bags of sandwiches?"

"Let's get everyone together and see what they have to say," Elimelech suggested.

During their short meeting, someone suggested and Asher agreed that he would lead everyone to a nearby kibbutz for a nature hike, picnic, and discussion about the meaning of religion in the twentieth century.

Thereafter, the children of Ahava referred to him as Asher the Rainmaker.

He returned to Yoqneam the following day. He had begun attending synagogue on Shabbat, but the pace was too much for him and too many unfamiliar words were used, despite his Hebrew studies at Kibbutz Hazorea.

Mr. Rotter, who was in charge of Yoqneam's synagogue, had agreed to allow Asher to attend services, which he found genuine and down to earth, with the congregants focused on the service rather than on socializing.

Rosh Hashanah approached and the essence of the services transcended his ignorance. What he had glimpsed for the first time over a fence from the Jordanian side of Jerusalem was all around him now, and inside him as well. Voices joined in praise of God's world, the bounties of nature, food on one's plate, and the new day itself. Voices, of which he was now one, praised and thanked God, along with a joining that had been missing from his life and which now lit him from within. Rosh Hashanah arrived with such joy, singing, and dancing that tears came to his eyes and prickles to his skin, as the worshippers gave thanks and begged mercy and forgiveness with one voice.

He read and studied his Hebrew Bible with renewed vigor and remembered differences in his previous readings he now saw were born of poor translations. He wondered if these were mistakes or purposeful changes and if so, had new religions been formed and wars fought over poor translations and differences of interpretation? The rabbi in Yoqneam, whose name was Harlap, worked with him, helping Asher to understand the Hebrew texts, and the two developed a lasting friendship.

Soon after the New Year, Hanni offered to acquire wooden barracks for Asher to live in. Adrian, ever the naturalist, dug himself a cave in the rocks higher up their slope. Each would continue tending his half of their fields and maintain his own fences against the ever-present threat of sheep and goats.

The truck driver Hanni had hired to deliver Asher's shack refused to haul it up the slope, so Isidore Jucker and some local men loaded it onto the Juckers' horse-drawn cart.

Asher fashioned a flat foundation of stone and mud, and, with the help of Isidore and the others, set the hut atop it and the roof atop that. As they pounded the final nails into the roof, the clouds let go with a driving rain which Asher enjoyed from inside his new home. It was small, barely four by four metres, but it was his and it was waterproof. He painted the walls white and the window molding and doorframes a light blue, which the Bedouins claimed would ward off evil spirits. Upon hearing the suggestion, Asher smiled, but the Bedouins explained that disease-carrying mosquitoes and flies were considered evil spirits and that shade of blue seemed to keep them away.

When his new home was complete, Asher invited everyone over for a vegetarian picnic. Quite a few, including the rabbi, walked all the way from the village to Asher's new hut and stayed for his meal. When asked how he could eat at the table of a non-Jew, the rav answered that he now knew Asher well enough to trust his strict vegetarianism.

24

Asher opened the door, and, after expressing initial surprise, invited the census taker into his hut.

"Ben-Gurion ordered our project some time ago. Weren't you expecting me?"

"This isn't exactly a big city. News travels slowly." He directed the olive-skinned young man to sit in one of two chairs at his little wooden table.

"I have some basic questions about your background, work and so forth."

Eventually they came to the matter of Asher's religion. "I'm honestly not quite sure how to answer that."

"Are you a Jew?" the young man asked.

"While I'm sympathetic and supportive, no, I am not."

"A Christian?"

Asher paused. "Well, I was born a Christian, but I don't think I want to be referred to as one now. I traveled quite a lot in India," he offered, "and I have a real affinity for eastern teachings."

The census man shook his head. "But you're not Asian in appearance and, in any case, you weren't born and raised a Buddhist, Sikh, or Hindu, were you? I'll have to register you as a Christian, despite your reservations."

"I suppose, if I were to die today," Asher mused, "I'd be buried in a Christian cemetery by a priest I'd never met."

The following day he visited Rabbi Harlap in Yoqneam. "I've decided to apply for a conversion to Judaism," he announced.

"Are you certain that's what you want?" the rabbi asked.

Asher told the rabbi of his experience with the census taker.

"I've been between religions and cultures long enough. Ever since the young man left, I've had that commitment Ruth made to Naomi running through my mind." Asher looked up, trying to remember the exact words. "Thy God is my God . . ."

"'Thy people shall be my people, and thy God my God; where thou diest, will I die, and there will I be buried.'" The rabbi sat back and appraised Asher, his head bobbing slightly as though assuring himself of something he had known all along. "I don't have to tell you this is no trifling matter. It's an involved process wherein we apply to the Rabbinic Court in Haifa, and then . . . a lot of waiting. It could take five years or more."

Asher's steel blue eyes never flinched. "Then the sooner we start, the better."

Overjoyed, Asher returned to his hut. He wondered about Jews who had come to Israel from places and backgrounds as diverse as Maroc and Poland, Yemen and Ireland; he remembered the Jews in Cochin, in southern India, where he had seen no trace of anti-Semitism. What was common to them; what brought them here, in this day and age? The nearby village of Elyakim, higher up in the hills of Menashe, had been established by Yemenite Jews. While the well-known Operation Flying Carpet of 1949 had brought the bulk of them, the first immigrants from Yemen had arrived two decades before. When Ezra, authorized by the famous Edict of King Cyrus (Ezra 1:1–4; Chronicles 36:23), called upon the Jewish diaspora or dispersed community in Yemen to come to Jerusalem, the argument was made that the time of the regathering had not yet come. Now, Jews the world over came with neither edict nor argument. Asher reasoned it was not merely anti-Semitism that drove them. There was more to it, divine work perhaps, as outlined by Moses and the prophets. Asher remembered when, at the bank in Frankfurt, he had thought of Israel as simply a new nation, like so many others after World War II. Now, Israel had become so much more to him. He thought of words he had read and which now took on new meaning: ". . . and they saw the great work which the Lord did . . ." (Exodus 14:30, 31). Like Ruth, he would not be merely sympathetic observer but active participant. While this entailed nothing supernatural, it was miraculous nonetheless. As Ben-Gurion had said: Whosoever in Israel does not believe in miracles is not a realist.

"Finish your fruit and we'll go outside," Moshe said. Moshe Negbi was a Holocaust survivor from Hungary with whom Asher had traveled to Haifa. "I have something for you."

Asher finished what was left of the fruit they had shared for lunch and followed Moshe outside. Leaning up against a tree was a new bicycle around which Moshe walked a circle, his arms folded. "Now you can take groceries home from Haifa."

Asher wasn't sure what to say; he didn't want to insult Moshe, who had become a dear friend. "What will people think of a forty-year-old man riding a bicycle all that way with bags of groceries?"

Moshe gave an amused laugh. "What will they think? Perhaps that he has strong legs. Tell me, have you given much thought to how others see us, Jews who would dare defend ourselves? You don't seem concerned about being associated with such audacious Jews. Now you're concerned about how others would judge you on a bicycle?"

"I'll put it to good use," said Asher, as he swung his leg over the bicycle, trying out its height. "I've been getting letters, you know, from my parents, urging me to return to Germany."

"Didn't they send money for your land?"

Asher nodded. "It's hard for them to get used to my living here, especially my mother. She wants me to get married and can't understand why she paid for law school since I'm living in a shack on the side of a hill, planting trees which are eaten by goats and sheep. Also . . . the gossip she hears around town about me is painful for her."

"I can see her confusion. Do you want to get married?"

"Who doesn't want to fall in love? But I haven't met anyone who interests me since, well, since I was in India, and even then I would have been afraid for the woman's safety if I were to bring her to Germany. This bike is perfect, by the way."

"I tried to set the seat and handlebars to your height."

Asher rode in circles around the tree. "I've told them my mind's made up. I'm staying here, but they don't seem to believe me."

"Parents can be like that," said Moshe. "Sometimes they need to be shown."

Asher hit the brakes, and the bicycle skidded a dark line in the dirt. "Maybe I'll invite them here. They'll see for themselves why I want to stay."

Almost immediately, Asher's plan was challenged by an assortment of acquaintances and old friends.

He was visited by an Austrian named Hermann who, while in

Europe during the Nazi years, had been in the resistance and had been imprisoned. He belonged to a religious group called the Friends of Man made up of Christians who had left the church but continued to follow the teachings of the New Testament.

Impressed by the man's background, Asher invited him to stay, and set about helping him buy a plot of land from Esther Krenski, from whom Asher and Adrian had bought their land. Asher was only too happy to have found a new friend and possible neighbor; Adrian's naturalistic life had grown more extreme and antisocial and Asher found him difficult, his behavior increasingly erratic.

Once he learned of Asher's conversion application, however, Hermann soured on the plan and on Asher himself. He accused Asher of being unfaithful to his religion, and would have no more to do with him, at least for the moment.

Soon after, Hedwig visited from Germany. Greyer and rounder, she brought the sad news that Heinrich had passed away. The beautiful Israeli countryside and Ahava's charitable works moved and inspired Asher's old friend and partner in charity, and they fell to discussing how Asher's new life had built upon their shared experiences. The visit was warm and comfortable until they came to the subject of Asher's conversion. As with the Austrian, Hermann, once Hedwig understood Asher's planned conversion, her eyes grew round with shock. "You would no longer accept Jesus?"

Asher looked faintly amused. "As what?"

"As your Lord and Savior, just as he always was."

He paused, deciding whether to allow himself to be offended. "I've made a choice for my future based on my own personal experiences and feelings." He looked her in the eyes. "I hope you can accept that."

She leaned toward him, her mouth set. "You're a baptized Christian, gone to Christian schools"—her voice began to rise—"raised by Christian parents in a Christian home."

Asher interrupted her. "Do you know how many have been killed in the name of Christianity?"

"We are charged with going out and preaching the Gospel all over the world. We're not charged with deciding if people want it."

Asher smiled sadly. "Really? I've learned that inaccurate translations lead to life-and-death problems, and what you said is an example of that. The original text reads 'Going forth you will teach the nations,' which means that the teaching would be in the way of life, not in proselytizing. It is a statement of fact that by going forth and living a good life you will teach by example; it is not an order to proselytize."

As though with great effort Hedwig took a deep breath. "Heinrich and I stood by our Jewish neighbors in the Nazi period, and you encouraged us to set up the Wapniarka Fund. So you know we sympathize with the Jews. This is still me, Hedwig. But I also know that not all people know what their souls need. That's why we must preach the Gospels, regardless of how they are received."

"Have you read," Asher countered, "about Elie Wiesel, who, when he saw his father being thrown into the furnace, claimed that he saw God being killed along with him? There are thousands here with similar experiences. And you want to offer them Jesus Christ as comforter of their souls? What they'll see, what I'll see is a church that at times has fostered anti-Semitism in his name. That was my experience. I was also taught, by that same church, that the suffering of the Jews was God's punishment for their infidelity. And this while changing our original calendar, holidays, and instructions. One no longer has to observe the Shabbat; one now has permission to eat shrimp and pigs and blood sausages. Don't you know that food containing blood is contrary to the Apostles? You yourself are vegetarian both for health and religious reasons. Whatever your motives, what Jews will see are the Crusades and the Inquisition, Good Friday pogroms.

These things happened; your good intentions cannot erase history. Besides, there are so many different missionary groups proclaiming to be the proper representatives of Jesus. These internal church conflicts have nothing to do with Israel. Live and let live." His features softened, became more sympathetic. "Please understand, your religion is fine for you and for so many others." He thought back to a conversation with Martin Buber. "It isn't so much Christianity; it's church history, after which your way cannot be forced on them. Look, I am not trying to offend you, but you must see how offensive this kind of missionizing would be to Jewish people." He paused. "And to me."

They looked at one another for a long moment. Then Hedwig stood up, looked down at her hands, murmured something to herself, and walked from the room. Asher would never see her again.

Asher was offered the use of a neighbor's vineyard during the *shmita* period, the sabbatical year when, by Jewish law, one must not tend his or her land. A Gentile, however, may work that land, and the fruit of the labor and land would belong to that Gentile. The arrangement benefited everyone, since the plants would be properly tended during the sabbatical, ensuring their healthy future. The offer had come from Mrs. Kremer, the widow of a Yoqneam baker. Asher accepted, and began working the little vineyard in her courtyard.

At harvest time he was congratulated for his efforts; the vineyard had been kept weed free, well pruned and so healthy that he was offered the job of working it the following year as well. Asher accepted, and soon a family living on the other side of the road, Mr. and Mrs. Moser, offered him the use of their vineyard.

Meanwhile, Adrian had developed the eccentric though not altogether unfounded idea that routinely discarded cauliflower trunks and cabbage centers were as nourishing as the rest of the plant, and suggested that he and Asher collect such unused vegetable parts from farmers. The response was overwhelming. Asher was surprised and moved that such generosity came from nonorthodox, even secular Jews, on behalf of a German.

The days of the week and seasons of the year had held a fascination for him all his life, from the time he had challenged his teachers about when the Sabbath ought to be observed, to his farmer's interest in the Hebrew calendar's relationship to the seasons. He learned through experience that faith in the wisdom underlying the calendar was central to understanding it.

An offering of green plants was due at Pesach, which came late that year. Asher and some of the local farmers discussed the fact that it was already late January and the plants had grown full and strong; by Pesach they would be dried out and past their time.

One farmer suggested that a late frost must be on its way, to keep the plants ripe until they were due to be reaped. Sure enough, in March, a chill descended into the plain, an unexpected snow he would never have believed if he hadn't expected it. The ground and all that sprang from it were frozen, both in temperature and time, ripe for cutting at Passover, exactly as predicted.

The new moon prayer between the third and tenth of each Hebrew month coincides with the prime sowing and planting dates for those flora that grow above ground, while beets and other plants that grow below are best sown after the full moon. The earth's water and the growth of plants corresponded directly, Asher noticed, to the moon's cycles. The Hebrew calendar takes the relationship into account, perhaps because those who invented or discerned the system were farmers. The Islamic calendar, he saw, "wandered backward through the Sun calendar" as the famous Ramadan saying went, without the added month that kept the Hebrew calendar tethered to the seasons. The western calendar, tied solely to the sun, reflects the lives of its adherents in all their walks of life but not, primarily, farming.

Israel, a society comprising elements from each of these histories and ways of life, was faced with the challenge of balancing all of these.

Asher's parents were coming to visit.

He showed the letter to Hanni and breathlessly explained what it meant, then traveled to Jerusalem and told Professor Bergman the news and encouraged him to tell the rest of his friends as soon as he saw them.

They were coming to satisfy their curiosity about their son's new way of life, for which he had left his promising legal career. After a stop in Egypt, their ship arrived at Haifa's port. He waved as they came down the ramp in their European attire, his father like a natty British lord and his mother in elegant mohair. Asher looked down at his own baggy khaki pants and short-sleeved shirt, and his stomach twisted with sudden anxiety.

His mother rushed at him, hugged him, then stepped back. "What's that on your head?"

He reached up and touched his hat, which was no different from those worn by most of the farmers in Yoqneam.

"A *kova tembel*," she shrieked at Wilhelm, who tried to hide his smile.

"It isn't a fool's hat," Asher protested. "This is how a farmer here dresses."

"Show us to a clothing shop so we can buy you something respectable, so you can look like a human being while being seen with your parents."

And they did. Asher used the time to revise his plan. Dragging his parents up a muddy hill to an unfurnished hut in the Yoqneam wilderness might not be the best way to begin their visit.

"Where are we going first?" Sophie asked, once she was satisfied with her son's appearance.

"Now that you've left Egypt, like the Israelis, we head for the desert. First the Negev in the south, to Beersheva, to see Roman ruins. It's a little primitive, only a one-star hotel. I hope you're up to it."

"Of course we're up to it," Sophie fluttered. "That's why we're here. To see the way it really is. We understand this is the desert."

The following day they all took a tour bus to Avdat and the Nabatean ruins, where his parents marvelled at the beauty of the desert, which was not at all monochromatic as they had imagined, but a rainbow of color. So taken were they with the landscape that they lost track of time and missed the last bus back to Beersheva. Sophie looked at her husband, as though his expertise might engineer a solution to their predicament. He shrugged. "It's the middle of the desert."

"We'll hitchhike, just as I've been doing for years," Asher said. "Someone's sure to pass, a cow, a Bedouin. Have faith."

They walked for some time, his mother holding her mohair coat gingerly over her arm. Eventually a Jeep approached and Asher flagged the driver down. Yes, he was on his way to Beersheva and they were welcome to ride with him, though the Jeep had only one upholstered seat, in the front next to the driver.

"We'll ride in the back," Sophie said, climbing in and spreading her coat on the dusty bench with a brave laugh. Wilhelm and Asher followed, looking at one another with wordless amusement.

The next day they toured Jerusalem, where Professor Bergman told Asher's surprised parents how impressed he was with their son's scholarship and humility. On their way out, Sophie turned to Asher and whispered, "A perceptive man, this professor. I'm beginning to see why you like it here."

They took note of the industrious, inventive spirit all around them, most visible in the countryside, where crops appeared to be harvested from solid rock and porous desert alike. Sophie warmed still further at Kiryat Bialik and Ahava; who would respond otherwise to a house full of orphaned children? She made fast friends with one family who worked there, the Blochs, referring to their matriarch as "the angel." Asher watched his mother warm to his new home; his father's reaction was still a mystery.

He decided they were as ready as they would ever be to see his home in the Yoqneam valley. Isidore Jucker offered to take them up the hill in his horse-drawn cart. After a polite visit with the Juckers, they bumped their way towards Asher's hut.

Asher was hypersensitive, listening for a phrase, a word, watching for a gesture that reflected on all he had worked for and sweated to build. His father's head swung to either side, taking in the landscape and finally the hut, looking it over from top to bottom, first from the outside, then scrutinizing its construction and materials from within.

They stayed an hour, chatting politely as though visiting family on a Sunday afternoon in Forchheim. Finally Sophie ran a fingertip along a strip of door molding and rubbed her thumb and forefinger together. "It's clean, and neat. I like it," she announced.

Wilhelm continued to scrutinize. Finally, he walked up to his son and stood close enough for a whisper to be heard, though he spoke in a normal tone. "Now I understand." A faint smile toyed with the corners of his eyes. "If I were your age, I'd live here, too."

Asher could hear his heart beating with gratitude; he had waited so long for this compliment.

"Of course," his father went on, "you have to make a living. What are your plans?" He waited.

"I have quite a few visitors here. I'm considering putting up a second hut with two rooms. I can put people up and make some income that way."

"What would a second hut cost?"

"I can get one from the children's home for eight hundred to a thousand marks."

"I see."

Because Asher's hut had no guest beds, Isidore, who had waited outside, took the Eders back to Yoqneam to spend the night. In the morning Asher hired a car to take them to see the countryside.

As they drove up through the Galilee hills towards the Lake of Tiberias, Sophie talked nonstop about the countryside, its history, and the future she hoped Asher would have. Wilhelm was silent, but his eyes absorbed everything. Asher watched them both and kept his feelings to himself.

His father finally tapped him on the shoulder. "You will win the next war, I think."

Asher's eyes opened as though he had been struck. "Why do you think there will be a war?"

"We've been doing a lot of traveling, not just here but before this, on our own. The Arabs don't agree with your existence."

"Why do you think we'll win?"

"I've been an engineer for more than forty years. I've seen what's here, I've seen what's in Alexandria. Take my word."

Asher's breath was short and high in his chest. Despite the mild weather, a sweat broke out on his forehead, evaporating as quickly as it appeared and leaving him with a chill. He had hoped Israel might follow Gandhi's lead and somehow avoid war. He had hoped Israel's neighbors would come to their senses. The thought of another war was like standing in a valley and watching the stirrings of an unavoidable avalanche in the hills high above.

The following day he took his parents back to Haifa and saw them to their boat, their good-byes at once warmer yet sadder than their greetings had been.

"Okay, so you're not among primitives," admitted Sophie.

His father's good-bye was less effusive but his steady look into his son's eyes was every bit as meaningful.

A week later Asher received a letter containing a check for a thousand marks and a four-word note in his father's handwriting.

"For the second hut."

25

Asher had been writing letters with the same energy he had put into studying the Bible in English, German, and Hebrew. He was writing to Europeans, most often Christian Europeans, and also to leaders, including Jordan's King Hussein. War, he wrote, must somehow be averted. Surely one must listen to a man from a country which had paid so heavily for starting wars, a former German soldier who had searched widely and carefully observed so much and who had such an avid interest in peace.

The responses were few and far between, and rarely contained views in line with his own.

In the early spring of 1967 he received a letter from John Boyd, an American reverend, who expected the outbreak of Middle Eastern hostilities at any moment. Take courage, Reverend Boyd counselled, and when asked to expand on his thoughts, the reverend wrote in early June that Israel would certainly retake the Gaza, Sinai, the West Bank and the Golan Heights, the hills between Syria and the Lake of Tiberias.

These were difficult days in which Asher tried to comfort frightened friends while struggling himself to remain calm. Egypt had rejected the presence of United Nations troops, and Israel was surrounded by enraged Egyptians, Syrians, Jordanians, Iraqis, and Lebanese.

The spirit fueling the logic behind Israeli perseverence was that God had not returned the Jews to this holy place to see them destroyed. Boyd's second letter arrived, predicting from Scripture exactly what was occurring at that moment.

On the second day of the war, Asher rushed to Kiryat Bialik to see to the safety of the children at the orphanage, whose caretakers he assumed were being drafted. He and a friend named Eliezer huddled close to radios and scrutinized newspapers for news of the war, but none came. They considered themselves part of the resistance movement, at once antiwar yet pro-Israel. Because he was not Jewish, Asher was not drafted.

On the third day Egyptian and Jordanian radio offered translations of broadcasts claiming that huge Egyptian contingents were advancing on Tel Aviv and that Haifa had been bombed and was in flames. Asher and Eliezer cried and strained their eyes across Haifa Bay but saw neither smoke nor fire. The stories must have been propaganda, they decided, their tears turning to derisive laughter.

Still, there had been no hard news.

On the fourth day the two friends presented themselves to the draft office, renouncing their former antiwar views. Their applications accepted, the two were told to wait for orders, which were sure to come within days.

Two days later they were still waiting when the Six-Day War came to an end with Jerusalem retaken, the Egyptians driven back, and the Syrians retreating from the Golan Heights under heavy fire. To Asher and his friend and many others it was a miracle the equal of any of old: the Chanukah miracle in which a small supply of oil lasted eight days; David's defeat of Goliath; and now, this six-day victory against utterly overwhelming forces. Who could say which was the greatest miracle?

Asher knew he had to tell his parents about his pending conversion; since they had taken the time, energy, and expense to visit him in his new home, Asher felt that he had to return the favor. He hoped and feared to bring up his application for conversion to Judaism even more than he had hoped and feared to show them his home when they had visited Israel.

He arrived on his birthday the following spring. Rather than allowing his anxiety to lead to procrastination as it had on the issue of their seeing his home in Yoqneam, he walked into his mother's kitchen, and after a few pleasantries announced that he had applied for conversion to Judaism.

His mother took a step backward, a palm pressing her chest. "But . . . you're a Christian. You can't become a Jew."

"What do you think Jesus was?" he answered quickly.

Her mouth opened, her eyes widened, and she took him by the shoulders. Then she pulled him to her and held him, swaying from side to side. She kissed him on the forehead. "You're right. Go now, and tell your father."

Wilhelm was bent over some papers at his desk, the lamp lighting one side of his face with a white glow while the other remained in deep shadow. Asher watched him from the door. "I have to tell you something. I've applied to a Hebrew court to become a Jew."

Wilhelm stood up and looked into his son's eyes for a long moment, his eyes solemn, his mouth grave. "Your religion is not my concern. You'll always be my son. Stay honest and straightforward, the way you've always been." He pulled a chair around from the other side of the desk and patted it, dipping his head to indicate that Oskar should sit, which he did. Father and son talked of Israel and Europe, of past and future, of fears and hopes. It was the longest, most thoughtful talk the two had ever had.

The following morning an urgent telegram arrived from Hermann, the Austrian with whom Asher had once hoped but failed to do business. Both of Asher's huts had burned to the ground.

Shaken, Asher asked his parents' advice. "Stay with us. You don't need to go back now," Sophie said. "You've nothing to go back to."

Asher considered the idea. "I appreciate the offer, but I can't let this get in the way of my application."

A few days later he flew back to Israel and found his huts in ashes; only his typewriter and a few bits of metal remained of any use. Isidore said Asher would be welcome to stay in an old watchtower in the village until his future was determined.

Hermann offered his sympathies and financial aid, but when Asher learned that the offer was in return for the two vineyards he had been given by the Kremer and Moser families, he rejected the offer with disgust. He had no titles to these vineyards, only the use of them. The vineyards had been freely given in acts of selfless generosity. The idea of including them in such a quid pro quo was so revolting that he considered not returning to Yoqneam because it would mean living so close to Hermann.

A few days later, Isidore told Asher that the villagers had agreed to collect money for him to use in rebuilding. Everyone had been deeply affected by his loss, and bewildered as to how such an isolated fire to two entirely unattached buildings might have occurred. Rumors and innuendoes had been circulating, with suspician of arson being the prevailing opinion.

Particularly painful was that the fires had been set at a holy time,

Erev Shabbat, Friday night. Even an atheistic Jew would have to hesitate before committing such a crime. When someone suggested that Adrian, whose behavior had grown increasingly eccentric, might have been responsible, Asher rejected the idea out of hand. He refused to accept that a friend, even a former friend, might have committed such an atrocity, no matter what his state of mind or mental capacity.

Another bit of innuendo that reached Asher was that when members of the Friends of Men, residents of Vienna and Berlin, learned about the fires, they sent money and clothing through Hermann. Now those who had extended their generosity were wondering why they had not been thanked or acknowledged.

None of the offerings had ever reached Asher.

Professor David Flusser was as animated as Asher remembered him from their first meeting in Jerusalem; the professor's round cheeks seemed always ready to burst with an opinion, usually one well supported by scholarship. When they had first met at the professor's home, the cut of his reddish hair had reminded Asher of his own father's.

After expressing sympathy for Asher's losses in the fires, the professor listened while Asher explained his hope to convert and his frustration with the Rabbinic Court in Haifa, which seemed endlessly delayed. Each time he contacted the court, he was told that the case was under review and results were expected soon.

For once, the professor was not so quick with an answer. He clasped his hands in front of him and appeared to search for the right words. "I'm not so sure this conversion is a good idea. First of all, if you live according to the seven laws of the Covenant of Noah you will have the same place in heaven as that of a Jew. Besides, you will have more freedom to speak on theological matters now, as a Christian who lives our way of life, than if you convert. People believe you now. They may see a conversion as a sign of pandering, as though you will be speaking from a Jewish point of view to curry favor."

Asher looked at the professor, his blue eyes unblinking. "I don't want to be a Christian for Israel. I want to be of Israel, in Israel, with Israel."

Professor Flusser's eyes softened and he smiled. "Then *baruch ha'ba*." They embraced. "Welcome!"

Was there any way of hurrying the court in Haifa? Asher wanted to know.

"The court will be suspicious," the professor said, "first of your background, that you might have some kind of criminal past you might be running from."

"Of course," Asher agreed, "very understandable."

"Then of your theological ideas, your Christianity, which to them will be nearly as serious."

"Well, I suppose if Israel can go through her trials and tribulations, then so can I. Perhaps as in the story of Ruth and Naomi it is necessary to reject a foreigner three times."

"I think this is a healthy point of view."

"I need two witnesses before the court. When it comes time, will you be one?"

Again the two men embraced.

"Since the court is taking so long, in the meantime it would be possible to have a *brit* performed as a sign of Judaism . . . "

"A circumcision?" Asher took a deep breath. "That was one way the Nazis determined whether or not one was a Jew." His smile showed both the irony and his own trepidation. "This would be done by a *mohel*?"

The professor shook his head. "Too dangerous. Because you're in your forties, you would go to the hospital for a few days. Surgeons would perform the operation."

The *brit* was performed on May 23, 1968, in Tel Aviv, by a doctor whose family had been killed in the Holocaust.

After several days, Asher returned to Yoqneam and, despite lingering pain, attempted to pursue his legal conversion. He was called before the Haifa court in a preliminary hearing and asked about his vegetarianism. Counselled by friends from Tel Aviv, Asher answered that Israel's first chief rabbi, Abraham Yitzchaq haCohen Kook, had himself been a vegetarian, though he did not promote the fact.

The court did not comment. He was told he would be asked to return for another hearing to be convened at a later date.

A multilingual drone of conversation surrounded him as the hall began to fill up. He looked around for the American clergyman who had invited him, but the Reverend Wendell Jones had not yet arrived. Asher had found himself a seat opposite the hall's entrance so he could watch people arrive. Whenever possible he wanted to remember the faces at gatherings such as these, of people who desired reconciliation and peace, in this case between Christians and Jews.

He studied each countenance as the guests entered the brightly lit hallway. Many were the light-complexioned faces of northern Europeans, chatting easily, at home in this international crowd. Mixed in with those were more than a few Semitic faces, and there, alongside that radiant woman, was . . .

"Cameroon!" He was out of his chair and waving before he realized what he was doing. The woman looked up and turned to her escort in surprise.

Asher waved an arm over his head. "Cameroon! Over here, it's Ash . . . Oskar, from India!"

Cameroon had changed little in the years since Asher had seen him. His face and beard had filled out and his smile was as luminous as ever.

"I can't believe it, Oskar. How did you end up here?" Cameroon clasped Asher's shoulders. "You look well. I guess you found what you were looking for in the East."

"No, I found it here, and my name is Asher now. I'm in the process of converting." He glanced at the woman with Cameroon and took a step back. "I am an old friend of Cameroon's. My name is Asher."

"Asher, this is Naomi."

The woman, who wore an elegant off-white dress delicately embroidered, Yemenite style, looked at Asher with expressive brown eyes. Her fine, focused features implied a decisive, discerning nature, while her prominent "Buddha ears" lent her face a unique intelligence and character.

They chatted for a few minutes about what they expected from the conference. Cameroon had begun looking from Naomi to Asher and back again, as the conversation died away. Naomi tipped her head forward and to one side. "Was there something you wanted to say?"

Cameroon hesitated, looked at Asher, then again at Naomi. "Why not?"

People had found their seats and the noise level had dropped, so he had to whisper. "You two have a great deal in common," he said to Naomi. "Why not invite him for a visit? And when you do, ask about the spiritual search that took him through India."

Cameroon was nodding emphatically towards Asher as the conference began. It was the first-ever open conference in Jerusalem on the subject of reconciliation between Christians and Jews, and the speakers were moving and profound, the questions and answers afterward heartfelt.

Afterwards, Asher and Naomi turned to one another and eagerly shared their opinions and feelings about the program's content, as though doing so were natural and comfortable. Asher was aware without thinking about it that this lovely woman was an independent thinker who took initiative and followed her heart.

While she did not say so, her features foreshadowed that she would take Cameroon's suggestion. Asher had no doubt that he would accept her invitation when it came.

He had never met anyone so appealing and attractive, not only physically but in her heart, mind, and spirit. Like two children discovering surprise gifts, they found more traits, experiences, and views in common, as the first visit quickly became a second and a third. Asher felt as though he were looking into a beautiful, regally feminine mirror. Each had been on a spiritual journey that had spanned the wreckage of Europe, spiritual India, and Israel, culminating with their finding one another.

They agreed that Israel faced a desperate challenge, more than that of a nation surrounded by enemies who bide their time, waiting for weakness. The greater challenge was from within, and they walked together and stayed up nights wondering how a country made up of such disparate orthodox and secular elements that seemed so diametrically opposed could possibly survive. They shared a desperate hope and faith that somehow it would.

While mutual respect, shared interests, and vast agreement endeared him to Naomi and her to him, it was something unseen yet forever felt, a unity of spirit, that made them certain that they would be together for the rest of their lives.

They had to wait, however, for the conversion ceremony.

The court, composed of three *rabbanim,* or rabbis who served as judges, gave its assent in March of 1969, with Naomi and two of Asher's new friends from Jerusalem as witnesses: Professor David

Flusser and Professor Zeev Falk, who had left Poland just before the war and now taught Jewish law at Hebrew University. The rabbis admonished Asher to refrain from writing treatises on biblical subjects for a number of years. To avoid being merely a sympathetic observer, he was to immerse himself in Jewish life and thought.

A drop of blood was taken, according to *halachic* law, and Asher was submerged three times in the ritual bath known as the *mikvah*, which for him was much more than a ritual. He was freed, liberated, accepted by the people and land he had grown to love, and accepted into "the Covenant of Abraham" as Asher Avraham Ben Avraham.

Neither Asher nor Naomi had any interest in a modern wedding with hordes of guests, dancing, and tumult. Instead they received permission to hold the wedding in an open courtyard on Mount Zion, traditionally referred to as the Tomb of King David.

On March 6, the seventeenth of Adar 5729 on the Hebrew calendar, one day before Asher's birthday, with his friends Professor David Flusser and Professor Zeev Falk serving as witnesses, Rabbi Adin Steinsalz pronounced Asher and Naomi man and wife.

EPILOGUE

After saying good-bye to his friends in Yoqneam, Asher and Naomi moved into her flat, a lovely penthouse in Jerusalem's Kaf Tet B'November Street, whose name commemorates the date (November 29) of the United Nation's decision in 1947 to recognize the State of Israel.

Years later, when asked about her husband, Naomi, who has since taken the name "Hannah," had this to say: "In spite of our different, even opposing, backgrounds, the common things were enough to bring and keep us together. Our differences posed a challenge for our growth. I was born Jewish but was not educated in our heritage due to the Holocaust. It was after my return from India, through Asher, that I found my way to my inner Jewish/Hebrew source.

"The Bible has several layers and components, including the *kabbalah,* and most of us come in contact merely with its surface level. It takes an inquisitive and penetrating mind like Asher's to explore its depth. Through him I came to see the beauty and innermost wisdom of my heritage.

"An acquaintance asked me once, why did I cause him to become Jewish? Didn't we suffer enough for our being Jewish? To this I replied: 'It was he who turned me Jewish in the real sense of the word.'"

The couple pondered what to do next, where Asher might work and what he might do that would be sustaining and fulfilling. He remembered a suggestion Hanni Ulmann had made in 1960 that he tour Israel with foreign volunteers, and help them understand the country.

Building on a long-held interest in writing about the original Bible, the Five Books of Moses, as a source for better understanding the Gospels, Asher began, in 1969, what would become a growing literary and academic phase of his life. That year he wrote a short pamphlet entitled *The Sayings of the Quran on the Arab-Israel Controversy*, which utilized his study of the Islamic holy book. An expanded version of the pamphlet entitled *Peace Is Possible Between Ishmael and Israel According to the Quran and Tanakh* was published in English, Hebrew, and Arabic (and, as of this writing, remains available at www.rb.org.il).

In 1971, Asher studied for and passed a course for tour guides and began a long, happy employment, traveling around Israel and occasionally abroad, teaching about his new home. Indirectly, this led to his meeting Leonard Levine, who was inspired by Asher's story and set out on his own journey to find an author to write it.

Although he was registered with Israel's army, Asher was too old for the draft. During the 1973 Yom Kippur War, he volunteered to transport soldiers and ferry supplies in his Volkswagen minibus to Jericho and throughout the Jordan valley.

In addition to numerous articles on the effect of religious texts on Israel's relationships with other countries, Asher has written the book *The Star of David: An Ancient Symbol of Integration* (Rubin Mass Ltd., Jerusalem, 1987).

In 1996, along with Muslim scholar and cleric the Sheikh Professor Abdul Hadi Palazzi, Asher founded the Islam-Israel Fellowship as a subdivision of the Root and Branch Association, Ltd., Jerusalem/Israel, with Sheikh Palazzi as Muslim cochair and Asher as Jewish cochair.

They hope that their work will eventually bear the fruits of peace and understanding.

BIBLIOGRAPHY

INTERVIEWS AND TAPES

The primary source for this book was sixteen audiotapes made during 2002 by Dr. Asher Eder and a series of follow-up letters and e-mails in which he responded to the author's questions.

Eder, Asher. Interview by author. Tape recording. Jerusalem, Israel, January–August 2002.

Levine, Judith. Interview by author. Long Beach, New York, fall 2001.

Levine, Leonard. Interview by author. Long Beach, New York, fall 2001.

Ulmann, Hanni I. Interview by author. Bellmore, New York, summer 2002.

Ulmann, Leonard. Interview by author. Bellmore, New York, summer 2002.

PUBLICATIONS

Ahmad, Hazrat Mirza Ghulam of Qadian. *The Philosophy of the Teachings of Islam*. London: London Mosque, 1979.

Artson, Rabbi Bradley Shavit. *The Bedside Torah: Wisdom, Visions, and Dreams*. Edited by Miriyam Glazer, Ph.D. Chicago: McGraw-Hill, Contemporary Books, 2001.

Berger, Peter L., ed. *The Other Side of God: A Polarity in World Religions.* Garden City, N.Y.: Anchor/Doubleday, 1981.

Bokenkotter, Thomas. *A Concise History of the Catholic Church,* 2d ed. New York: Doubleday, 1990.

Borg, Marcus J. *Reading the Bible Again for the First Time.* New York: HarperCollins, 2001.

Calef, Noel. *The Israel I Love.* Tel-Aviv, Israel: Nateev Publishing, 1977.

De Riencourt, Amaury. *The Soul of India.* New York: Harper & Brothers, 1960.

Epstein, Lawrence J. *Questions and Answers on Conversion to Judaism.* Northvale, N.J.: Jason Aronson, 1998.

Feiler, Bruce. *Walking the Bible: A Journey by Land Through the Five Books of Moses.* New York: HarperCollins, 2001.

Fischer, Klaus P. *Nazi Germany: A New History.* New York: Continuum Publishing Co., 1995.

Fulbrook, Mary. *A Concise History of Germany.* Cambridge: Cambridge University Press, 1990.

Goldhagen, Daniel Jonah. *Hitler's Willing Executioners: Ordinary Germans and the Holocaust.* New York: Alfred A. Knopf, 1996.

Greeley, Andrew M. *The Catholic Why? Book.* Chicago: Thomas More Press, 1983.

Hagen, Steve. *Buddhism: Plain & Simple.* New York: Broadway Books, 1997.

Heck, Alfons. *A Child of Hitler: Germany in the Days When God Wore a Swastika.* Frederick, Colo.: Renaissance House, 1985.

The Holy Scriptures. Revised in Accordance with Jewish Tradition And Modern Biblical Scholarship. New York: Hebrew Publishing Company, 1930.

Israel Information Center. *Facts About Israel.* N.p.: 1995.

Jungk, Peter Stephan. *Shabbat.* Translated by Arthur S. Wensinger and Richard H. Wood. New York: Random House, 1985.

Kolatch, Alfred J. *The Jewish Book of Why.* Middle Village, N.Y.: Jonathan David Publishers Inc., 1981.

Ludhiana Tribune. Chandigarh, India: N.p., 2000.

Read, Anthony, and David Fisher. *Kristallnacht: The Nazi Night of Terror.* New York: Random House, 1989.

Rempel, Gerhard. *Hitler's Children: The Hitler Youth and the SS.* Chapel Hill: University of North Carolina Press, 1989.

Renard, John. *The Handy Religion Answer Book.* Canton, Mich.: Visible Ink Press, 2002.

Singh, Nikky-Guninder Kaur. *Sikhism: World Religions.* New York: Facts On File, 1993.

Shirer, William L. *The Rise and Fall of the Third Reich: A History of Nazi Germany.* New York: Simon & Schuster, 1959.

Swami, Shri Purohit, trans. *Bhagavad Gita.* Annotations by Kendra Crossen Burroughs. Woodstock, Vt.: Skylight Paths Publishing, 2001.

United States Department of Energy. *The Berlin Blockade and Airlift.* Funk and Wagnalls Infopedia 2 CD Rom, 1992-6 Softkey Multimedia.

Von Der Grun, Max. *Howl like the Wolves: Growing Up in Nazi Germany.* New York: William Morrow & Co., 1980.

Weigel, George. *The Truth of Catholicism.* New York: Cliff Street Books/Harper Collins, 2001.

Wolpert, Stanley. *A New History of India,* 4th Ed. New York: Oxford University Press, 1993.

Young-Eisendrath, Polly, ed. *Awakening to Zen: The Teachings of Roshi Philip Kapleau.* New York: Scribner, 1997.

WEBSITES
Information can be found on the following websites.
Ahimsa information on www.sivanandadlshq.org;
Ahmadiyya information on
     www.islamworld.freeservers.com/ahmedis;
Mt. Athos information on www.poseidon.csd.auth.gr/athos;
"The Hugo Bergmann Family Papers," assembled and presented by
     Adolf Dasha Bergmann, Copenhagen, Denmark (author's note:
     Professor Bergman's name appears in references as both
     Bergman and Bergmann) on
     www.jewishgen.org/BohMor/hugo.html;
Bruderhof information on www.Bruderhof.com;
various Biblical information on www.bibleplaces.com;
Church of the Holy Sepulcher information on
     www.israel-mfa.gov.il;
dervish information on www.travelintelligence.net;
information about German war planes on
     www.warbirdsresourcegroup.org;
India geography on www.kamat.com and
     www.indiatouristoffice.org;
India and Israel sacred site information (various) on
     www.sacredsites.com;
Ramakrishna-Vivekananda information on the website of the Swami
     Adiswarananda, Ramakrishna-Vivekananda Center of New York,
     www.ramakrishna.org/sv_sa.htm;
regathering of the people of Israel on www.focusonjerusalem.com;
Albert Schweitzer information on the official website of the Nobel
     Foundation,
     www.nobel.se/peace/laureates/1952/schweitzer-bio.html;
Sevagram Ashram information on www.mkgandhi.org;

Shivananda Ashram information on
    www.philtar.ucsm.ac.uk/encyclopedia/hindu/ascetic/shivan.html;
Sikh information on www.photon.bu.edu;
Subhas Bose information on www.Calcuttaweb.com;
Tubishvat information on www.knesset.gov.il/tubishvat.

ACKNOWLEDGMENTS

My heartfelt thanks go to the following people: Ellen, whose research and reading were crucial, and always so loving and graceful; my parents, brother, and sister; Asher and Hannah (Naomi) Eder, who trusted me with their life experiences and worked so hard to help bring this project to fruition (much of the book's structure and more than a few phrases are owed to Asher's insight, hard work, and thoughtful scholarship); Leonard and Judy Levine, who brought me Asher's story and have been so supportive and helpful throughout the process of writing this book; Craig Gill, Anne Stascavage, the entire staff at the University Press of Mississippi, and copy editor Carol Cox; Hanni Ulmann, the former director of the Ahava Orphanage in Kiryat Bialik, Israel, her son, Jonathan I. Ulmann, and daughter-in-law, Anna, and Dr. León Gniwesch for their knowledge, experiences, input, and insight; the Long Beach, Oceanside, and Lynbrook, Long Island, public libraries and their staffs; Grace and Saul Gluck, the Schnitzer family, David Baram, Joy Bashevkin, Mike Burns, Carole Butler, Saj Craig, Don Draude, the Drew University Department of History, 1975–1979, Barbara Fischkin, Steve and Nancy Goldberg, Ruth Marconi, Jim Mulvaney, Margaret Oliver, Florence Ondré, Ruth and Bob

Safranek, the Long Beach, New York, Artists in Partnership, and Matthew and Daniela Schab for their ongoing support; and the Hyman family, who helped make all this possible.

—David E. Feldman

I will extol Thee, O Lord . . . [T]hou has brought up from the nether world my soul . . .
        —Psalms 30:1, 3

I want to take the opportunity to express my thanks and gratitude to: my parents; all those Christians, Hindus, Muslims, and others who have been instrumental in teaching me, and helping me, in my life's journey; the Jewish men and women whom I could befriend, whether they are mentioned in particular in this book or not, and the Jewish people in general for being there, steadfast, throughout history, in spite of all the slander and persecutions, thus by their very being witnessing the Lord G-d of the Fathers; the Jewish people, religious or secular, for receiving me as one coming from the enemy's camp into their fold; my wife and life's companion, Hannah, for being with me, and supporting me, lovingly; Yehudah Levine for his friendship and his efforts to find a suitable author for my story; David E. Feldman for writing in the empathic and beautiful way he has. May his work be enjoyable and enriching to you, dear reader.
        —Asher Avraham Ben Avraham (Asher Eder)
        Spring 2003
        Jerusalem